Fundraising For Dummies
2nd Edition

P9-BYS-353

Resources that Keep You in Touch

- *The Chronicle of Philanthropy* (www.philanthropy.com)
- *Foundation Reporter 2005,* a comprehensive guide to foundations (www.taftgroup.com/taft/fr.html)
- *The Foundation Directory,* published by the Foundation Center (http://fdncenter.org)
- *Philanthropic News Digest,* published by the Foundation Center (http://fdncenter.org/pnd/current/index.html)
- To take a look at the many offerings on the Foundation Center's periodicals list, go to http://fdncenter.org/newyork/ny_periodicals.html
- *Giving USA,* published by the American Association of Fund-Raising Counsel (www.aafrc.org)
- *Nonprofit Times* (www.nptimes.com), a publication for nonprofit management.
- BBB Wise Giving Alliance, a clearinghouse for information to inform donors (www.give.org/)
- The NPT Top 100, a study of America's largest nonprofits; go to http://www.nptimes.com/Nov04/sr_npt100.html to download a copy.
- Publications in your field of service

Organizations You Can Join (Or Make a Presentation to)

- Your local chapter of the **NSFRE** (National Society of Fund Raising Executives), www.nsfre.com
- The **Council on Foundations,** www.cof.org
- Your local **Donors Alliance** or **Community Foundation**
- Your local **Arts Council**
- The **Rotary** and **Kiwanis** in your town
- **Associations** of organizations in your service area
- Your local **lawyers' association**
- Your local **accountants' association**
- **Association of Fundraising Professionals,** www.afpnet.org

Fundraising Basics

- Assess your resources and sources of income.
- Write and remember to state your case.
- Develop a fundraising plan.
- Choose a dynamic leader.
- Create and maintain a donor and prospect list.
- Build relationships with your donors.
- Follow up on each donation.
- Revisit your case statement regularly and revise as needed.
- Communicate your mission and integrity to the public.
- Sustain your services and agency with the fruits of your labor.

Copyright © 2006 Wiley Publishing, Inc.
All rights reserved.
Item 9847-3.
For more information about Wiley Publishing, call 1-800-762-2974.

For Dummies: Bestselling Book Series for Beginners

Fundraising For Dummies,® 2nd Edition

Cheat Sheet

Knowing Your Income Sources

Before you begin fundraising, you have to know where your money is coming from and where you're missing out on a potential market. Use the following chart to list the sources of your income in the past fiscal year (total dollars raised from each market). If you've had little or no income from one of these major sources, consider targeting that source as a growth opportunity this year.

Markets	Total Amount Received	Percentage of Funding
Board	_____	_____
Individuals	_____	_____
Clients or Customers	_____	_____
Corporations	_____	_____
Foundations	_____	_____
Others (list)		
_____	_____	_____
_____	_____	_____
_____	_____	_____

Assessing Your Fundraising Resources

Unless you can clearly state what aspects of the fundraising plan you already have in place and what you still need, you can't get underway. List what you need in the table, using the descriptions below as your guide:

- ✔ **Money** includes current assets, known incoming contributions, and pledges.
- ✔ **People** includes your board, paid staff, volunteers, and people you serve.
- ✔ **Time** involves the total paid and nonpaid hours worked in a week, plus the amount of time between now and your fundraising deadline.
- ✔ **Materials** includes all hard goods you need to carry out your objectives, donations, and in-kind contributions.
- ✔ **Space** is your physical location.
- ✔ **Record-keeping** is the way you manage data, such as donor list, financials, personnel data, and publications.

Resources	Resources in Place	Resources Not in Place
Money	_____	_____
People	_____	_____
Time	_____	_____
Materials	_____	_____
Space	_____	_____
Record-keeping	_____	_____

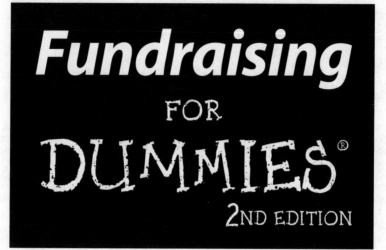

Fundraising
FOR
DUMMIES®
2ND EDITION

by John Mutz and Katherine Murray

WILEY

Wiley Publishing, Inc.

About the Authors

John Mutz: John Mutz is a fundraising expert and speaker who has an extensive array of fundraising credits. He was named 1997 Volunteer Fundraiser of the Year by the Indiana Chapter of National Association of Fundraising Executives. In 1999, John served as Chairman of the United Way of Central Indiana, which raised more than $36.5 million. From 1996 to 1998, John served as Chairman of the Indianapolis Zoo, where he chaired a $14.5 million fundraising campaign for White River State Park Gardens. From 1989 through 1994, John was the president of the Lilly Endowment, one of the nation's five largest private foundations, which supports the causes of religion, education, and community development. The Endowment included in its grant-making activity special grants intended to improve the financial viability of nonprofit organizations. It was also during his time there that the Lilly Endowment made the grant that brought the Fundraising School to the Center on Philanthropy at Indiana University Purdue University at Indianapolis (IUPUI).

In 1988, John was the Republican Candidate for Governor of Indiana, during which time he raised $4 million for the campaign. He is also co-founder of the Indiana Donor's Alliance, a statewide organization of Community Foundations. In addition to his board positions, John serves as a regular speaker for the Executive Leadership Institute (National Society of Fundraising Executives), the National Council of Foundations, and The Center on Philanthropy. He has also been a speaker for the Rocky Mountain Council of Foundations and Hillsdale College and has given dozens of speeches to community foundations. John served as Indiana's Lieutenant Governor from 1980 to 1988 and recently retired as president of the state's largest electric utility.

Katherine Murray: Katherine Murray has written dozens of books on a variety of topics, ranging from computers to parenting. From her early *Introduction to Personal Computers* (1988, Que Corporation) to *Discovering PCs* (1997, IDG Books) to *The Working Parents' Handbook* (1996, Park Avenue Productions), Katherine has specialized in writing how-to books for general audiences. A number of years ago, Katherine's "how-to" writing led her into the nonprofit world, when she volunteered her research and writing skills to help selected nonprofit organizations with missions close to her heart. Since that time, Katherine has completed a certification in Fundraising Management from the IU Center on Philanthropy and become a kind of "fundraising coach" for small and struggling nonprofits.

Today, Katherine continues her work as a nonprofit consultant — often working as a volunteer — helping organizations return to their missions, compose attention-getting case statements, develop fundraising plans, create publishing and media strategies, and research and write grant proposals. In addition to her nonprofit work, Katherine is the Publisher of KIDSRIGHTS, a company in Indianapolis, Indiana, that publishes and distributes materials for children and families in crisis. KIDSRIGHTS materials are often used by nonprofit professionals who serve families facing the difficult issues of domestic violence, child abuse, rape recovery, teen parenting, and drug and alcohol addictions. It is Katherine's hope that *Fundraising For Dummies,* 2nd Edition, will give those organizations what they need to make their fundraising more effective and serve a greater number of families than they ever have before.

Dedication

To the thousands of volunteers who give of their time, effort, and wealth to support nonprofit causes throughout the world. These people truly are the individuals who possess the "habit of the heart" that Alexis de Tocqueville wrote about in his great book *Democracy in America*.

Authors' Acknowledgments

We would like to thank a number of people who have helped us by volunteering their anecdotes, fundraising tips, editorial prowess, and technical expertise during the writing of this book. First thanks go to Burton Weisbrod, Betty Beene, Robert Payton, Ken Gladish, Peter Goldberg, Jeff Bonner, and Ken Bode, for their professional expertise and insights. Thanks also to the folks at Wiley, in particular Tracy Boggier and Jennifer Connolly, for helping to shape this book's first edition into a magnificent updated second edition. Special thanks go to our families, for encouraging and supporting us in the midst of late nights, long hours, and looming deadlines.

Lastly, heart-felt thanks go to all the volunteers, staff members, and leaders in the many nonprofit organizations we have served throughout the years. We've been touched and inspired by your dedication and persistent work to make this world a better place, and we hope that this book makes your goals seem more reachable than ever. Special thanks goes to Carolyn Mutz for getting us together to write this book.

Publisher's Acknowledgments

We're proud of this book; please send us your comments through our Dummies online registration form located at www.dummies.com/register/.

Some of the people who helped bring this book to market include the following:

Acquisitions, Editorial, and Media Development

Development Editor: Nancy Stevenson

Project Editors: Jennifer Connolly, Kristin DeMint

Acquisitions Editor: Tracy Boggier

Copy Editors: Jennifer Connolly, Carrie A. Burchfield

Technical Editor: Matt Eldridge

Editorial Manager: Michelle Hacker

Editorial Supervisor: Carmen Krikorian

Editorial Assistant: Hanna Scott

Cover Photos: © Wiley Publishing, Inc.

Cartoons: Rich Tennant (www.the5thwave.com)

Composition Services

Project Coordinator: Maridee Ennis

Layout and Graphics: Carl Byers, Joyce Haughey, Barry Offringa, Erin Zeltner

Proofreaders: Leeann Harney, Stephanie D. Jumper, Jessica Kramer, TECHBOOKS Production Services

Indexer: TECHBOOKS Production Services

Publishing and Editorial for Consumer Dummies

    Diane Graves Steele, Vice President and Publisher, Consumer Dummies

    Joyce Pepple, Acquisitions Director, Consumer Dummies

    Kristin A. Cocks, Product Development Director, Consumer Dummies

    Michael Spring, Vice President and Publisher, Travel

    Kelly Regan, Editorial Director, Travel

Publishing for Technology Dummies

    Andy Cummings, Vice President and Publisher, Dummies Technology/General User

Composition Services

    Gerry Fahey, Vice President of Production Services

    Debbie Stailey, Director of Composition Services

Contents at a Glance

Table of Contents

Introduction

*N*obody begins working with a nonprofit saying, "Gee, I've always wanted to ask people for money!" The involvement usually begins with a need — a need we become aware of, whether it's homeless families, or arts cutbacks, or public policy issues. We hear or see something, our hearts are touched, our minds open. Sometimes our checkbooks do, too.

Whether we wind up helping as a volunteer, joining a staff, or serving on a board, we align with an agency because we believe in what it is doing, first and foremost. And at some point, assisting the agency means trying to help the nonprofit get the funding it needs to keep the doors open, keep the services coming, and get people help. We realize that somebody has to raise funds. You may be reading this book now because you are "the somebody" that your organization is counting on.

But there's no way around it — fundraising today is a challenge. Agencies have incredible competition for the donor's dollars. Volunteers, staff, and board members come and go, which means that there's always a new crop of people to train. As the media — print, broadcast, and Internet — gets faster and more insistent, we find ourselves competing with all sorts of voices clamoring for attention. How will we get our agency noticed? Who will we approach? What do we have to do to ensure our survival in the years to come?

Fundraising For Dummies, 2nd Edition, answers those questions with practical, tried-and-true offerings, friendly insights, and colorful examples. Whether you run a one-person office or chair a 20-member board of directors, this book walks you through the process of getting ready to raise funds, preparing a far-reaching fundraising plan, gathering your resources, and putting the plan in place. Additionally, you discover a wealth of fundraising tools and discover how you can use them most effectively.

About This Book

This is the type of book you can dip into to find just what you need. You don't have to read it cover to cover to get value. If you know all about what's covered in Chapter 2, skip ahead and get what you need in Chapter 10.

We do suggest that you read over Chapter 1, which gives you some fundraising basics, including some basic terminology. But then wander where your interests and most urgent needs lead you. When more information about a topic is included elsewhere in the book we include a cross-reference, so you can easily jump over there to beef up on the areas that interest you most.

Throughout the book we strive to make ideas and lingo easy to understand, putting things in simple terms with advice straight from the school of fundraising hard knocks. The idea is to get you going with effective fundraising techniques fast.

Conventions Used in This Book

There are a few conventions we've used consistently throughout the book that you should know about.

- New terms appear in *italics* and are closely followed by an easy-to-understand definition.
- All Web addresses appear in `monofont`.

What You're Not to Read

Sidebars are just that — side topics that may be intriguing but aren't exactly essential to getting familiar with the topic of fundraising. They may point out the background of a term or practice, for example. If you want to speed through and skip sidebars, go ahead, no guilt required.

Foolish Assumptions

We've gone ahead and made some assumptions about our readers in writing this book. We think that

- You're a current or aspiring fundraiser.
- Whether you have 20 years of experience or are just starting out, you'd like some fresh ideas and advice.

✔ You may be anyone from a full-time staff member to a volunteer charged with fundraising tasks.

✔ You don't have a huge staff or open-ended budget.

✔ You have a mission that you are raising funds for that is important to you.

✔ You don't have time to waste; you need to get to work right away with ideas and tools that can help you succeed.

How This Book Is Organized

Fundraising For Dummies, 2nd Edition, is organized into six different parts, with chapters arranged to walk you (more or less) through the process of preparing for, creating, implementing, and evaluating a cohesive fundraising system.

Part 1: Putting Your Fundraising Ducks in a Row

Part I is all about your readiness — as an agency — to set up a fundraising system. Long before you start taking those checks to the bank, you need to make sure that your organization is ready to raise funds. What is your mission? Why do you do what you do? Who is helped by your agency? What does your board do? This part of the book will help you evaluate these questions — and more besides — to make sure that you are, in fact, ready to roll out your own fundraising plan.

Part 11: Finding — and Winning Over — Donors

Part II introduces that all-important person: your donor. Who are your donors and where can you find them? What motivates a donor to give? How can you lessen your chances of hearing "No!" on your donor calls? How equitable is the agency-donor relationship? This part introduces you to these aspects of a fundraising system and helps you play donor and agency roles to prepare for your — eventual — dialog with the donor.

Part III: Assembling Your Fundraising Toolkit

If you are new to fundraising, you may be thrilled to discover that there are actual tools that will help you be successful on the job. Yes, everybody needs a stapler, but that's not the kind of tool we're talking about here. You have at your disposal dozens of ways in which you can get — and keep — attention for your agency, whether that attention translates into volunteer hours, funds raised, grants awarded, or successful phone campaigns. This part helps you take advantage of those resources and put them to work for you.

Part IV: Leveraging the Internet

It's an online world today, and your organization had better be up to the challenge. Everybody who's anybody has a Web site, and so should you. In this part, you discover the ins and outs of how to maximize your Web site to promote and brand your group and even collect donations online. You explore the possibilities of e-newsletters and e-mail for gaining visibility and soliciting funds.

Part V: On the (Fundraising) Campaign Trail

As you become acclimated to the fundraising environment, you quickly discover that different campaigns are run for different purposes and there are different types of donors. Your year-in, year-out operations are funded by your annual fund. A special event might purchase new playground equipment. The new library building goes up on the dollars raised for the capital campaign. You can go after major gifts from corporations and foundations, or decide to build an endowment for longer-term financial security. This part explores the different campaigns and approaches to fund building and provides advice about when you should use each, what to expect, and how to sidestep trouble when it comes walking your way.

Part VI: The Part of Tens

In typical *For Dummies* fashion, this part of the book lists a collection of ten items, grouped around a particular subject. Some will be tongue in cheek;

others will be vital. Whichever the case, be sure to read through the ones that suit you best. You may want to start with "Ten Great Opening Lines." You never know when one may come in handy.

Icons Used in This Book

If you have ever used a *For Dummies* book before, you know that each book has a lot of little pictures stuck on the pages, showing you what's special and important about a particular paragraph. The icons used to represent what is special and important vary from book to book. Here are the icons we've chosen to include in *Fundraising For Dummies,* 2nd Edition.

Basic "how-to-do-it-better" ideas appear with this icon so you can do things correctly from the start.

We use a "remember-this" icon for concepts and practical information.

Steer clear of the information listed with this icon, or your fundraising campaign could be a bomb.

Where to Go from Here

Well, you could take the afternoon off and go watch the Cubs play . . . but more than likely you are now fired up and ready to tackle some of the fundraising issues you face. Before you begin, however, review the following fundraising truths:

- ✔ Fundraising starts with passion.
- ✔ People want to give.
- ✔ You help donors achieve their goals.
- ✔ Fundraising is a noble endeavor.

Don't believe it? By the time you're done reading, you will. In the meantime, sit back, feel confident that you're not alone out there, and enjoy your trip through *Fundraising For Dummies,* 2nd Edition.

Part I
Putting Your Fundraising Ducks in a Row

The 5th Wave   By Rich Tennant

"Robin, some of the men thought our mission statement, 'Steal from the rich. Give to the poor.', didn't quite cover it, and would like to include, 'Forest Conservation, Wilderness Survival, the Advancement of Recreational Archery, Ambushing Techniques, Bird Watching...'"

In this part . . .

*B*efore you can start bringing in the big bucks to fund your organization, you need to know some of the basics about effective fundraising. In this part, you get an up-close look at the foundation of your fundraising efforts. Where's your passion? What's your mission? Who's on your board? How good are you at mobilizing volunteers for fundraising? Use this part to answer these basic questions and put your fundraising house in order.

Chapter 1

Identifying the Fruits of Your Fundraising Passion

*F*undraising folks have an old saying: "People don't give to causes. People give to people with causes." This saying means that, in essence, you're the important part. Your inspiration, your perspiration, your passion. So that brings us to the Big Question. . . .

What are you passionate about?

Chances are, passion for some cause led you to fundraising in the first place. Oh, sure, you find professional fundraisers out in the field who are interested first and foremost in turning a fast buck. But those people are few and far between in our experience. People are drawn to organizations because they see a need — perhaps up close and personal — and they feel compelled to do what they can to make a difference.

That spark of passion makes you want to help. Your passion is one of the best tools to use as you fan the embers of possibility into a full fundraising flame.

In this chapter, you take a look at having and staying in touch with that initial spark — the spark that brought about the birth of your organization, the spark that keeps it going, and the spark you caught and are helping to flame. We also show you how to fan the flame to ignite others for your cause, give you the rundown on some basic fundraising lingo, and attach fundraising at large to a dollar figure (so you know just how vast the industry is). And for newbies just breaking into the nonprofit world, we highlight the various types of these organizations, give you some advice on maintaining the buzz, and share a few tips for the road on marketing your new venture.

Sparking Fundraising Action

As anyone who's ever had any experience with trying to raise money can attest, *fundraising* isn't a pretty word. In fact, it's a tough term to confront, a kind of "oh-no-here-comes-the-pitch" sounding word. Some people say that fundraising is really "friend-raising," but that's like putting a bit of polish on an otherwise slippery word.

Nonetheless, fundraising is a necessary part of a nonprofit organization — the part that puts the hinges on the doors so it can open and the part that keeps the blankets on the beds and the food in the pantry. It pays the salary for the midwife and provides the day-camp scholarships for inner-city kids.

But fundraising isn't the main objective of a nonprofit organization, although you may sometimes feel that it gets the bulk of the focus. Fundraising is the means to the end, the way of fulfilling your mission, whether that mission is reaching homeless people in need, healing the sick, or promoting the art or music you're passionate about.

Chapter 2 deals with the important issue of ethics in fundraising — how you think about what you do. In that chapter, you consider the biases, apologies, and reactions that you battle against — within yourself and from the general population — when you set out to raise funds.

Remembering why you signed on

You may be involved with fundraising today, or you may be considering a request for involvement, but the initial spark is what we're talking about here. Like the Olympic flame, your spark gets carried from person to person and warms the very lifeblood of your organization, whether you're a volunteer, staff member, or board member.

Knowing your spark story is important for several reasons:

- ✔ When you share it, it inspires others.
- ✔ When you remember it, it inspires you.
- ✔ When you recognize its importance, it helps you remember your priorities.
- ✔ When you keep it in mind, it provides a common ground where you can meet — and enlist help from — others you bring into your organization's cause.

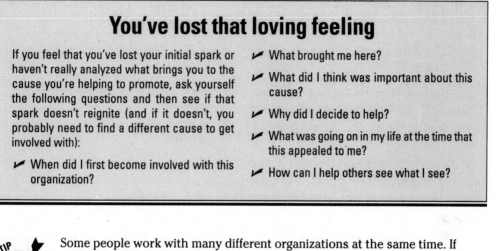

You've lost that loving feeling

If you feel that you've lost your initial spark or haven't really analyzed what brings you to the cause you're helping to promote, ask yourself the following questions and then see if that spark doesn't reignite (and if it doesn't, you probably need to find a different cause to get involved with):

✔ When did I first become involved with this organization?

✔ What brought me here?

✔ What did I think was important about this cause?

✔ Why did I decide to help?

✔ What was going on in my life at the time that this appealed to me?

✔ How can I help others see what I see?

TIP

Some people work with many different organizations at the same time. If you're charged with fundraising for your nonprofit group — whether your role is a volunteer, paid staff member, or board member — chances are that you work with a select few, just given the amount of time and effort that solid fundraising requires. Even if you work with several nonprofit organizations, take time to remember why you selected them over others. Knowing why you care about these causes is important to keeping you motivated — even if you're overextended, time- and responsibility-wise.

Helping your donor catch the spark

We talk in this chapter about the importance of knowing what brought you to nonprofit work in the first place. That spark shows in your eyes and your smile. It carries in your voice and makes your story ring true. It shows in the manner in which you promote your organization and in the personal pride you take in your relationship to your work or your cause. This section presents a few key fundraising philosophies and tools that can help your donor catch the spark that you hold. For more specifics about working with donors, visit the chapters in Part II of this book.

The best thing you can do for your donor is believe in the mission you're representing. When you're gung-ho for your cause, others see it and are encouraged to join. They start to imagine themselves working for a solid cause, a good effort, a positive change.

Today's philanthropy realizes that you can't always see or touch the person who needs the help. Nonprofit organizations arose to help people help others

How many people volunteer?

Do you think that volunteering is only for those few people who don't have any other commitments? Think again. The Independent Sector, a coalition of nonprofits, foundations, and corporations supporting philanthropy, cites the following statistics in its 2001 study, which surveyed more than 4,000 Americans:

✔ Eighty-nine percent of households give money to charitable organizations.

✔ Forty-four percent of adults volunteer their time.

✔ Forty-two percent of adults both gave and volunteered.

✔ 15.5 billion hours were spent volunteering nationwide.

whether they live down the block or on the other side of the world. These organized bodies provide the channels for your help to get to Rwandan refugees, Kosovan orphans, or the homeless families in your neighborhood, which enables you to do something concrete to help change the world for the better.

As a fundraiser, remember that you're the all-important link that helps a caring donor give to others. When you view what you do in this way, you recognize the importance of your role as a service provider. You also see how that spark can pass from one to another. And suddenly, the conversation is no longer about simply raising funds.

Making friends with fundraising

Before going any further, we need to clearly define the terms we bat around in fundraising. We offer the following definitions, with our own commentary added. You see and hear these terms again and again as you proceed to raise money for the causes you believe in:

✔ **Philanthropy:** Actions and giving that attempt to improve the lot of people.

In the fundraising field, one standard definition of philanthropy is "voluntary action for the public good," meaning any action one takes — with or without a financial component — that is an act to make life better for someone else. When you tithe at church, it's philanthropy. When you drop coins in the container on the counter at the local convenience store, you're a philanthropist. When you include your local theater or your alma mater in your will, you're practicing philanthropy.

✔ **Gift:** Something you offer to somebody else with no thought of compensation.

A gift may appear in many facets of life. When Aunt Mildred gives you her parakeet, it's a gift. In fundraising, a gift may mean that any number of things that build on this basic definition.

- You may hear about a *lead gift,* which is the first, usually sizeable, gift of a capital campaign. Go to Chapter 20 for more about capital campaigns.

- A *major gift* is another type of large gift that a donor may give in order to support a particular program, launch a campaign, further a cause, or be applied in another specific area. Check out Chapter 21 for more on major gifts.

- A *general gift* is one a donor gives to an annual fund or contributes to operating expenses.

Still, a gift is a gift, freely given, with no theoretical arm-twisting and no product or service given in return.

✔ **Fundraising:** Collecting money for a cause.

Another definition may be as follows: Fundraising is the intentional and strategic activity of acquiring contributions for support and growth. Those contributions can include money, time, services, labor, donations of hard goods, or in-kind contributions.

✔ **Volunteer:** One who freely gives of his or her time to render a service.

In other words, at a basic level, a volunteer is someone who works for no monetary payment. As a volunteer, you get other benefits — the ability to help build something you believe in, acquire new skills, forge new relationships, and more. Head to Chapter 4 for more on finding and recruiting volunteers.

✔ **Annual Fund:** A yearly fundraising effort.

Most organizations run a yearly fundraising campaign, in addition to any program specific efforts. This annual fund is often earmarked for ongoing operational expenses. See Chapter 18 for more about annual funds.

✔ **Endowment:** A substantial fund that generates ongoing income from its investment.

An endowment is usually a large sum of money that can be invested, and the profits from those investments, or even the interest the money generates, help to support an organization. See Chapter 23 to discover more about how endowments work.

Philanthropy as a right

Although philanthropy isn't a new concept, U.S. residents get an additional perk when they give that residents of other countries don't: The United States is the first country in the world to include a fundamental philosophy that encourages charitable giving. When you give, you get a tax break. That's not some loophole that someone figured out how to wriggle through — it's intentional. Lawmakers highly regarded the practice of philanthropy. It's part of your heritage. It's part of your right — and, some would say, part of your obligation.

Fundraising today — and in the future

Fundraising is Big Business. In 2004, the American Association of Fundraising Counsel (www.aafrc.org) released fundraising figures for 2003 in the latest edition of *Giving USA*, the annual report on philanthropy in the United States. Total contributions to nonprofit organizations weighed in at $241 billion, a 2.8 percent increase over amounts in the year 2000. You may think that's one heck of a lot of hot meals. Or free condoms. Or community leadership seminars. Or tithes.

When you look at the societal statistics about who fundraisers are, where fundraising is going, and where you spend both your energies and your dollars, you may be surprised to find that Americans are living in a philanthropic age. Americans volunteer their time; they give blood; they write checks; they build houses. In this time of media hype, "negativism," and preoccupation with social ills, just seeing the flip side of that negativity in increased involvement, higher levels of giving, and a greater number of human service organizations — of all different flavors, springing up to make life better for generations today and tomorrow — is reaffirming.

We are also at a time when fundraising is changing. For example, giving is becoming more global, with gifts given across borders at times of national strife such as disastrous weather or terrorist attacks. Estate planning will grow as baby boomers retire and determine where to leave their wealth. These and other trends make this an interesting time in the world of fundraising. (See Chapter 24 for more predictions about future trends in fundraising).

Building Nonprofit Organizations

The nonprofit organizations (NPOs) you care about were born from passion — a response to an identified need in the local, national, or international community. The very frame of philanthropy rests on the idea that "when people work together, they are stronger" — that when you share your resources,

---

What about political fundraising?

You may notice that in this chapter (and even book) we don't mention the fundraising your favorite political candidate does in order to secure your vote and fund his or her trip to office. Political fundraising is the unappreciated stepchild of the fundraising field. Because of widely publicized political fundraising abuses, people sometimes blame fundraising for corrupting or, at least, preoccupying the minds and intentions of candidates.

In fact, if political fundraising would more openly apply the good practices and ethics used in charitable fundraising, the standards would improve, the money would be raised, and good people of varying income brackets could get into office. The areas aren't so different, after all: When you raise funds in the nonprofit world, you're working for a cause you care about. When you raise funds for a political candidate, you believe in the person or the platform. The skills you discover in nonprofit fundraising are directly transferable to the political arena — and may lead you to contribute to the public debate and thus to the political system.

---

whether those resources are your wealth, time, effort, or ideas, others can benefit. Basically when people provide help, comfort, education, and more to people in need, society as a whole benefits. But putting together solutions is hard work — and passion and hard work are essential ingredients to carry the idea from that initial spark of recognized need to the realization of a program that achieves its mission.

Recognizing the many nonprofits

NPOs exist to battle every imaginable ill — from environmental to health to human service issues. And don't forget animals, arts, and political groups. Your organization undoubtedly falls into one of the following categories:

- ✔ Arts/cultural organizations
- ✔ Educational organizations
- ✔ Environmental organizations
- ✔ Health organizations
- ✔ International aid and relief organizations
- ✔ Public policy/social benefit organizations
- ✔ Religious organizations
- ✔ Social service organizations

Three nonprofits built from passion

Looking at examples of how passion has been at the core of fundraising efforts can be enlightening and inspiring. Here are a few:

✔ **MADD (Mothers Against Drunk Driving)** was created when mom Candy Lightner lost her 13-year-old daughter Cari in an accident caused by a repeat-offender drunken driver. Though it benefited from a few large corporate gifts at its inception, the organization continues to be largely a grass-roots organization calling for heightened awareness and tougher punishments for alcohol- or drug-impaired drivers. MADD has grown to more than three million members worldwide because of Candy's original passion, her perceived need for an organized effort to combat drunk driving, and the spark that spread to others. What's amazing about MADD is that it illustrates perfectly what passion applied to a cause can do: Beyond simply growing in numbers, MADD grew in voice, becoming instrumental in changing the values and very perspectives with which people view drinking and driving in today's culture. You can visit the MADD Web site at www.madd.org.

✔ **Habitat for Humanity** grew out of a passion sparked in the mid-1960s when founders Millard and Linda Fuller visited Koinonia Farm, a small, cooperative farming community in Georgia. There they began discussions with farmer and scholar Clarence Jordan about the possibility of partnership housing, in which those in need of homes would work together with volunteers to build solid, affordable homes. Since Habitat's founding in 1976, more than 200,000 homes have been built in more than 100 countries. Check out the Habitat Web site at www.habitat.org.

Some years ago, John (one of your humble authors) had the good fortune to meet Millard Fuller and spend some time with him. He shared his vision of how people become unified in a good cause. Whether the volunteers who range from doctors, construction workers, healthcare professionals, or stay-at-home parents pick up the tools and drive the first nail, they're joined together in work that helps build a life. His challenge, said Millard, was to get people to hammer that first nail.

✔ The spark that would flame into the **Children's Defense Fund** was ignited in Marian Wright Edelman during her work as a private civil rights lawyer in Mississippi in 1964. According to her book, *The Measure of Our Success* (HarperCollins), she began a fight for the hungry, homeless, illiterate, and economically disadvantaged children as her primary focus. Today the Children's Defense Fund has celebrated its 30th anniversary and is an active advocate for the child on the local and national level. You can find the Children's Defense Fund on the Web at www.childrensdefense.org.

All in all, more than 1.23 million charitable organizations are in the United States, (give or take a few hundred), according to the Independent Sector's survey, "Giving and Volunteering in the United States." Luckily, there are also millions of people wanting to help, most of whom are also willing to give.

Competing for dollars

So if tons of people are giving, then doesn't it follow that many people are also receiving? How many people are doing what fundraisers do — raising funds for your various NPOs? How many of these organizations exist today, and how does that compare to a decade ago? In other words, what does your competition for fundraising dollars look like?

The IRS reports that the number of charities that filed tax returns with the government rose from 180,931 in 1995 to 240,559 in 2001. That's a pretty hefty growth in only six years! By comparison, between 1999 and 2000 the number of private foundations filing during that period grew 7 percent, for a total of 66,738.

So what form do all these nonprofit organizations take? Typically, your competition will be one of two kinds:

- **501(c)(3)** is one section of the IRS code that defines and qualifies nonprofit organizations for special treatment under today's tax laws. Having 501(c)(3) status allows nonprofits to be tax-exempt and to accept donations for which donors receive tax deductions. A nonprofit with 501(c)(4) status is a nonprofit in the social welfare arena.

- **Independent sector,** or **third sector,** is a phrase used to describe the group of charitable organizations that include both 501(c)(3)s and 501(c)(4)s.

A mixed bag of contributions

Many nonprofits receive funds from a variety of contributors. An arts organization, for example, raises a percentage of its funds by selling tickets for its exhibits, applies for grant monies from selected foundations, solicits both charitable contributions and in-kind gifts from corporations, and develops a planned giving program to help longtime donors work out bequests that continue to fund the organization after the death of the donor. (See Chapter 21 for more on planned giving.)

In some agencies, especially those involved in health and human services, government funding is a part of the package. Other NPOs sell a product and thereby are responsible for some taxable income in addition to their charitable contributions.

Whatever the funding patterns for your organization may be, get to know your income sources. Evaluate them, assess them, and know where your strengths and challenges lie. Strengthening this part of your program can help you discover major funding possibilities that you may be missing now.

Although the increasing number of 501(c)(3)s is a good thing, which spotlights the growing awareness of and responsiveness to human need, a downside to all this growth exists: increased competition. Missions overlap. Different organizations seek to serve the same populations. Donors are pulled in different directions, recognizing that their dollars may be coveted by a number of similar organizations addressing similar needs.

The sad fact is that a nonprofit mortality rate does exist. Each year, nonprofits fold up their 501(c)(3) umbrellas and disappear. The level of competition for today's fundraising dollars means survival of the fittest. In order to survive, you need to stay on your toes, ready for anything. Sometimes you may even ask yourself, "Is this service worthwhile? Are there other organizations repeating our services?"

Keeping your organization going

What does this competition mean to you? For starters, if you want to keep your agency active and growing:

- ✔ **Know your mission statement inside and out.** A crystal-clear "why are we here?" mission statement (also called a case statement) helps keep everyone focused on the organization's vision. If your statement's language is outdated, be willing to speak in terms that reach your constituents' hearts. See Chapter 3 for more on creating this case statement.

- ✔ **Be different.** Be sure that you stay plugged into your environment. Be active in local fundraising groups — know who else serves the population you serve. When possible, work with, as opposed to against, other agencies so that you both can complement and not duplicate each other. Then you need to differentiate your cause from other similar organizations: Many opportunities abound for giving, but not so many that duplicating services is okay — at least not for the long term.

- ✔ **Know what's out there.**

- ✔ **Be responsive to the people you serve.** The ever-changing world presents you with opportunities for refocusing and retooling at every turn. If the social ill you battle is no longer viable, step back and reconsider your clients' needs.

- ✔ **Ask the tough questions.** Does your organization meet today's needs? For instance, 50 years ago, an agency created to provide lodging to unmarried pregnant women was much needed. In today's climate, programs exist in many places to help young women, and single pregnancy no longer carries the same crippling social stigma it once did. An organization that asks itself the hard questions, such as whether what it's doing is really necessary and then changes based on the answers, won't be left in the dust when the world around it continues to grow.

✔ **Be willing to change.** Yep. You read it right. After you answer those tough questions about your organization, you have to be willing to make the necessary changes. Especially for large, unwieldy organizations with a vested power structure and a bureaucratic bent, change is resisted at the board table. But populations, needs, and services change. Be willing to change with them. Doing so can help protect your agency's existence.

✔ **Put your best foot forward.** People generally dislike crisis appeals — if you're always crying "Wolf!" to bring in funding from various donors, sooner or later people are going to tire of the continual pleas. Instead, if you can show your donors that you're part of a winning organization, a force that works for good in the world, you may not only keep their interest but also inspire them to join you in your winning campaign. (See Chapter 7 for ways to show and tell your cause to donors.)

Getting Attention — and Money

So just how do you get started raising funds? You can approach fundraising in several different ways, all of which we discuss in various chapters of this book. If you read Parts I and II and you perform the outlined groundwork to understand your own mission and goals and research potential donors, then you're ready to spread the word and ask for contributions.

To help with those contributions, review Part III for a discussion on using print materials and direct mail, writing grant proposals, working with the media, and fundraising over the phone. Part IV looks at ways you can leverage the online world to run e-mail campaigns, to keep people aware of your mission with an e-newsletter, or to offer information on your own Web site.

Chapter 2

Finding the Right Perspective: Fundraising Issues and Ethics

*T*he happiest fundraisers love what they do. They believe in their cause, and an air of invincibility surrounds them. They may not be the biggest moneymakers on the block right now, but something inside them recognizes that one day they may be. They have the power of belief, the pride of profession, that inner conviction that what they do makes a difference.

That's one place where your spark comes in handy.

This chapter explores the issues that may hang you up when you first begin fundraising. Not only is the understandable dread of asking someone for money something to combat (nobody we know is too fond of rejection) but also a kind of built-in stigma exists — deep, in those unspoken attitudes we have about money — that comes with the territory. Here you find out how to face some of those demons head-on and recognize that they are simply misguided impressions you may have about fundraising. When you shine the light on those demons, they disappear like the illusions they are.

Sacrificing or Selling: The Fundraising Debate Continues

Part of the stigma of fundraising is a social issue. We used to shy away from talking about things like sex, religion, and money. Today we're still shy about religion and money. Taboos keep the reins on too much familiarity, keeping us from asking "prying" questions about another's finances, barring us from being so bold as to "peek" into another person's checkbook while we're standing in the checkout line at the grocery store. The person who does that for a living is, so the unspoken perception goes, violating a kind of personal privacy we each, as individuals, want.

Another part of the stigma is simply bad rep (as in reputation). To illustrate, we'll tell you a story:

Jimmy is a part-time used car salesman. He knows every trick in the book for getting you to buy that car. He overlooks the fact that the car has *lemon* written all over it. He somehow blinks away the idea that he's trying to sell you a two-seater and you've got a family of five. He nods understandingly when you tell him that you were barely able to pay your electric bill last month and certainly don't need a little yellow sports car that will put you even further into debt. As you sign the purchase agreement, he smiles a big smile, assuring you that all your troubles will just blow away as you do 90 mph through the desert. His gold tooth gleams.

Jimmy isn't a fundraiser. And he's not an ethical car salesman, either. Jimmy is interested in one thing: getting your money. And that's not what's at the front of a fundraiser's mind. All the textbooks and professional organizations will tell you: Fundraising is a noble endeavor. People who have been in this business for the span of their careers affirm it: Good work gets done; doors get opened; programs help, heal, feed, and house because of the dollars they raise.

In business, we don't blanche when we read books that exalt the salesperson. A sale, after all, provides the lifeblood of a business. In sales, you might argue, you have an exchange of goods or services. In fundraising, you have an opportunity for people to walk the talk of their beliefs.

Telephone solicitors who call in the middle of dinnertime can hardly be accused of altruistic behavior. Who knows, though? Maybe they're giving up their dinner to call.

Living with the stigma

If fundraising is such a noble profession, where does the fundraiser's black eye come from?

Unfortunately, for some people, the word *fundraising* means, "I'll try anything to get your money." This mentality taints the fundraising process for all fundraisers who then have to get past that stigma when approaching possible donors.

For ethical fundraisers, doing whatever it takes to get money couldn't be farther from the truth. Instead, you offer potential donors not the sale of a product or a palpable "warm fuzzy," but rather the opportunity to join a group of people working in an area you care about. You offer a chance to make a difference, an opportunity to "start where you are, use what you have, and do what you can," as the saying goes.

An ethical fundraiser doesn't sell a lemon of an organization to a donor. So, to be an ethical fundraiser, you need to remember that

✔ The match needs to be right between the donor and the organization.

✔ The donor needs to have the ability to give (if the electric bill was a problem last month, major philanthropic giving is out of the question this month).

✔ The transaction that takes place has to be a good one for both parties because this is the beginning of a long-term relationship, not a hit-and-run experience in which the fundraiser stuffs the check in his pocket and heads on down the road, grinning his gold-toothed smile.

Combining selling with ideals

Parts of fundraising are similar to — and informed by — good salesmanship. You need to develop certain skills to be a good salesperson:

✔ Communicating with your customer

✔ Being a good listener

✔ Helping a customer find the right fit

✔ Closing the deal

In fundraising, these skills translate into

- ✔ Communicating your mission and passion to your donor
- ✔ Listening to your donor's concerns and interests
- ✔ Helping your donors find the giving level and program that match their interests
- ✔ Getting the donation so it can start doing good right away

Use tools of research that help you prospect for the people who will care about your cause (you can discover more about these tools in Chapter 6). If you identify people who have a real interest, then approaching them isn't selling them something they don't want; it's providing a connection they crave.

If you can see sales as an honorable profession, you can embrace the need for using sales skills in an honorable way to fundraise with even more conviction.

Do some people work for organizations they don't believe in? Sure. But if you're reading this book and want to grow in your professional or volunteer ability to fundraise, we assume that you're willing to make the investment of time and effort you need in order to master the art of fundraising. Even if you're not crazy about what you do right now, you can benefit by acquiring the skills you need for the day when you're working in a cause that really gets those fires raging.

Understanding the Ethics of Fundraising

If you caught the spark of fundraising as a noble endeavor, start talking about the standards by which you determine the "right" ways to fundraise. If you're new to the area of fundraising, perhaps involved for the first time through volunteer efforts, board membership, or a new development job, you may be beginning to soak up some of the attitudes present in nonprofit work. You'll find that ethics and accountability are important ideas in the nonprofit sector.

What are ethics? And what do they have to do with our views about what we do? *Ethics* deal with the study of what's right and wrong and developing a moral code you can live by. Everybody in every walk of life at some time or other has to measure what they do for a living with what they feel is right and wrong.

Finding ethical standards organizations

So who sets the ethical standards for fundraising, and how are they governed? A number of professional organizations exist to help set the standards we use

Paid by commission: A hot ethical topic

One issue continually batted about by professional fundraisers — those working in development for an organization and those serving as consultants — is whether a grant proposal writer should be paid by commission. Industry ethics say no. In fact, in the 501(c)(3) language, it says "no part of the net earnings of which inures to the benefit of any private shareholder or individual." In at least one interpretation, this means our income should not be directly tied to the funds we raise.

The argument for paying grant proposal writers a percentage comes from those cases when a small organization needs a good grant writer in order to secure major funds to keep the doors open. (Other things should be in place here, but let's stick with the percentages discussion.) If a grant proposal writer is paid a percentage after the grant is made, the organization can defer payment until it secures the funds and the grant proposal writer is paid what she's "worth."

Although this argument continues and many consultants — especially for small organizations — do agree to work for percentages, this position is considered unethical by professional fundraising organizations.

to guide ethics in fundraising. You can contact these organizations to find out about membership and meetings in your area:

✔ **Association of Fundraising Professionals (AFP):** AFP is a professional association of individuals responsible for generating donor support for a wide variety of nonprofit charitable organizations. With more than 172 chapters, AFP is the largest (26,000 members) professional organization in fundraising today.

AFP includes chapters in all major cities, nationwide. Groups meet monthly to discuss issues with their peers, hear speakers, and find out more about their craft and their industry. Contact your local AFP office to find out about the groups closest to you.

Association of Fundraising Professionals
1101 King Street, Suite 700
Alexandria, VA 22314
703-684-0410
www.afpnet.org

✔ **Council for Advancement and Support of Education (CASE):** CASE is an international professional organization for "educational advancement officers," that offers resources and training opportunities to its members.

Council for Advancement and Support of Education
1307 New York Avenue NW, Suite 1000
Washington, DC 20005-4701
202-328-2273
www.case.org

✔ **Association for Healthcare Philanthropy (AHP):** AHP is an international association that serves healthcare through philanthropy by developing the competency, professionalism, and productivity of its members.

Association for Healthcare Philanthropy
313 Park Avenue, Suite 400
Falls Church, VA 22046
703-532-6243
www.ahp.org

✔ **American Association of Fund-Raising Counsel (AAFRC):** AAFRC was started in 1935 to help ensure ethical principles in not-for-profit consulting agencies. Member firms are carefully screened to ensure their practices meet AAFRC standards.

American Association of Fund-Raising Counsel
4700 W. Lake Avenue
Glenview, IL 60025
847-375-4709
www.aafrc.org

Familiarizing yourself with the fundraiser's credo

As you continue thinking about ethical and responsible approaches to fundraising, you may want to familiarize yourself with some of the industry standards:

✔ The document "A Donor Bill of Rights" was developed by a number of the professional organizations (including the AAFRC, AHP, CASE, and AFP). This document gives you an idea of the type of exchange valued in an ethical relationship between donor and organization. It's worth taking the time to read the most current version online (go to the Web site of the AFP — www.afpnet.org — to read the full document). Notice how many of the items have to do with clear, honest communication between parties.

✔ Another standard established by the National Committee on Planned Giving (NCPG) details the practices that should be following by ethical charitable gift planners. Check out the "Model Standards of Practice for the Charitable Gift Planner," available on the NCPG Web site: www.ncpg.org.

Debunking Fundraising Myths

This section exposes four myths of fundraising that can hinder fundraisers from optimal performance in their work. Building on the idea that fundraising is a noble profession and that professional ethics drive what you do, you can set about getting rid of some of these attitudes — your own or those of others — by imagining yourself in the anecdotes in the following list. The attitudes reflected in these anecdotes aren't unethical; rather, they are close calls that depend on your attitude about what you do and how clearly you understand your priorities. Following each myth, we propose some ethical guidelines for that type of situation.

The four myths of fundraising covered in the following sections can really get in your way when trying to solicit those donations, so dispel them now!

Myth #1: It's all about the money

Some people say fundraisers only care about money, others consider that fundraisers care about helping others. Which is true?

Making money the whole point

You have a lunch appointment with Mrs. M. You have spoken on the phone with her twice in preparation for this face-to-face meeting, and both times Mrs. M. sounded pleasant but cautious. You review your notes from your donor files as you drive to her house: her personal net worth, her other philanthropic interests, and her personal information. You know that she was widowed last year and that two months ago her son Ted made a substantial contribution to the capital campaign of his alma mater. As you pull into the landscaped drive, you return the donor file to your briefcase — no need for her to see your resource materials as the two of you drive to the restaurant.

You ring the bell and the housekeeper answers. She asks you into the foyer. Moments later, Mrs. M. comes down the stairs. She smiles and extends her hand. You shake her hand and introduce yourself; then compliment her on the dress she's wearing. She flashes you a wry gaze. Perhaps the dress comment was too much, you think. Oh come on, her glance tells you. We both know this is all about money. What will you do to show Mrs. M. otherwise?

Sharing concerns and a willingness to help

Instead of being all about money — seeing the donor as a dollar amount — fundraising is really about the relationship you create with another person — a hand extended, saying "come join our cause."

Not everyone shares your concerns about recycling, music, or the college of your choice. Some people care more about political activism, fighting cancer, finding homes for the marginalized, or getting runaway teens home. When you find someone who shares your heart and welcomes your cause, you've got a potential ally. With some good communication from you and the right conditions for the giver (including a link to your cause, interest in what you're doing, and the ability and willingness to give), helping is a natural next step.

Find the right connection with Mrs. M., one that benefits her as well as your cause, and you can easily demonstrate that this relationship is about much more than money.

If you believe that how you use your time is a sacred endeavor, then how you spend your money, making that choice, is also a sacred endeavor. It's noble to raise money for something you care deeply about. But you still need to sit back and reflect often on what you do.

Myth #2: Lying to get what you want

It's sometimes tempting to tell a little lie or exaggerate to try to get to your goal. In fundraising, insincere tactics don't get you far in the long run. Is a short-term leap in honesty worth a long-term donor relationship? See what you think as you read this anecdote.

A white lie for a good cause is okay

You're sitting with a board member at his house on a personal call with a major donor. You're beginning a capital campaign and hope to secure a lead gift. Tom R. has a reputation for being a great local philanthropist — he has supported everything from the arts to human services to education. Your organization is one he has supported on lower levels for many years. But this is the first time you have approached him for a major gift.

The conversation is not going as well as you had hoped. He is firing questions at you left and right about specific uses of his gift and about guarantees that it will be used the way he wants it to be. The focus from the board was specific about where lead gifts would go, but he wants a personal guarantee from you that he will be able to determine how his money is used. You glance at the board member; she says nothing. You decide to fudge a little, hoping you can figure out what to do later. "Okay," you say, finally. "If you're willing to agree to this lead gift today, we'll let you choose the designation."

What will you say to the board member when you get back out to the car? How will you handle the situation when the donor realizes he can't control the way his funds are applied?

Slick may sell, but authenticity wins the day

The truth is, fundraising is actually a long-term activity. A firm hold on your ethics and priorities, and a clear statement from your board about what to accept and what to resist, helps you fight the temptation to "give in" when a gift you've been pursuing is right in front of you and is yours for the taking — if only you bend a little.

Fundraisers create opportunities for people who care to help others through our organizations. Our ability to communicate that clearly, honestly, and with enthusiasm is not lying — that's spark (see Chapter 1 to read more about spark!).

The right thing to do with Mr. Major Donor in the preceding situation is to be honest about what you can and can't do; if you think the board would make an exception, offer to ask them and get back to the donor tomorrow.

Myth #3: Your donor owes the world something

Do you go after donations with the attitude that people with money owe you something? Or do you try to build a mutually beneficial relationship where you and the donor help each other?

It's about time the rich started giving to the poor

Elias Q. Smith has been the richest man in town since he inherited his family's fortune. He has a reputation for being miserly, and other fundraisers you've known who have approached him have come back with their tails between their legs. You made it a goal more than a year ago to approach Mr. Smith for an upcoming campaign — you have worked extensively on building what you think is a foolproof presentation.

When you arrive at his office, his secretary informs you that Mr. Smith is tied up in meetings all afternoon and won't be able to meet with you after all. He has requested that you reschedule the appointment for another day. You tell the secretary you'll wait. She shakes her head and returns to her work. You sit there, stewing about Mr. Smith's miserly ways. It's about time he gives something back, you think. It's not right to sit on all that money and not do something with it.

What do you say when Mr. Smith opens the door after his current meeting adjourns? Will the look on your face show your feeling of entitlement? How much respect have you shown for Mr. Smith and his choices by not rescheduling your appointment as he requested?

The best donations benefit both the giver and the organization

People give for all kinds of reasons, and nothing is wrong with that. Maybe the donor wants to be part of your organization because of a good experience he or she once had with the same type of organization. Maybe your cause is good for his business. Maybe she wants the recognition a named giving opportunity presents. Maybe he's trying to prove something to his mother. Who are we to question motives?

The most important thing to remember is that the donor/organization relationship is supposed to be a win-win arrangement (to use modern business-speak). Both parties gain something. You create the relationship with a donor who believes in your cause and can help you further it through money, goodwill, word of mouth, and maybe hands-on effort or in-kind donations. The donor gets the satisfaction of helping a cause he believes in, maybe getting a fountain named after him (or his mother), having something to tell the folks at the Rotary club, and enjoying the warm fuzzies from having done something for his community.

The organization benefits from the donor's gift or services, and continues building the relationship by keeping the donor informed about the organization, remembering to say thank you, and generally honoring the relationship.

Give Mr. Smith the chance to find out about what your organization does and respect his right to make his own choice about whether there's a match of interests. If there's not, thank him for his time to protect any future relationship if he has a change of heart and move on.

Some donors are shy

Some people have problems with the idea that if they give to your organization, their name may be added to the engraved nameplate in the foyer. Some people aren't comfortable with banquets and recognitions and fountains and programs named in their honor. These people make great anonymous donors.

Myth #4: Wining and dining donors is all you do

Some folks consider that fundraisers spend their donor dollars on lengthy lunches with major givers. The fact is that most fundraisers have to be very accountable for the money that they spend and how they spend it. Which side of the debate do you come down on?

Fundraisers schmooze for a living

You have a lunch scheduled every day this week. A new contact on Monday, a fellow fundraiser on Tuesday, a board member on Wednesday, a planned gift prospect on Thursday, and your top giver for 2005 at Le Chateau (your favorite!) on Friday. It's going to be a great week. On your way to lunch, you try not to think about the look on your executive director's face when you told her your lunch schedule.

"I'm concerned about the amount of money we're spending to make money," she said. "I'd like to talk about this later this week."

You shrug off the concern and have a pleasant lunch with the new donor. She is actively involved in children's issues and made a trip to Namibia last year to visit an orphanage. The waiter brings the check and you pick it up quickly. Your prospective donor glances at the credit card you pull from your wallet. "Is the organization paying for this?" she asks. "Oh, of course," you respond. Her next question blindsides you. "Is that where my donation will go?"

Fundraisers are accountable for what they spend

Behind the "get-the-check-and-I'm-outta-here!" mindset is the slick manipulator who has his eye on the cash rather than on the value it brings the organization. This type of fundraiser, you may think, is likely to use the funds for the fancy lunches, the trips to St. John, and the pay raises he gives himself. But in truth, nonprofits are called to a high level of accountability. The slick manipulator probably wouldn't get away with it. And the verification on nonprofits' accountability is increasing all the time.

Before a foundation makes a grant in your direction, it wants to see what you do with the money you have, what you've done in the past, and what you're planning to do in the future. Likewise, before a donor even gets close to giving a major gift, she's going to have her financial advisors and lawyers check you out — look closely at your financial statements, your tax filings, and the giving levels of your board.

The donor in this situation has a legitimate concern. You have two issues to deal with here: one, see if there are ways in which you should cut down your spending on lunch checks and so on; and two, explain the structure of your fundraising budget and planning to show that, though a certain percentage of operating funds go towards fundraising costs, the lion's share of donations support the actual programs.

As of June 1999, IRS rules require U.S. tax-exempt organizations to make available to the public copies of their exemption applications and their three most recently filed annual information returns.

Chapter 3

Making Your Case Statement: Your Agency's Reason to Be

This chapter isn't about writing grant proposals — you may read that in Chapter 11. Nor is this chapter about making life interesting for board members. Instead, this chapter is about something even more important — the fabric from which all your other documents, including grant proposals, are cut: the case statement.

You may not be — nor do you have any intention of becoming — an attorney, but there's something to be said for being able to make your case. When you can describe the mission of your organization, your goals, your objectives, your programs, your staff, and your plans, all in one cohesive, well-thought-out document, your donors will be impressed. The people working with you will be impressed. Even others in the fundraising community will be impressed. And all the while, they'll be thinking, "There's an organization that has its act together!"

Stating Your Case

Before you can write your case statement (see "Ten Steps to Writing the Case," later in this chapter), you need to understand what your case is and how you use the case statement. This section lays the groundwork so you're prepared to state your case effectively.

Understanding what the case statement is and how you use it

The case statement, done well, provides the basis for all your other published materials as well. The message you generate in the case speaks for itself through presentations, brochures, newsletters, annual reports, and more. The tone, flavor, style, and focus of this information, carried from one piece to the next, help build the identity for your organization. The fact that you aren't saying one thing in one way in this brochure and saying it another way in that brochure won't be lost on your potential donors. Consistency carries a message.

Another use of the case — especially a good-looking case statement — is the effect it leaves behind. You can't be everywhere at once, and you can't always be the one to represent your organization. But when you want to put the best face possible on your contact with your clients, you can visit them and then leave your printed materials behind. A well-written and nicely produced case statement gives the potential donor the facts of your organization — in more detail than you can or would offer in a face-to-face meeting.

The case statement left behind serves as a reference to the donor: "What did he say that their budget was for summer camp last year?" The case also provides a list of ways the donor can help your organization. The donor can — and hopefully will — look through the materials to find out more about you, your mission, your programs, your history, and your plans for the future.

A case statement is

- ✔ A clear statement of the need your agency addresses, how you address it, what makes you unique, and how others can help
- ✔ A document you can use in drafting all your other publications and presentations
- ✔ An item that requires your board and staff to communicate with each other about the central vision of the organization

A case statement is not

- ✔ Everything there is to know about a specific program
- ✔ Something the board uses to show off its talents
- ✔ A long-winded grant proposal
- ✔ A work of fiction

Getting started with your case statement

Unfamiliar with case statements? Don't worry — here are some questions people often ask as they begin to draft a case statement for the first time. These inquiries give you a quick idea of what goes into a case statement:

- ✔ **How long should the case statement be?** This is an easy one: As long as it needs to be. Now, before you start groaning, check out the steps in "Ten Steps to Writing the Case" later in this chapter for a listing of the items you need to include in your case statement. The actual length of the sections themselves are determined by how much you have to say in each one.

- ✔ **How often should you write a case statement?** Theoretically, you write a case statement one time from scratch — but you update it as needed. Because you have sections for programs, budget, and more, some parts of your case may need revising every year. Other parts, such as the staffing section or the history section, need revision less often, only as changes warrant them.

- ✔ **Who should write the case statement?** Ideally, a person who has a clear sense of the vision of your organization — someone with spark — should write the case statement. But this type of writing can be difficult, and the drier the text, the less likely donors and evaluators will make it all the way through to the end. If you have someone on your board or your staff who is a talented, lively writer, solicit that person's services; otherwise, draft the person most likely to get the job done and then have a committee of reviewers go through the draft and offer opinions, make suggestions, and add information as needed.

- ✔ **Should you include pictures and charts in a case statement?** Your board or leadership group should decide the way in which you publish your case, but, in general, it never hurts to look good. Don't overwhelm your readers by providing too many charts, using too many or conflicting type styles, or shouting at them with headlines that are too big. Simple and understated are best. But a few photos — especially of a program in progress, your new facility, or your cheerful staff — can help hold the reader's interest and build a bit more recognition for your agency.

- ✔ **Would your case statement make a good video?** More and more, as the cost of video production drops and computer capabilities increase, businesses and nonprofit organizations alike are beginning to put their messages on video. You can show the spark you want to communicate to your viewers, linking images — emotional, hopeful, or heart-wrenching images — with your cause in your donor's mind. This can be helpful for corporate and foundation grant applications, as well as introducing your organization to potential donors in another state or country, or on another continent. Consider having your video play whenever somebody hits your Web site (but provide a button to 'Skip the Introduction' for those who have seen it too many times).

✔ **Should you make your case statement available on the Web?**
Absolutely! The more information about your organization the better — for both your donors and your organization. One suggestion, however: Hold back any sensitive financial data from the general public eye. Provide a link so that any visitors who want to see your financial data can send you an e-mail request.

A new IRS ruling requires nonprofit corporations to make available their exemption applications and three annual information reports. If you make this available from the Web (in downloadable PDF format, perhaps), you can save yourself the hours and expense of printing and mailing the documents each time they're requested.

Ten Steps to Writing the Case

Okay, are you ready to get your writing tools out and start writing that case statement? No? You need to prepare to do a little stream-of-consciousness writing.

First, get a legal pad and a sharp pencil, or sit down at your computer and start your favorite word processing program.

This section assumes that you're the person responsible for writing the case statement — the first draft, anyway — and that the document will then be reviewed by your board, your focus group (we talk about them later in this chapter), and staff members you've selected to help with the review process. Of course, if your organization does everything by committee and you'll be drafting the document as a team, take each of these steps, multiply them by the number of people on the team, and pad whatever schedule you set for your tasks (which will vary depending on your goal and the size of your organization) to provide extra time for each additional cook who will stir the pot.

When doing the first draft, write quickly. You can go back and correct or edit later. Just get something down on paper. That's the first step.

In the following steps, we walk you through the process of writing a case statement, using the organization StreetReach, a young nonprofit that serves homeless teenagers, as an example.

Step 1: The mission — why are you here?

The first step is to draft your mission statement. The best mission statements all have a few things in common:

- ✔ They're clear, concise, and easy to understand.
- ✔ They capture and hold the reader's interest.
- ✔ They include a call to action that gives the reader a reason to respond now.

Your mission statement should draw readers in and hold their attention. Start out strong. Be compelling. Describe the issue you're addressing; then tell your solution; then specifically describe your organization and show how it uniquely addresses the problem you opened with. The process looks like this:

- ✔ Big picture (problem)
- ✔ Zooming in (solution)
- ✔ Close up (the specific ways in which your organization addresses the problem)

Getting a clear view of your mission

Perhaps even more important than what the outside world will think of you is what your organization understands about itself. Drafting a careful case statement helps bring a wide range of thoughts into a focused purpose, which enables everyone connected with your organization — donors included — to get a better picture of what you do and what you need.

For example, you know that it's your organization's mission "to identify and reach out to disenfranchised teenagers in the Baltimore community, offering fun, educational, and safe activities that help them build better relationships with peers and parents." But when asked about the mission of your organization, here are some examples of how a few different board members respond:

> *"We're here to serve the needs of youth."*

> *"We help teens in trouble."*

> *"We get kids off the street."*

Although none of the board members is dead wrong in the summary of your mission, none of them hit the nail on the head, either. When people have different ideas of what the organization does, they may be pulled in different directions, which can mean wasted effort, money, time, or something worse. When you define, and stick to, a clear, specific mission for your organization, you assure that everyone's efforts are spent in pulling the organization down the same path.

Board members of StreetReach all have different ideas of what the agency is all about. The agency hires Jane as its first full-time development director. (A development director is in charge of fundraising for an organization.) One of Jane's responsibilities is to draft a case statement. Consider how Jane handled each of the elements described in the preceding section in the StreetReach mission statement:

- ✔ **Big picture:** Homeless teens. Living under bridges, in abandoned tenements, in boxes and doorways in every major city nationwide. Homeless teens often run away as young as 12, learn the prostitution trade weeks later, and eat only every other day, surviving on the scraps left by those who have homes, and families, and futures.

- ✔ **Zooming in:** You may want to think that a city as progressive as Baltimore doesn't have teenagers living on the streets. You may want to think that, but you'd be closing your eyes to a real problem in our city today. Last year more than 350 teenagers lived under bridges, in abandoned buildings, and in the doorways of our community. They lived on the streets along with the shadows of drug addiction, horrendous poverty, illness, depression, and the haunting nightmares of sexual abuse and exploitation.

- ✔ **Close up:** StreetReach is a 501(c)(3) organization that was started with the simple mission of getting help for these kids — whether that means connecting them with their families, giving them bus fare home, finding sufficient counseling services, providing occupational training, or moving them into transitional housing. StreetReach reaches out and offers a hand and a heart to hurting teens, giving them a home, a chance, and the skills they need to create a life free from the horrors of homelessness.

The resulting mission statement should look something like this:

Homeless teens. Not a problem here? Better look again. Come join us and help us get these kids back home to their beds, their rooms, and their families. And for those kids who don't have a home to go back to, you can provide a means for them to complete their educations and pick up the tools they need to enter the workforce, which gives them a real chance to succeed in an adult world.

If you already have a published mission statement for your organization, use it. You may want to tweak it a bit to fit the case statement format, if you like, but remember that ultimately the board will have to support it, too.

Rewriting and refreshing

What is your mission? Can you summarize it in seven words or less? Could you print it on a T-shirt? A bumper sticker? Your agency letterhead? The mission statement of the Children's Defense Fund has several different phrases, but the one we remember most is "Leave No Child Behind," which the Fund has made a registered trademark.

Thousands of nonprofit organizations are out there today — what's special about what you do? If you can't answer that question for yourself and your agency, you're going to have a hard time convincing someone else to join forces with you and fight for your cause. As the competition for fundraising dollars becomes fiercer (which it has), the need to determine "What's special about us?" grows ever greater.

Is it time to rethink your mission? If your analyses of other nonprofits in your area show that you're overlapping services with other agencies, it may be time for a retooling. That requires a lot of thought, vision, planning, and debate, but positioning your agency to ride the waves of change and meet the real needs of your clients ensures the life of your organization and the continued fulfillment of your mission in the future.

Step 2: The goals: What do you want to accomplish?

After you've established the "why" of your organization — the mission — you need to think about the "what." What are you trying to accomplish? Your non-profit organization's response to the need you focused on in the mission statement makes up the goals you want to achieve. Here are a few examples:

- ✔ For an animal shelter, one goal might be to increase public awareness of the importance of spaying and neutering pets, so fewer stray animals live on the street.
- ✔ For a medical research think tank, a goal might be to create a forum for top-level scientists to discuss the latest advances in cancer research.
- ✔ For an arts organization, a goal might be to preserve and promote classic and contemporary art through interactive exhibits in public schools.

The goals for the StreetReach organization for which the mission statement was composed (see Step 1, in the preceding section) are these:

- ✔ To get teens off the street
- ✔ To help teens get home whenever possible
- ✔ To enable teens who can't return home to become self-sufficient

Remember to think "organizational" goals here. You may want to open the new family center by fall of 2010, but if that's still in debate, you can't include it. Better uses of goals are the bigger challenges you seek to address through your agency, such as helping to preserve the natural waterways in your area, improving the reading skills of recovering addicts, or taking arts education into private schools by the year 2010.

Similar but not the same

When you first begin working with the mission statement, goals, and the objectives, the different areas may seem to mush together in your mind. Don't panic — that's normal. There is an important, albeit subtle, difference in each of these very important areas:

✔ The mission statement explains the need that your organization addresses.

✔ The goals are general ways in which your organization seeks to respond to that need.

✔ The objectives list the specific, measurable ways your organization will meet its goals.

And although not a defined section in your case statement, your organization's accountability needs to come through loud and clear throughout the entire document. Your donors and other major stakeholders will get a sense of your accountability, especially in the sections about the leadership of your organization, evidence of financial responsibility, and long-range planning.

Although your organization will have only one mission statement and a few goals, you may have several objectives for each of your goals.

Step 3: The objectives: How will you reach your goals?

While your goal may be to get homeless teens off the street, your objective might be to work with local agencies to find housing for 25 teens a year. Objectives give you a way to tell the people who read your case statement how you will accomplish the goals you defined in the last section.

Make your objectives specific, measurable, and attainable.

Here are a few examples of objectives:

✔ For a community college with a goal to increase enrollment, one objective might be to enroll 100 new students for the fall semester of 2007.

✔ For a farming cooperative with a goal to provide low-cost organically grown produce to the community, one objective could be to organize an annual fundraising dinner.

✔ For an Internet research organization that seeks to provide a forum for debate on Internet thought, one objective might be to host a symposium on free speech on the Internet in the fall of 2007.

✔ For a child-advocacy organization with a goal to improve the educational environment for young children, an objective might be to ensure that each preschooler has a healthy breakfast.

The objectives Jane comes up with for StreetReach (the example organization from Steps 1 and 2, in the preceding sections) show specifically how the organization plans to work toward each of its goals.

Goal 1 is to get teens off the street, so the objectives are as follows:

- ✔ Research and report on the extent of the homelessness problem among teens by June 1, 2007.
- ✔ Develop a trained volunteer group of 30 adults to begin outreach services by September 1, 2007.
- ✔ Provide, as of September 1, 2007, transitional housing, food, and clothing to ten teens coming in off the street.

Goal 2 is to help teens get home whenever possible, so the objectives are

- ✔ Establish links with national agencies for runaway and homeless teens by June 30, 2007.
- ✔ Establish a fund to provide transportation home for teens by June 30, 2007.
- ✔ Identify and contact programs in family mediation in Baltimore and surrounding areas by July 30, 2007.
- ✔ Publish materials for teens and parents on healing relationships by July 30, 2007.
- ✔ Hire two counselors to provide counseling services for teens by September 1, 2007.

Goal 3 is to enable teens who can't return home to become self-sufficient, so the objectives are

- ✔ Offer six-month residency program for teens who can't return home beginning October 1, 2006.
- ✔ Provide occupational evaluations for teens by October 1, 2006.
- ✔ Tutor teens (through use of volunteer time and talent) in areas of need by October 1, 2006.
- ✔ Establish links with occupational counselors to place teens in part-time employment while they complete the residency program by September 1, 2006.

Here are some questions you should be able to answer "yes" to as you write your objectives:

- ✔ Are your objectives brief?
- ✔ Are your objectives measurable?

✔ Did you set a date by which the objectives will be achieved?

✔ Do the objectives answer the question "How will we meet this specific goal?"

✔ Have you included specific program information?

If your organization is using an existing case statement, find out when the objectives were last updated. Because objectives are measurable and tied to programmatic responses to your organization's goals, they will — and should — be revised every year.

Step 4: Programs: What, exactly, do you provide?

Ah! After completing Step 3, you've made it through the rough part — it's all downhill from here. In the remaining sections of your case statement, you get to pull from existing facts instead of focusing on the philosophical whys and wherefores behind your mission.

In the Programs section, you get to pull out the stops a bit and toot the horn of your organization. What are your most effective programs? What are you most proud of? This section enables you to talk about what your organization does and how it helps the people it serves.

In Jane's case, she writes about the TLC Program that StreetReach currently offers, taking medical supplies and basic food and clothing items to kids living on the street. The major parts of her program, which include links to area agencies, reuniting teens with families, and residential training for kids who can't return home, are all programs StreetReach plans to launch this year to further their mission.

Be sure to include a paragraph about each of the programs your organization offers. Then, when you need to use selected paragraphs in a grant proposal (grant proposals are discussed in Chapter 11), for example, you can simply remove the paragraphs that don't apply and leave those that do. See? A minimum effort and economy of work. The case statement helps you write it once — powerfully, and say it infinitum.

Step 5: Governance: What is the anatomy of your board?

Not all prospective donors are board-savvy, but you can be sure that any donor considering giving you a large gift, or any foundation reviewing your grant proposal, will want to know how your organization is governed. Who comprises your board? What different areas and interests do they represent?

Be sure to include the following things in your Governance section:

- ✔ The legal status of your organization. Do you have 501(c)(3) status?
- ✔ An overall picture of your board, including number of members, how members are selected, terms of service, and committee structure
- ✔ Specific information about key people on your board
- ✔ Information about the administrator, or executive director, of your organization

What is a board supposed to do? You may be surprised to see how different one board is from the next — a variety of personalities and methodologies comprise the bigger picture of the nonprofit board. Painting with broad strokes, however, the board makes sure that the organization keeps on track with its philosophical, legal, and financial goals, but for the most part leaves the day-in, day-out running of programs and services to staff members. We talk more about boards in Chapter 4.

Step 6: Staff: Who are the people behind your services?

The next important step is to include information on who actually provides the services to the people you serve. In this section of the case statement, include both general information about how your staffing system is set up and specific information on the duties of key roles. You may want to include summarized job descriptions to give readers an idea of which tasks go with which roles.

In addition to the general talk about the hats your staff members wear, you need to talk about the staff members themselves. It's a good idea here to stick to the key staff members in your organization — people in roles unlikely to change often, such as the executive director, the director of development, and so on. Also introduce key volunteers and people who have been ready, willing, and able to take on leadership for your organization's cause.

Staff will be an important section in all grant proposals you submit. Along with those proposals, you will want to attach the resumes of key people in your programs. As you create your case statement, you may want to request copies of those resumes so you have them on hand later.

If you are a startup NPO, you may not have staff yet. That's okay. In your staffing section, mention that you're a startup organization, describe any current staffing conditions, and mention where you envision your staffing to be a year from now.

Step 7: Location: Where do you live and work?

The Location section describes where you provide the services you offer. You may have a traditional office in a traditional part of town, or you may be an Internet-based 501(c)(3) that does its work in the home offices and computers of various board and staff members. You may work out of a museum or out of a delivery van. Whatever your location, describe it. Explain how the location is right for the services you provide. Show how it helps you meet your goals. And include any plans for improvement and/or enhancement you have for the facility (and be sure to illustrate how that will speed you on your way to meeting your service goals).

In the Location section, include

- ✔ Your address and information about your neighborhood as it relates to your mission

- ✔ Specific information about the location's unique applicability to your function (for example, StreetReach is currently operating in offices at a Community Development Center, which give them access to office support services and a connection with a local job training professional on staff there)

- ✔ The number of people who can be served at your location

- ✔ Plans for improvement and/or expansion

Step 8: Finances: Is your organization financially responsible?

Are you a numbers person? If not, don't hesitate to ask someone who is to help you with this section. The way in which you communicate the finances of your organization has much to do with the credibility your potential donor perceives.

Summarizing your financial picture

Although the Finance section includes your current financial statements, one of the most important things a donor looks for is an explanation — a summary — of your financial picture.

Your summary should include

✔ The way in which your organization now receives income

✔ The expenses you have

✔ Your current financial picture

✔ Your projected financial picture

The most important thing to remember about your Finance section is to write it in understandable terms. Not everybody is an accountant, but everybody knows that 1+1=2.

Where do you get your funds? You may sell tickets, get project grants, have special events, sell memberships, and charge for services. Where do your funds go? Your expenses may include your staff salaries, your location costs, costs of current programs, expenses for special projects, and more.

Getting tips for writing the Finance section

Talking about money is a tough thing to do, and writing about it can be worse. If you remember that you are still simply telling the story — explaining the need, but this time with numbers — you can get beyond financial phobias and get the important information down on paper. In general, remember to

✔ **Fight the desire to detail to death.** Especially when talking about money, people tend to show specifics to the *n*th degree. It's more important in this financial narrative to give the reader a big picture of your finances. The financial statements you provide can fill in the detail for those who want them.

✔ **Remember, it's all about people, not numbers.** Numbers and people aren't mutually exclusive — talk about your numbers in the context of the people they help. For example, use a statement like, "We were able to feed 250 preschool children breakfast on 180 school days at an average cost of 56 cents per child."

✔ **Show and tell.** Charts are helpful in giving readers a quick impression of your overall financial picture. Create charts that are easy to understand, and be sure to title and label them in such a way that readers can get the message quickly.

✔ **Evaluate and revise.** Your board will be reviewing your entire case statement, of course, but you may want to have your financial advisor review the finances section before the initial review. Having a professional take a peek at the numeric data can help you catch any errors or inconsistencies early.

Step 9: Development: What will you do in the future?

What are you doing to ensure your organization's future? Do you have a development plan in place? What does the five-year plan for your agency look like? How does your organization evaluate itself? How do you know when you've met your goals?

Anyone thinking of contributing to your cause wants to know that you will be around tomorrow. If they donate $1,000 to your symphony today, they want to know that they will be able to come hear Mozart in the summer series. The development plan you describe in this section shows your prospective donor the following things:

- ✔ That your organization has a vision for the future
- ✔ That you have a specific plan for carrying out that vision
- ✔ That you have checks and balances in place to ensure accountability
- ✔ That you have credible people monitoring programs, finances, and growth
- ✔ That you have a means of evaluating your own progress and revising goals as needed

This section requires big-time board input. If you're the lone development person or a volunteer putting together a case statement for the first time, you may not know how these things work in your particular agency. Not all organizations have a system of self-evaluation, although everyone seems to agree it's a much-needed facet of nonprofit management. If you're in the dark about these things, request a meeting with your executive director and/or board chairperson. Asking and answering questions about the way your programs get evaluated may just start a domino effect that causes your board to think about these things seriously for the first time.

Step 10: History: What successes are you building on?

Many charitable organizations — especially those that have been around for a long time — want to tell you their history. They'll keep you rooted in your seat for hours, describing great people, events, and influences that came about because of their existence in your community. They'll be glad to show you photos of past volunteers and produce a timeline of significant achievements.

There's only one thing wrong with this approach — it puts your donors to sleep.

Today's donors want to know the highlights that show you have mome
and accomplishments to build on, but their focus is all about today's is:
History is all well and good and is important as a means for gauging how
organization has lived up to its promises in the past, but people giving m
today want to know where the money will go today. They want to join with you
in solving a need today. And they're also interested in doing something today
that will help make things better for tomorrow. For this reason, the History section comes at the end of the case statement, not that it's unimportant.

There's power in history — a reconnecting energy that summons the best of
the past with the hope for tomorrow. Your past successes are essential in
convincing donors that their money will actually accomplish something. The
people involved with your organization catch the spark first ignited by your
agency's founders when they relive the history of the need, the mission, and
the people. But the viability of your current request doesn't lie in its past.
You're raising money today because there's a need for what you do — today.
Speak to that need. Put real faces on the need, describing people whose lives
improve because of your mission.

Polishing Your Case Statement

It's time to sit down and write that case statement. This part is pretty much
like any writing process: You have to craft a well-written draft, evaluate it
objectively to make it tighter and stronger, and then run it up the flagpole
and see who salutes. Then you go back and tighten it some more.

Each of these steps makes for a more powerful and direct written tool for your
agency and takes the load off of you so you don't have to write in a vacuum.

Discovering ten tips for writing a great case statement

After you have the framework for what goes in to your case statement, you
need to polish it up and make it readable. Here are some tips that should help:

- **Make it clear.** Focus your mission statement, goals, objectives, and program information so readers get a well-defined picture of what you're
  saying.

- **Make it urgent.** With so many causes competing today, you need to give
  your reader a reason to care about your cause now. What's urgent about
  the problem your agency seeks to solve? Be sure that the reader knows
  why today is the time to act.

✔ **Make it complete.** Remember the five Ws for news stories — who, what, when, where, and why — and include them in your case statement. Be sure to include these facts in the Executive Summary, as well. That section may be the only part decision makers read, and the answers to those questions are the ones they will want to know first.

✔ **Make it interesting.** Tell stories when you can — both success stories and heart-tugging stories capture the emotions of your reader. Hearing about how parents used your counseling services to help their teenage daughter recover from a suicide attempt is much more effective than listing teen suicide statistics.

✔ **Paint images in your readers' minds.** Remember that visual words and action words activate your reader's imagination. Did your client smile when she received her graduation certificate? Say so — paint the smile in your readers' minds.

✔ **Don't overdo it.** Tugging on heartstrings requires an even hand. Don't gush or overstate. People can only hear so much about Trina's lost limbs and then they start to turn away. Explain, describe, but don't go overboard on the heart-wrenching stories.

✔ **Do your homework.** Make sure that the facts of your statement — financials, program design, staff info, and plans — are accurate and well researched. Have a complete set of case information for board members to review well in advance of the next meeting. That way, people can come to the meeting with a complete set of data, some opinion about what they've read (don't expect a standing ovation the first time out), and a few suggestions of their own. If you have all the facts in place, others can concentrate on helping you shape what you started with.

✔ **Summarize.** Using understandable language is an important part of an effective case statement. Don't let your budget speak for itself — it won't! Write a budget narrative, to explain in real-world terms what your numbers mean. Don't hesitate to summarize and clarify when some good old-fashioned straight talk will erase a few question marks in the reader's mind.

✔ **Include a call to action.** After you get your readers all worked up about your programs and your agency, don't just leave them sitting there — give them a way to help. Your case statement should include ways the reader can join with your cause. Make sure that you talk about how much that new program costs, what you need in the way of hardware to start it, what talents you'd welcome, and more. Invite people to participate.

✔ **Reread, revisit, revise.** This case statement business isn't a walk in the park. Even if you've been writing for a while and you're fairly confident in your communication skills, you'll find that writing a good case statement takes an open mind, a willing heart, and a very small ego. It's meant to be a team effort — something that is forged only after considerable conversation and, sometimes, debate. So draft your best shot, take two aspirin, and ask for reviews — from past donors, from volunteers, staff, and the board — and await the next meeting when everyone gets a turn at being Editor (the one with the Big Red Pen). Don't take corrections and changes personally, either — remember that the ultimate goal is a sterling, clever, but most of all heart-felt and engaging case statement that will represent the passion and purpose of your organization.

Evaluating your case statement

After you've finished the draft of your case statement, put it in a drawer for a day or two (if you have the luxury of time) and then reread it with fresh eyes. When you do, read it with the following ideas in mind:

✔ Is the need compelling?

✔ Are your goals communicated clearly?

✔ Do your objectives seem realistic?

✔ Are your programs described fully?

✔ Does your board appear competent and ready for growth?

✔ Is your staff well equipped and capable?

✔ Does your location provide what you need to carry out your services?

✔ Is your financial section complete and written in understandable terms?

✔ Does your board have a method of evaluating itself and the organization's progress?

✔ Does your History section tell the lively story of your organization?

Who's at stake?

A stakeholder is someone who has an interest in your organization — whether that person is a donor, a volunteer, a staff member, or a board member. When you begin to discuss case statements, it's a good idea to test the primary ideas — such as your mission statement — with a sampling of your stakeholders. Be sure to have clients represented as well as those people who serve them. One arts organization created to support a local symphony forgot to count the musicians among the stakeholders from whom they invited input. Oops. Be sure that when you ask for opinions and suggestions, you ask a wide range of people who care about what you do — not only those responsible for securing the funding for it.

If you have all the basic questions answered, you can take one more look at the case statement before you release it for your board's review. This time, focus on the language used:

- ✔ **Try to paint pictures in your reader's mind.** Images last longer than abstracts. Describe the light in the eyes of the elderly patient, not just the medical supplies she receives.

- ✔ **Write with passion.** Your words will read with passion. "The masterful chords of Rachmaninoff sounded through Sandinsky Hall, pounding powerfully from the fingers of 14-year-old piano prodigy Anna LaFuentes . . ."

- ✔ **Use "alive" language.** The verbs you choose carry the movement of the images. Flash strong words wherever possible. "The Clean Needles program brings healing to an ailing neighborhood in downtown Detroit . . ."

- ✔ **Keep people in front.** Your case statement is, on one level, the story of your organization; but your organization is the story of people in need and your response to that need: "Where did you first learn to read? In a big overstuffed armchair in your family's living room? In your grandmother's lap? Sitting, well fed and warm, in your first grade classroom? Or did you learn the way 12-year-old Eric did, cold, unfed, and dirty, trying to teach himself to read while crouching under a bridge to stay dry on a blustery fall day . . ."

Finally, when the case statement is drafted and it's as good as it's going to get, print it and deliver it to your board for review. When you get the document back, don't be disheartened to see red marks all over it — the case statement is organic, the growing vision of an organization that evolves and changes.

This would be a great time for a board retreat, which we discuss in Chapter 4. Think of it: Your board schedules a weekend away, at a retreat center in the foothills. The leaves are beginning to change — the crisp promise of fall is in the air. Board members review the case statement, debate points, focus their vision, and come back with the completed case — and renewed vigor — to apply to the future of the organization.

Testing your ideas

The case statement gives you a creative way to (1) think through your ideas; (2) get them down on paper; and (3) test them with the people who care about your organization. Testing your case periodically is a good idea, even after you've written a sterling case statement you plan to use to infinity. Reviewing and testing your case helps you determine the following things:

- Is the case still pertinent for your organization?
- Is the need still real?
- Are your solutions timely and effective?
- Are you well staffed?
- What does your board involvement look like?
- How sound are your programs?
- Have others given to your cause?
- Have any prominent members of the community given?
- Are your long-range plans still on target with your goals?

One great way to test your ideas for your case is to bring in a group of people for a focus group. A *focus group* is any group of people you bring together to focus on a particular task, document, problem, or program. Focus groups are often used to test a new idea with a sampling of people and can be very valuable in gauging things that are best not left solely to the "inside" perspective of those who work with your organization on a day-in, day-out basis.

You may want to set up a focus group early in the case statement process, as you're assembling information. You can set the rules for your focus group, but in general follow these guidelines:

- Have something to show the group, such as a draft of your case statement or an outline so they have something to respond to.
- Give simple instructions about what types of evaluations you are looking for.
- Review the case and ask for questions before you turn the group loose to discuss their ideas.
- If you have a large group, let the group divide into teams of three or four.
- Have each group select a representative who will write down the ideas.
- Leave plenty of time for group discussion when the smaller groups reconvene.
- Thank the participants (and send follow-up thank-you cards).

Building on a legacy

Maybe you'll be lucky and you won't have to write a case from the ground up. You may already have the information you need printed in other places, in other forms. Be sure to do some sleuthing before you begin writing things from scratch. You might look for already-published information in your organization:

✔ History booklet

✔ Information brochure

✔ Annual report

✔ Membership brochure

✔ Program overviews

✔ Past grant proposals

Of course, after you find the information you seek, you still need to make sure that the information is up-to-date and reflects the needs of your organization today. The same testing ground should still be in place so that you can show the case statement to trustees, donors, selected clients, and trusted volunteers.

Although focus groups can be helpful in getting a feel for issues you need to address in more depth, don't mistake them for a representative sampling of public opinion. If four out of six people in the group think that your idea is a great one, for example, you can't take that to mean that the same percentage of the general public will feel the same way. Test your ideas, throw them out in a focus group, and listen carefully to the ideas and suggestions offered. Then you can use the preliminary information you've gathered to target and launch a more in-depth investigation, if needed.

Although you may find it easier for someone from your organization to conduct the focus group, having an independent third party facilitate the focus group, especially someone who has experience doing so, can be useful. Individuals deeply involved with your organization may not as easily pick up on nuances as a properly briefed third party. You don't necessarily have to pay a third-party facilitator — friends or acquaintances can often play this role for free because they care about you or your organization.

Remember that inviting people to help is a great way to help them feel included, valued, and worthwhile. Choose a cross section of your favorite donors, people who have invested time, money, and care in your organization and your cause.

Don't ask other people's opinions unless you're willing to accept their input graciously and make use of it.

Printing and putting the final case statement to work

After your case statement is final, edited, revised, and approved, what do you do with it? Print it up in a professional format. Here are some ideas for creating a nice-looking but low-key case statement:

- ✔ **Use a readable typeface.** Remember that the people reading your case may be young, old, or anywhere in between; so don't make the print (also referred to as a font) too small. Generally setting your word processor to 12-point Times Roman is a good choice.

- ✔ **Make your headlines stand out — but not too far out.** You will have headings for each of the major categories, and you need to choose a type size and style that lets readers know that you're changing tracks. A larger font, like Arial 16 bold, accomplishes this. Consider using built-in styles for consistency.

- ✔ **Avoid using too many type differences.** The flexibility of word processing gives you so many different typefaces and formatting choices to play with that you can drive yourself — and your readers — batty by using too many bells and whistles in a single document.

- ✔ **Include charts if necessary.** Charts are a great way to show complex information at a glance, but don't include them if you don't need them. Including visual effects gratuitously may seem like a good idea in the name of holding people's attention, but unneeded information in a case is just a waste of everyone's time.

Finally, after you have the case statement in its final form, you can reuse what you've created in a number of different publications. This isn't only a smart use of your time; it also helps build the credibility of your organization because all your publications are consistent. You can use the information you created in your case statement in virtually everything you publish about your organization, including brochures, newsletters, grant proposals, campaign plans, appeal letters, speeches, press releases, and on your Web site.

Always keep a master copy of your case statement updated with changes, revisions, and ideas that others suggest. You may find that as the years go by, some ideas work better than others, some programs are explained better than others, and some foundations request more information in certain areas because your case isn't quite detailed enough on some points. You can make those over time, improving the case as you go along. Your case statement, like your organization, is an evolving, growing entity. Remember to keep it up-to-date as your agency goes through its life cycle.

Chapter 4

Organizing Your Team: Board Members and Volunteers

• •

In This Chapter

▶ Getting to know your board

▶ Knowing how your board functions

▶ Finding board members

▶ Detecting board problems

▶ Jump-starting your board with retreats

▶ Taking a volunteer multiple-choice quiz

▶ Knowing how volunteers make a difference in fundraising

▶ Finding volunteers

▶ Getting the most out of your volunteers

▶ Tapping into the power of retiree volunteers

• •

*I*n this chapter, we show you how to work with two of your most valuable assets: your board and your volunteers. Your board helps you set your goals and strategies. They can provide tremendous support for fundraising efforts. Volunteers are the people in the trenches who lick stamps, go door-to-door, or process donations. These two groups of people provide the answers to the why and how of any fundraising effort.

Starting with a Good Board

Start by asking yourself a few questions:

✔ What do you do when the board looks to you for answers?

✔ How are boards put together?

> ✔ What are their responsibilities?
>
> ✔ How can you ensure that prospective board members come on board in a role that's right for them?

The board is a very important part of your organization, so you will need to understand who these people are and what they can do for you. Recruiting the best members for your board is one of the most important steps in starting to fundraise.

As a development person, you may wonder what your role with the board should be. If you are the development director or executive director, of course, the board hired you. If you are a volunteer, you may have grown through the ranks into a position of volunteer leadership, which means that you have some involvement with your board.

As the person in a key fundraising position, you may want to know some of these basics about your role in relation to the board:

- ✔ **Share the fundraising.** You are not — nor should you be — the Lone Fundraiser for your organization. The board is responsible for overseeing the mission, development, implementation, and evaluation of the work that's carried out. Each person involved in the leadership of the organization should be willing to be involved in securing the funds necessary to fulfill the mission. If fundraising is not part of your board members' job descriptions, it should be.

- ✔ **Identify prospective board members.** Even if your role doesn't include recruiting board members (in some organizations, recruitment is done on a peer-to-peer basis), your role is key in identifying people who would add experience and assets to your board.

- ✔ **Keep the spark alive.** Part of your role as a development person is to help your board catch the spark if they've lost it (see Chapter 1 to read about the spark); you can do this by providing information, running retreats, or suggesting new roles and committee structures.

- ✔ **Train and educate new members.** Another part of your work with the board involves training new members and educating them about fundraising opportunities, keeping abreast of new ideas and avenues, and apprising the board of needs, changes, and the status of current campaigns.

As a development person, you may find a big difference in your relationship with the board in small, medium, and large nonprofits. In a small agency, you may have a close, team-like relationship with the entire board. In a larger organization, you may work only with the development committee, and even that relationship may have a formal feeling to it.

Understanding Board Dynamics: Wimps Need Not Apply

Being a board member isn't all about prestige and power. It invo_ __.1011, dedication, hard work, and all the responsibility a person is willing and able to handle. Some of the most important duties of a board include recruiting and hiring the CEO; approving the mission statement, the budget, and the fundraising plan; and developing the policies that make the staff accountable to the organization. This section explains the various responsibilities of the board, which can be divided into three major areas (see Figure 4-1):

✔ Organization governance

✔ Community interaction

✔ Growth and vision

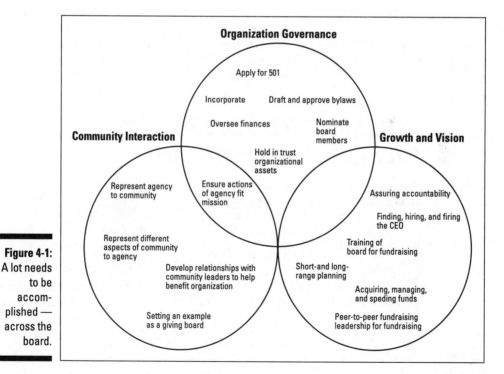

Figure 4-1:
A lot needs
to be
accom-
plished —
across the
board.

Organization Governance

Apply for 501

Incorporate   Draft and approve bylaws

Oversee finances   Nominate board members

Community Interaction   Growth and Vision

Hold in trust organizational assets

Represent agency to community   Ensure actions of agency fit mission   Assuring accountability

Finding, hiring, and firing the CEO

Represent different aspects of community to agency   Training of board for fundraising

Develop relationships with community leaders to help benefit organization   Short-and long-range planning

Acquiring, managing, and speding funds

Setting an example as a giving board   Peer-to-peer fundraising leadership for fundraising

Making sure that you're legal

The board of directors for your organization has the responsibility of governing the agency, both in terms of legal issues and in answering the question, "Are we being true to our mission?" Board members are charged with the stewardship of the organization's assets — financial and material — holding these items in trust for the stakeholders. Some of the legal responsibilities of the board include the following:

- Making sure that the organization qualifies and applies for 501(c)(3) status
- Incorporating the organization as a nonprofit corporation
- Drafting and adopting the corporate charter
- Drafting the organization's bylaws
- Ensuring that the organization operates within its legal requirements
- Overseeing and ensuring the payment of financial responsibilities
- Determining that actions of the agency fit the organization's mission

If you're with a new organization preparing to draft its charter and bylaws, you may want to talk to some of the attorneys in your area. Lawyers often take pride in doing *pro bono* (free or at-cost) work for nonprofits.

Assessing what the community thinks of your organization

There was a time when a family's honor was tied to the family name. A member of the family was thought to represent the entire family in public, in business, in life. Honor was at stake. Reputation was important.

Your organization's reputation is also important. One of the roles that your board plays is representing your organization. Your board members *are* your organization to the community. The choices the board makes — on behalf of the organization or not — reflect on you and your mission. As a group, they are responsible for evaluating and leading the public persona of your organization.

Everyone wants their boards staffed with high-profile members — the people who are asked to serve on everything, the people who have power, money, and friends they can bring to your donor base. As important as these very real assets are, however, is the credibility a respected member of your community brings to your organization. When others see that a known and respected person aligns with your mission, they begin to see your organization in a different light.

NPOs are tarred and feathered with the same brush

Your board is ultimately responsible for moral and ethical issues as far are your nonprofit is concerned. When the board abdicates its responsibility to monitor what's going on in the organization, disaster can strike and the recovery can be slow and painful.

A now legendary fall from grace in the nonprofit community happened almost 15 years ago at the United Way. The CEO at that time had served a number of good years with the agency when he lost sight of his mission and began making unethical and unwise choices. When the fiscal abuses came to light, the whole of the United Way — and, in fact, the entire nonprofit community — was tarnished. Donors wondered whether their money was going to fund flights to Europe or hidden agendas.

After an extensive evaluation of the situation, it was discovered that the board, which had appeared to be the best possible board an organization could have, dropped the ball in this situation. No one knew what was going on. No questions had been asked. They had abdicated their role as guardians of the ethical standards for the organization, and in doing so had enabled a situation that had a negative impact on public perception.

There's a dual side to this community liaison role: the way in which your board represents the community to your organization. Your board may be comprised of folks who represent all sorts of different interests in the community you serve — you may have people who benefit from the services you offer as well as service providers, lawyers, bankers, educators, policy makers, business leaders, and more. They help make sure that your organization meets the needs of the community it serves.

In the old days, the message given to boards was "your main responsibility is to hire and fire the Chief Executive." Now boards have a responsibility to serve their stakeholders as well. And along with the responsibility to stakeholders may come a personal or legal responsibility. Case in point: An arts organization in Chicago recently sued a board member who pledged a major gift and then refused to carry through with the pledge. The moral? Think carefully about what you expect from your board members and be sure that everyone understands these expectations.

Running an effective board meeting

Who runs the board meeting? The staff does. If you're the paid staff, you create and circulate the agenda, you keep the meeting running, and you come up with creative ideas to keep the board sparked and moving forward. Even if another worker in the organization runs the general meeting, when it's time for the fundraising discussion, you're probably up to bat.

Here are ways to get your board meetings off snooze control and wake them up to a new level of productivity:

- ✔ **Set your agenda.** Nobody wants to sit through a board meeting that drones on for hours covering lots of territory that could more effectively be dealt with in committee. Better to be focused, goal oriented, and achieving instead of wheel-spinning, confused, and ineffective. Set your agenda, circulate it before the meeting, and come equipped with ideas to keep the discussion moving forward when it begins to stall, or reel it in when it begins to spin off course.

- ✔ **Be creative.** Talking isn't your only means of communication in a meeting. You can do a conference call with a member of your national office; you can show a video on board fundraising; or have guest speakers, consultants, or clients who receive your services come in and speak to the board. If they can't come in, use online videoconferencing software to pull them into the meeting.

- ✔ **Bring in the other guys.** What's wrong with bringing in the CEO of a competing nonprofit and having him share his ideas with your board? People do it all the time. And often, in the nonprofit community, those achieving are willing to share their ideas. The chairman of the art museum board comes in to speak to the symphony board. The person in charge of the biggest homeless shelter in town goes to talk to the newest shelter. When you invite someone with a fresh perspective to your meetings, your board members begin to ask themselves, "Why haven't we tried that?" or "Is that something we should think about doing next year when we launch our capital campaign?"

- ✔ **Ask tough questions.** The best CEOs are willing to hear bad news. What isn't working? Where do your services fall down? What's being done to improve them? Opening up to hearing not only the good reports but also the bad ones presents some interesting — and perhaps lively — debate.

- ✔ **Build in time to brainstorm.** So many board meetings get mired down in the mundane. Don't just have monotonous business talk — build in brainstorming time. You can reserve 15 minutes as a matter of course to brainstorm on one area of your organization that needs attention. Choose the brainstorming topic when you send around the agendas. A successful brainstorming session leaves your board members thinking, and gives them inspiration to carry through to their next tasks.

Advancing your cause by using your board

Is your organization on track to realize its vision? It's up to your board to oversee all strategic planning: setting goals, drafting objectives, and developing

action items that move your organization in the direction it wants
is what the board is expected to do for your organization to keep it on tr

- ✔ **Hiring, evaluating, and maybe firing an executive director:** A major
  part of making sure that the organization is headed in the right direction
  is the selection, recruitment, and hiring of the executive director. Of
  course, the board's responsibility also includes the evaluation and, occa-
  sionally, the dismissal of the executive director.

  When the board evaluates the executive director, whose input should it
  invite? A recent online discussion in a nonprofit group batted around the
  pros and cons of involving staff in executive director evaluations. Some
  members felt that it was most effective to have peer reviews for executive directors as well as reviews from the executive director's immediate
  reports. Others weren't so sure. One worry is that someone with an ax
  to grind may take a swing at the executive director. The consensus
  among industry professionals was to welcome input from key staff members but remind the board to use its discernment in determining issues
  and courses of action.

- ✔ **Setting up systems of accountability:** The board is responsible for setting up systems to test the credibility and accountability of the organization. This involves financial audits and on-site visits. It's not enough to
  count on the assurances of the executive director — board members
  need periodically to see with their own eyes what's going on at the loca-
  tions where services are provided.

- ✔ **Raising funds for the organization:** Boards are integrally involved in
  raising funds for the organization. They are charged with making sure
  that the resources are there for the mission to be carried out. This
  includes all sorts of tasks related to the acquisition, management, and
  spending of funds.

- ✔ **Making individual contributions:** An important aspect of board leadership involves board members making their own donations. Some members feel that the donation of their time and effort should count as their
  "donation." But many foundations, as well as high-level donors, want to
  see, before they give, that you have "100 percent participation" of your
  board. That means that all your board members contribute financially to
  your organization.

- ✔ **Approving the fundraising plan:** The board is also vitally important in
  approving the fundraising plan for the organization. You may draft it, but
  the board okays it and holds you to your milestones, too. (See Chapter 5
  for more on developing your fundraising plan.)

Recruiting Board Members

What people make the best board members? First and foremost, they're people who care. A board member who has been affected by the illness your nonprofit fights or touched by the services you offer makes a great ally. Hopefully, your board also comprises people who bring the richness of experience, the expertise of their professions, and financial, social, and strategic resources to the organization, the board at large, and the individuals served by the organization.

Profiling the ideal board member: Diversity counts

Although you do hear a lot about board members' financial resources in any given discussion on boards and fundraising, note that board service isn't only for the wealthy. Some board members are selected, at least in part, because they can give the organization access to donors in a certain income bracket. But this, also, is not true of the entire board. A healthy board needs to be diverse and should include some people who receive the services your organization offers.

Are all board members volunteers? Most, but not all, nonprofit boards are staffed by volunteer board members. In a few high-profile organizations, however, board members are paid for their services.

Wouldn't it be nice if, when you need a new board member, you could just stop into Board Members "R" Us and pick one out? Unfortunately, it's not that simple. Here are a few ideas on where to start looking:

- ✔ Businesses who serve the same clients you reach out to. Make alliances with these companies.
- ✔ Stakeholders in the organization itself. Look at clients who have received services or family members of clients
- ✔ Board members in other NPOs in your city. Get a list of 501(c)(3)s and look for those people who may have an affinity for your organization's mission.
- ✔ Annual reports from organizations with complementary missions. For example, if you know that Mrs. Goldenrod is a benefactor of a local art gallery, she is a logical match for your Community Arts Council agency.

Great board members come from all walks of life. The best board members have passion for your organization, the expertise or insight that is needed on your board, some experience in fundraising, and the willingness to commit their time and to work hard. Over 90 percent of all symphony board members have played an instrument. It all comes back to passion.

Picking the perfect-size board

So just how big should a board be? The answer depends on the size of the organization. A small nonprofit may have few members — maybe 8 to 12. A large organization may have 75 active board members, but that group is divided into a number of committees charged with handling different responsibilities in the organization. In a large board, the primary committee is called the Executive Committee; other committees may include both voting and nonvoting members.

A board that's too large can be unwieldy. Simply scheduling a board meeting with 25 people can be a nightmare for a small group with few, if any, paid staff. Have enough members to bring the skills and diversity you need, but not so many that managing the board is a full-time job.

Whether you're dealing with a large or small board, having a committee structure enables the board to divide up responsibilities and make more effective use of its members' already-limited time. The Executive Committee may meet, say, quarterly throughout the year, and the other committees, which are organized to fulfill different parts of the organizational responsibilities, can meet in the interim as needed or as scheduled to accomplish their specific goals. Table 4-1 lists types of committees that often are part of the bigger board structure:

Table 4-1	A Primer of Committees
Committee	*Description*
Executive Committee	Comprises board officers and the chairs of your committees. The Executive Director meets with this committee.
Finance Committee	Responsible for the financial commitments and investments of the organization.
Nominating Committee	Organized to identify, recruit, and nominate prospective board members and officers.
Governance Committee	Oversees the way in which the organization is run, evaluated, and supported.
Program Committee	Responsible for overseeing the organization's programs.
Public Relations Committee	Acts to establish and build the organization's identity in the community through Public Relations.
Development Committee	Establishes, leads, and evaluates fundraising efforts for the organization.

Building a successful board

How can you, as a development person, help make sure that the right people are in the right roles on your organization's board? You can keep several things in mind as you review your board and evaluate the types of roles you need to fill:

✔ Note the age of your clients and constituents. Does the average age of your board members reflect the people you serve? Is the board all of the same generation or does it represent a mix of ages?

✔ At least some members should be deeply involved in the mission.

✔ At least some members should have a business background.

✔ You should have a written job description for board service as it applies to your organization.

✔ You should have a committee structure that gives prospective members a range of options for involvement.

Setting expectations for your board members

When you prepare to talk to a prospective board member about a vacancy on your board, first get focused on what you are asking for and what you expect from a board member. The more specific you can be, the better for all involved. This enables the prospective board member to understand what the role involves, how much time it requires, what the financial considerations are (such as how much he is expected to raise and whether he is expected to give), and how long he's expected to serve.

When you are recruiting a new board member, you need to communicate, however diplomatically, that board members are expected to

✔ Be giving members of the board

✔ Fundraise

✔ Attend meetings

✔ Participate in at least one committee function

Do you have to be wealthy to be a board member? Although it may sometimes appear that board membership is an opportunity for the rich, in reality, a nonprofit is best served by having all its stakeholders represented in its board membership. Most boards don't demand a certain "bottom-line" contribution from board members (although some do); instead, giving to an organization — based on your ability to do so — is what's most important. Later, when you turn in those grant proposal applications, it's important to be able to say, "We have a 100-percent giving board."

In small nonprofits, board members often have to wear many hats. Be sure to identify the qualities you need — links to major givers, money management skills, strategic planners — before you begin the process of scouting prospective board members to fill open seats.

Presenting your case to prospective board members

The link between board member and organization is an important one, similar to that between donor and organization. A donor, after all, needs to catch the passion and be willing to act. A board member needs not only to catch the passion and be willing to act, but also to be willing to get things done and shoulder considerable responsibility over a specified term.

Just as the link between donor and organization should benefit both, the relationship between board member and organization should be an equitable one. To get that synergy, you have to find the right fit. People who have the talent you need and the time to invest make happy, effective board members. People who feel coerced into taking a role or sign up for the wrong slot may be less than satisfied with their role and, ultimately, with the organization.

When you talk to a prospective board member about his or her involvement, be sensitive to the board member's language — both physical and verbal. Is she worried about the time investment? Is she horrified by the idea of fundraising? Is she overcommitted as it is?

By offering board members a range of options, you can give someone the opportunity to gracefully decline a role that would be too much for him, but still keep him involved and invested in your cause. For example, one small nonprofit has a number of different categories for its board:

- ✔ Honorary members who have contributed effort or income or both at a high level and are recognized for their ongoing involvement
- ✔ Advisory members who serve to advise the board in specific areas related to the organization's mission
- ✔ Founding members who function as an advisory council to the executive board
- ✔ Executive members who are the voting members of the board

Spotting the Red Flags

The world of the boardroom in the nonprofit community is diverse. As different as the organizations they serve, boards often develop unhealthy practices. Here are a few bad board symptoms to watch for:

- **Members thrive on micromanagement.** Your board should *not* be in the micromanagement business. Although the board is responsible for recruiting and hiring the Executive Director; for approving the mission statement, the budget, and the fundraising activity; and for developing policies that make the staff accountable to the mission, it should not be providing services. Board members should not go in and tell the staff how to do their jobs.

  Repeat after us: Policy is the job of the board. Administration is the job of the staff.

- **The executive director is the Big Cheese.** Although it's not unusual to find an executive director who also serves as board chairperson, in general, this is not a great idea. Having your exec on your board could one day take its toll on the organization's accountability. If the executive director isn't doing his job and he's also the chairman of the board, who's going to call the meeting to fire him?

- **Meetings are stuck in the past.** If you find yourself spending all your time in the executive committee meeting rehashing old issues and going over things already decided, ask yourself why. Are there new plans on the horizon? Are you moving forward? Be sure to schedule brainstorming time at the end of your meeting, and give yourself the time you need to focus on the forward motion of your organization. Brainstorming gives your board members something to mull over between meetings and ends the meeting on a progressive and inspiring note.

- **Members are no-shows.** What kind of board attendance do you have? If attendance is dwindling consistently, you may have a big problem. Do board members know what's expected of them, meeting-wise? Do you schedule too many meetings? Are your meetings so far apart that members forget where they left off? Do you need a better method of notifying members about upcoming meetings? You can't have a healthy, active board unless your board members are willing to spend time and effort. Keep an eye on attendance and be ready to start tracking it if there seems to be a problem.

Re-energizing Your Board with a Retreat

If someone walked up to your desk and gave your organization a check for $2,000 to spend any way you'd like, what would you do with it?

One organization used a donation to plan a board retreat and came away thinking that it was the best way they'd ever spent their organization's money.

One of the problems built into board service specifically and in nonprofit work in general is that you don't seem to have any time left over at the end of the day to do that all-important planning and brainstorming. "We spend so much time rubber-stamping what we've already done," said one development director, "that we never think about where we're going."

If you haven't had a board retreat in the last year, you probably need to plan one. A retreat, whether it lasts a day or a weekend, gives the board and key staff members time to reflect, get perspective on what they're doing, and perhaps turn your organization in a much-needed new direction.

When's a good time for a board retreat? As with anything that isn't part of your day-to-day putting out of fires, it sometimes seems that there's never a good time. Still, you may want to schedule a board retreat when you are

- ✔ Drafting your case statement
- ✔ Identifying your constituents
- ✔ Doing strategic planning
- ✔ Preparing your annual review
- ✔ Launching a new initiative

Try using these tips for your next board retreat:

- ✔ Suggest the idea of the retreat to the board weeks before you want to plan the event. This way they can free up their calendars and prepare mentally for the meeting.

- ✔ Hire an outside person to facilitate the meeting. If you do, you can participate in the brainstorming rather than lead the discussion.

  Where can you find a good retreat facilitator? You may want to look into an organization whose mission it is to provide just such support to nonprofits. However, if you want to select an individual, look for someone with a background in nonprofits, fundraising, or management. Of course, good interpersonal and communication skills are a must.

What results should you see come from a board retreat? You should see some specifics, such as objectives, action plans, and assignments. You should also see renewed vigor and a more unified vision, plus a flare in your collective spark.

You can use a number of analytic models to help you determine what your organization has to work with and what it needs to work on. SWOT (Strengths, Weaknesses, Opportunities, and Threats) is one such method of evaluation that helps you and your board brainstorm about the various assets and liabilities in your current organization and gives you the information you need to develop an informed and effective strategic plan. Visit www.quickmba.com/strategy/swot/ to study the basics of this approach.

Checking Your Perspective on Volunteers

How important are volunteers? Are they just the people with nothing better to do who donate their time to your organization for free? Do you give them the jobs the paid staff doesn't want to do? Do they come and go as they want, involved or not as the mood strikes them? What, if anything, do volunteers have to do with the fundraising efforts of your organization?

In school we all feared quizzes. So why as adults do we gravitate to them when one shows up in a magazine or on a Web site? Who knows! Take the following quiz so you can understand your attitudes toward volunteers as well as get a take on the proper perspective. (Taking the quiz is voluntary, of course.)

1. The agency needs volunteers because

    A. We can't afford to pay people for all the work we need done.

    B. Volunteers help us extend our effectiveness.

    C. Using volunteers is the right thing to do.

    D. Having a strong volunteer corps looks good on the grant proposals that we submit.

    E. All of the above.

Although each of these answers may be true to some degree (with the possible exception of C — utilizing volunteers is "right" for your organization only if they are needed in order to fulfill your mission), the correct answer is B, "They help us extend our effectiveness." Volunteers aren't around to do your drudgework or to do the things the paid staff doesn't want to do. They fulfill a useful, vital role in your organization, which can enhance and increase your fundraising effectiveness.

2. Volunteers should be expected to

    A. Submit to an interview

    B. Go through training

    C. Show up as scheduled

    D. Communicate with staff if something isn't working

    E. All of the above

Pretty easy one, eh? It should be. A volunteer should be expected to do E, "All the above." Because it's important that volunteers value what they contribute, they need to treat a job as a job, paid or not. Having good, trained, capable volunteers is important for your organization both in terms of the work that gets done and the way your organization appears to the outside world. Interviewing, training, and evaluating volunteers are as important as those tasks in the paid world of employment.

3. Volunteers should not be expected to

    A. Fundraise

    B. Recruit other volunteers

    C. Rearrange their schedules

    D. Play a leadership role

    E. All of the above

The correct answer here is C, "Rearrange their schedules." When someone volunteers time and talent, it's common courtesy to allow them to choose their time of service. If you really need someone in a certain time slot, it's okay to ask, of course. Your best bet is to give a volunteer a range of times in which to serve — people honor commitments more consistently when they've had a say in defining them.

At first glance, you may have opted for A, "Fundraise," but who says that volunteers shouldn't fundraise? Your board members do it all the time, and most (but not all) board members are volunteers. Volunteers can be very effective as fundraising team members. In fact, at one point in our fundraising experience, we brought in a team of volunteers to raise $125,000, giving each of them the responsibility of raising $5,000 through their own donations, friends, families, and peers. Each volunteer was carefully selected and trained, and every one met his or her fundraising goal.

Before you approach a volunteer, know what kind of work you want done. Have a specific plan. Nobody wants to hear, "Oh, we just need warm bodies. We'll appreciate any help you can give us." That sounds as though anybody can do the job, which isn't what the volunteer really wants to hear. Volunteers want to feel that they fill a unique need and that their time and talents are valuable.

4. Happy volunteers are likely to benefit the organization by

    A. Giving monetary gifts of increasing amounts

    B. Remaining dedicated to the organization over time

    C. Attracting friends to the organization

    D. Improving the public perception of the organization

    E. All of the above

This answer is E, "All of the above." Does that surprise you? Studies have shown that volunteers who are happy with an organization want to get closer — and that means taking on more volunteer work, perhaps taking a leadership position, and giving donations that are higher than average. The benefits of a happy volunteer are obvious and many. Friends who see your happy volunteer wonder what's going on at your place that's so fulfilling. People at fundraising events who encounter your volunteer are struck by the image he or she presents — "Here's an organization that is moving in a positive direction."

Do your volunteers wear many hats? In a small organization, a single volunteer may be worked so hard he burns out in a short amount of time. Watch out for the 80/20 rule — 80 percent of the work is done by 20 percent of the people. People carrying the 80 percent can tire quickly, which doesn't do you or the volunteer any good.

5. Unhappy volunteers are likely to

    A. Come to you and tell you what's wrong

    B. Honor their commitments to your agency

    C. Talk about their unhappiness with your organization outside your organization

    D. Work through it on their own

    E. All of the above

The correct answer for this one is C, and you need to act to avoid that. In our experience of both leading corps of volunteers and serving as volunteers ourselves, we have seen few volunteers take the initiative to approach the leadership when something is going wrong. Most likely what happens is the volunteer suddenly disappears, won't answer calls, doesn't show up for scheduled times, and avoids organizational functions. And you can bet that the volunteer's friends are hearing about the problem, even if you aren't.

If you suspect a volunteer is unhappy, address the issue. Call him and let him know that he's been missed. Give him the opportunity to share his feelings with you. After you know what the problem is, you have a better chance of addressing it directly. And, odds are he's not the only one feeling this way, so working through the problem with one person lays the groundwork for fixing the problem entirely.

6. Agencies should recognize volunteer efforts by

    A. Saying "thank you"

    B. Having volunteer dinners

    C. Recognizing efforts with certificates, plaques, and so on

    D. Inviting the volunteer to participate at a higher level

    E. All of the above

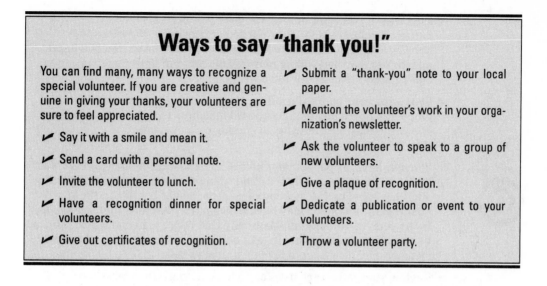

Ways to say "thank you!"

You can find many, many ways to recognize a special volunteer. If you are creative and genuine in giving your thanks, your volunteers are sure to feel appreciated.

✔ Say it with a smile and mean it.

✔ Send a card with a personal note.

✔ Invite the volunteer to lunch.

✔ Have a recognition dinner for special volunteers.

✔ Give out certificates of recognition.

✔ Submit a "thank-you" note to your local paper.

✔ Mention the volunteer's work in your organization's newsletter.

✔ Ask the volunteer to speak to a group of new volunteers.

✔ Give a plaque of recognition.

✔ Dedicate a publication or event to your volunteers.

✔ Throw a volunteer party.

Yes, it's another E, "All of the above." Volunteer recognition is a big part of any agency with a solid volunteer group — if the company wants to keep the group solid. As you know (and, we hope, practice), "thank you" may be the two most important words at your disposal. Say "thank you" to your clients, to each other, to your funders, and especially to those people who practice true philanthropy — the volunteers who give voluntarily of their time, talent, effort, and resources for the benefit of the greater good.

Although the absolutely greatest asset to any charitable organization is its donor base, don't forget that your volunteers are part of that base. A happy volunteer not only gives more, but he also talks about your mission to other people, providing an important link between your organization and friends you haven't yet met. Remember: The biggest reason people give to organizations is because they are asked to give by someone they know.

Seeking Volunteers

Where do you find these wonderful volunteers? This isn't a small task: Whole committees exist to build a volunteer base — to build it, lead it, and grow it. We hope that you've already acquired a thriving volunteer group, and you can start with the list you've created and build on it. But if not, here's how you can find good volunteers:

✔ **Know what — and who — you need.** Identify the areas in which you want to enlist volunteer help. Have specifics, jobs, times, tasks, and relationships in mind. The more you plan these areas, the better your chances of finding — and keeping — just the right volunteers.

✔ **Plan where you want to look for your volunteers.** Where would you find good volunteers for your particular charitable organization? Looking in a vet's office for volunteers for an animal shelter is a logical match. You may find willing participants for your literacy organization among schoolteachers or local writers.

✔ **Start with your board.** Introduce the idea of building your volunteer group at a board meeting. Ask board members to suggest people they know who may be interested in serving on a committee or volunteering their time.

You may have, as part of your board, a nominating committee that is in charge of identifying and recruiting volunteer board members. Additionally, depending on the makeup of your particular board and the size of your organization, you may have a committee that identifies, builds, and trains your volunteer staff. Make sure that they are in communication. A volunteer who isn't willing to take on all the responsibilities of a board member may be willing to take on a smaller task.

✔ **Review your volunteer list.** Take a look at your existing list. Do you see patterns in the volunteers' other activities that would provide access to other volunteers — for example, do some volunteers belong to a gardening club that may be a good place to make a presentation for your organization? Do some belong to a fraternity? A civic group?

✔ **Target families of volunteers.** Often the families of volunteers are a good place to find not only donors, but also to find volunteers. For example, volunteerism among teens is growing and presents a great opportunity for progressive-minded charitable organizations.

According to Giving and Volunteering in the United States, 2001, high-school volunteering reached its highest level in the past 50 years.

✔ **Consider the people served by your organization.** Have you considered your clients as a possible source of volunteers? If you work for a small business development center, it would be a logical step for someone who has mastered valuable business techniques to be interested in passing them along. If your immunization program for preschoolers reaches neighborhood parents, you may find moms and dads who have benefited from your services to be receptive to helping others.

Using Your Volunteers as Fundraisers

As you become more aware of who your volunteers are and what they're doing, you notice that a select group may be of great help to you in fundraising.

Following, we list a few of the ways that a volunteer can get directly involved in fundraising:

✔ Serving on a development committee

✔ Helping you find sponsors for special events or publications

✔ Writing, printing, or addressing letters

✔ Working in a phone campaign

✔ Serving at a special event

✔ Being part of a donor visit

✔ Hosting a donor luncheon

How do you know which of your volunteers would be helpful in your fundraising efforts?

Look for the following qualities in your ideal fundraising volunteer:

✔ A contagious passion

✔ The ability to lead others

✔ Strong organizational skills

✔ A friendly, open manner

✔ The ability to follow through

✔ A talent for working in a team

Remember that involving your volunteers in fundraising efforts takes training. You don't want to send Tammy out into the world to begin cold-calling on people for donations. You do want to think about Tammy's talents, identify where they would be most useful, and then create the plan that would match her talents with your needs.

So let's say that you decide that Tammy would be a great phone person in your annual telethon. Remember that you need to give her plenty of information about her role. Specifically, you want to prepare Tammy for the telethon by

1. **Showing her how to use the phones (yes, some people don't realize you have to dial 9 to get an outside line).**

2. **Giving her a script and going through it with her a few times.**

3. **Giving her an instruction sheet that includes her script, the hours she's agreed to volunteer, and points to remember.**

4. **Remembering to say "thank you" after the telethon.**

5. **Letting her know how she did and inviting her to be part of next year's effort.**

You can find more details about training for phone solicitations in Chapter 13. The point here is the importance of training. Poorly trained volunteers can sink your campaigns and your organization. Not to mention, your volunteers may have a frustrating experience and disappear forever.

Fundraising isn't for everyone. Even if a specific volunteer is a great speaker, an outgoing person, and a valuable member of the community, if he isn't comfortable asking for money, the donors he approaches won't be comfortable either. Part of respecting the volunteer-agency relationship means using the talents volunteers want to offer, which doesn't involve coercing people into roles they don't want to play.

Making Use of Baby Boomers: Retirees as Volunteers

In the next 20 years or so you could tap into a gold mine of volunteer talent. A generation of the population is entering retirement years and has skills you need (think computer and business savvy), good health and energy, and time to commit to your cause. This generation has also paid their corporate dues and longs to get back to the altruistic orientation of their younger years. What are you waiting for?

Here are some things to consider in attracting senior volunteers:

- ✔ These people want to feel their continued value to society. Volunteering is a structured way to feel like part of something worthwhile.

- ✔ Some retired people use volunteer work as a way to reproduce the role they played in a paying job.

- ✔ Older volunteers may need special considerations in terms of asking them to do certain types of work (lifting 50 pound boxes is out!) or needing handicapped access to your facilities.

- ✔ Never underestimate these vital, energetic, and intelligent people who are smart and have life skills to contribute to your mission. People in their 60s and 70s are much more active and productive than they have ever been.

How do you find these folks? Go make a speech at the local senior center, connect with somebody at an adult condominium community, or do a mailing to the homeowners in a more affluent housing development that is known to be home to many retirees.

Chapter 5

Creating a Winning Fundraising Plan

*W*hat do you really need in order to raise funds? Sadly, you can't survive on your good intentions and good will. No donor wants to give to a disorganized organization.

You may work for the best cause in the world, but if you can't demonstrate (1) what you have, (2) what you need, (3) how you'll go about getting it, and (4) how you'll account for it after you receive it, you won't raise much money. In addition to supporting your cause, you have to support the clients, staff, and operations of your organization.

In this chapter we talk about the fundraising plan, your road map, a modus operandi for the resources that will no doubt come pouring in after you get your plan together and begin putting it in action. You find out the various steps involved in putting the plan together. Then we can bat around a few ideas for ways that you can evaluate your plan's progress and improve the plan as you go.

Getting Familiar with Fundraising Terms

Don't get bogged down in fundraising semantics. Here we present some terms that you're likely to see in any discussion of a fundraising plan:

- **Market:** This simply means where you look for funds. Do you count on churches for the bulk of your support? Do you reach out to foundations for your dollars? Does your existence depend on individual donor gifts? The market is the area you turn to in order to fundraise.

- **Vehicle:** In the real world, you choose a different vehicle depending on where you want to go. If you need to go to the corner store, you use your feet — or a bicycle. If you're going off road you need an SUV. In fundraising, different vehicles take you different places, too. You might choose the annual fund (discussed in Chapter 18), the capital campaign (covered in Chapter 20), or planned giving strategies (check these out in Chapter 21) to build different aspects of your organization and meet different needs.

- **Strategic analysis:** This sounds like what it is — strategic analysis enables you to analyze your strategy — or develop one if you do not yet possess one — and find out what your fundraising needs are, what resources you have available, and what kind of plan will help you achieve your goals.

Drafting the Perfect Plan

Remember the case statement (see Chapter 3 to read about the case statement)? The fundraising plan is a different document; it includes the case statement but also several other types of information. While your case statement explains the philosophical need and response your agency provides to that need, the fundraising plan goes further and lists specific steps you take to raise the funds to serve your clients. You need a fundraising plan

- To help you recognize what you have to work with
- To define what you need
- To select your market
- To choose your fundraising vehicle
- To organize the steps required to put the fundraising plan in place
- To demonstrate to the outside world that you are organized and businesslike

As you write your plan, you should include the following items:

1. **A clear statement of your mission (your case statement)**

2. **Your fundraising goal (what program or other goal you are raising money for)**

3. **Your needs statement, explaining what your fundraising market and resources are**

4. **Your financial target**

5. **Your selected vehicle**

6. **Your targeted markets**

When you write up the plan you will include specific information, such as the overall timeframe, the benchmark goals you want to make during that period, resources you will be using, information on campaign leadership, and the fundraising budget for the campaign. (Not sure about that last part? Read on . . . the last section in this chapter titled, "Budgeting Your Fundraising Efforts," deals with creating a fundraising budget.)

Starting with the case statement

The first step in building your fundraising plan is to write your organization's case statement — your carefully expressed reason for being, which we discuss in Chapter 3. If you don't have a copy of your organization's case statement right there in front of you, go ahead and get it. We'll wait.

Starting with the case statement is a must. This statement includes the goals and objectives you set for your organization (see Chapter 3 to read about creating goals and objectives for your organization). Why do you need a case statement before you can create a fundraising plan? Before you can make sense of how to find money to support your purpose, you have to identify what your overall purpose is.

Identifying your goals

Now that you've identified your mission with the case study, it's time to identify what your organization wants to fund. Do you need to generate money for programs? Are you raising funds for operating costs? Perhaps you want to expand your offices or build an endowment.

Most nonprofit organizations have four primary fundraising goals. They need funding for

- ✔ Programs
- ✔ Everyday operations
- ✔ Capital enhancements
- ✔ Building an endowment

Identifying your specific fundraising goals is key to setting up your plan. Just saying "We have to raise money — for everything!" isn't going to take you very far. Whatever your fundraising goal, apply these three questions to that goal:

- ✔ Why do we want this?
- ✔ What tasks are involved in achieving this goal?
- ✔ How much will it cost?

Your answers to these questions need to be focused and specific. What you come up with eventually becomes your goal statement.

Building a needs statement

After you create the case statement laying out your mission, and identify your specific fundraising goal, you have to answer the question, "How do we meet our mission and reach this goal?" The answer to that question is really a list of questions that help you define the big picture of your fundraising plan:

- ✔ What resources do you have?
- ✔ What resources do you need?
- ✔ Which fundraising vehicle is the right one?
- ✔ Which market do you want to approach?

Armed with the answers to these questions, you can create a needs statement that summarizes how you go about raising funds in the first place. You also begin to see a clearer picture of which of these factors you already have in place that you can draw from and what you still need to do before you can go further in implementing a fundraising plan.

Be sure that the people who will carry out the plan are part of creating the plan. Nobody wants to hear, "We just decided that our goal is to raise $1,000,000 this year. Do you think that you can do that?"

Assessing your existing resources

The case, goal, and needs statements lay out your overall approach, but the next step in your fundraising plan is to assemble specific information to include in it and people to help drive it. In most cases you don't have to start a fundraising plan from scratch. You probably have a lot of information and people already available. If your agency has done fundraising in the past in any sort of organized way, you may be able to find the following essential items:

- The donor list
- Histories of how much your donors have given in the past
- Fundraising strategies used in the past — and how effective they were
- Any market studies done by your organization gauging public awareness of your organization
- Public relations materials used in the past (membership brochures, annual reports, copies of press releases, and so on)
- A list of potential donors
- Volunteers or staff who have participated in past fundraising efforts
- Board members experienced in fundraising
- A detailed, specific program or campaign that directly addresses the needs statement

Before you start writing a fundraising plan you have to get into fact-finding . . . also known as getting all your ducks in a row. Investing some time now to investigate what's been done before can save you valuable time and help you focus your efforts and resources. If you discover, for example, that a program appeal fell flat two years ago, you can carefully investigate the "whys" behind that bomb before you launch something similar. Likewise, if you happen across a volunteer who turns out to be a whiz at making connections, you may have a great ally that you otherwise may have missed.

Determining what resources you need

After you have a sense of what resources you already have, you can determine what resources you need. What might you need in order to get organized to raise funds? Following, we list items and people you need to add to your resource list before beginning your organized effort:

- Updated mission statement and goals
- A development committee (not a must, but helpful if you have the people power)

✔ A complete slate of board members (if there are empty seats, fill them!)

✔ A donor list

✔ A development staff person

✔ Training for your board in fundraising

✔ An assessment of public opinion regarding your organization

Setting your financial targets

How do you know how much money you need to raise? The leadership of your organization — the board, the executive director, and the program director — should be the ones to provide that information. You may be in on the discussions, of course, especially when they get to the "Do you think that this is doable?" part, but the financial targets are really up to them to decide.

As you think about your fundraising financial goals, fight the temptation to get stuck in the present moment, considering your immediate — and perhaps emergency — needs. If you are in a situation in which you are worried about keeping the doors open, it may be hard to consider a three- or five-year funding plan. However, having a far-reaching vision is one of the best insurance policies for reaching a distant destination. If you can't see it in your future, you can't plan for it.

Not long ago, working on an annual campaign for a major nonprofit organization, we were aiming at a goal of $300,000, which was made up mostly of small gifts. But twice during that campaign, people walked into the office, took out their checkbooks, and said something like, "You know, I've been coming here for more than five years and just love it. Here's a check for $25,000." We were floored both times. The moral of the story? Count on the smaller gifts, but don't forget to cultivate the major gifts along the way.

Plan your fundraising targets for

✔ The present, which may be funding for a summer program, the acquisition of a van, or the salary of a special speaker

✔ The short term, which may be the next semester, the next year, or until a specific program ends

✔ The long term, which may be a five-year plan or a plan for an endowment fund

Some organizations do extensive testing before they set and announce a fundraising target. In a capital campaign, for example, much of the work is done — and a good portion of the money already raised through major lead gifts — before the campaign is announced publicly. Why? Because success breeds success, and people like to give to a campaign that is going well.

When you can announce your $5 million capital campaign and present graph that illustrate that you are already 35 percent of the way to your financial goal, you inspire others to give.

The all-powerful Gift Range Chart

One tool that is extremely helpful in planning for the realization of your financial goal is a Gift Range Chart. These charts are often used for large campaigns like a capital campaign. They enable you to determine how many large gifts you need in order to reach different benchmarks in your target amount. For example, suppose that the first benchmark of your three-year fundraising plan is to raise $250,000 the first year. The Gift Range Chart can help you find out how many gifts at various levels you need in order to reach that goal. Table 5-1 charts it out for you:

Table 5-1	Gift Range Chart		
# of Gifts	**Size of Gift**	**Raises**	**Cumulative Total**
5	$10,000	$50,000	$50,000
10	$7,500	$75,000	$125,000
14	$5,000	$70,000	$195,000
18	$2,500	$45,000	$240,000
Many small gifts	Varying sizes	$10,000	$250,000

Although an old fundraising joke goes, "It's easy to raise a million dollars! Just find a willing millionaire to write you that one big check!" — in reality, it is the multitude of smaller gifts, along with those well-cultivated major gifts, that bring you to your goal.

Getting the right vehicles on board

A fundraising vehicle is any of the campaigns, events, grants, and so on that you use for your overall fundraising strategy. When you begin a fundraising campaign, you decide where you want to go — what your fundraising goals are. The vehicle is the means of reaching your goals. If you know that you want to increase your donor base by 12 percent, for example, and hit a fundraising goal of $300,000 by year's end, you have established the end point. What you then need is to choose the right fundraising vehicle or vehicles to get you there.

Goal-setting tips

Here are some tips to help ensure that you set attainable goals:

✔ Make sure that those involved in the fundraising are involved in the goal setting as well.

✔ Be specific about how much you want to raise. Do not use vague phrases such as, "as much as we can get."

✔ Set benchmarks for the campaign. Know how many $1,000 gifts you want to obtain by a certain date, for example.

Understanding the different vehicles

What are the standard fundraising vehicles?

✔ **Annual campaign:** A yearly fundraising campaign to raise support for operating expenses

✔ **Major gifts:** May be a one-time gift or repeated large gifts given to support a particular program, project, or improvement

✔ **Capital campaign:** Adds to an organization's assets, for example a building

✔ **Planned gifts:** Adds to the endowment of the organization

How do you choose a fundraising vehicle? The answer depends on your needs statement. If you are raising funds for day-to-day operations, you want to create an annual fund campaign to reach that end. If you are focusing on building an endowment for your organization, think of the planned giving vehicle. Table 5-2 gives you a quick look at the different types of vehicles used for different fundraising purposes.

Table 5-2   Fundraising Campaign Vehicles and Their Destinations

Vehicle	Destination	Comments
Annual campaign	Operational funding	The annual campaign may employ a number of fundraising tools, including direct mail, telephone solicitation programs, membership drives, and special gifts from individuals and corporations.

Vehicle	Destination	Comments
Major gifts	Special needs such as programs	Major gifts can also be "lead" funding, special capital needs, "special" gifts in capital campaigns, or contributions to an annual fund.
Capital campaign	Increased assets for the agency	The capital campaign is an extensive fundraising program that calls for high-level gifts often paid over a number of years.
Planned giving	Endowment funding	Planned gifts are major gifts made from the donor's estate; these gifts are traditionally large and carefully planned.

Direct mail appeals or telephone soliciting programs are not campaigns. In some discussions, you may see these types of fundraising programs referred to as vehicles, but they are really tools that you employ while you're working with one of the vehicles listed here. For example, you may use a direct mail or telephone approach for your annual campaign. We talk about direct mail in Chapter 10 and phone solicitation in Chapter 13.

What about special events? We didn't forget the black tie and tails you have hanging in the back of your closet. Special events can be great fundraisers if done right. When you generate a windfall with your special event, unless you've publicized that the proceeds will be used for a particular purpose, the moneys you raise can go wherever you need them: the operating fund, the capital campaign, a special project, programming, or the endowment fund. We talk more about special events in Chapter 19.

Creating a vehicle comparison worksheet

If you have a track record to use, look back through your fundraising budget for past campaigns. How much did you raise for your annual fund? What did you spend raising that amount? Compare and contrast similar numbers for your direct mail campaign, your donor renewal program, and your special events. Where did you break even? Where did you make significant money? Where did you take a loss? Use Table 5-3 to help you think things through.

Table 5-3	Vehicle Comparison Worksheet		
Vehicle	*Income*	*Expenses*	*Percentage (Income Divided by Expense)*

Discovering fundraising markets

The next step is to identify your markets: From where do you raise the majority of your funds? Again, if you are an existing organization, you have data that gives you that information pretty quickly. If you are just starting up, you need to put some thought and planning into where you should begin.

If you work in a large organization, you are at an advantage because you most likely have all the data you need on past campaigns and their fundraising results. Look through the data carefully, but don't get stuck in the past. Think about current economic trends, community issues, and the cultural climate before deciding on the right market and the right vehicle for your effort.

The best fundraising plans don't focus too heavily on any one area, but mix and match constituencies to make sure that they are raising both short- and long-term funds all the time. Consider the markets in Table 5-4 and think about the amount of time it takes to receive a gift from each.

Table 5-4			Markets and More
Market	*Short-Term*	*Long-Term*	*Description*
Individual donors	✔	✔	Donors comprise the biggest category of givers; short-term donors may contribute to the annual fund; long-term donors, through a cultivated relationship with the agency, may develop into major givers and donors interested in making a planned gift. The goal is to get repeated gifts to the annual fund and cultivate donors into other giving programs as well.
Affinity groups	✔		Affinity groups, such as professional associations or special interest groups, are usually a source of short-term, programmatic funding; a specific time period is usually applied.
Churches	✔	✔	Depending on your relationships with sponsoring churches, you may receive specific program support or ongoing operational support. Although you may receive small to medium gifts from many churches consistently, the likelihood that you will get a major gift from a church is small. The best market for major gifts is in your relationships with individual donors, which may come to you through a church contact.
Corporations	✔	✔	Corporations are often more interested in funding a specific program — something they can see their name on — than in providing for operational expenses or endowment concerns. For a short-term relationship, corporations may supply program or equipment grants; a long-term relationship can be developed with a corporation that serves as a partnering relationship.

(continued)

Table 5-4 *(continued)*

Market	Short-Term	Long-Term	Description
Foundations	✔		Foundations, by and large, are interested in helping provide solutions, which means programs, programs, and more programs. Generally, foundations do not want to fund either annual fund campaigns or the "bricks and mortar" of capital drives. In thinking about your funding needs, coming up with a great grant proposal for a specific program that fits the mission of a foundation is a great way to meet short-term funding goals.
Government	✔	✔	Similar to corporations (but with a lot more red tape), government may be able to provide your organization with program-related moneys, staff salaries, and perhaps even ongoing operational support. Long-term involvement is possible, although you will not build a sizeable endowment from the support of government grants.

Where may you raise funds for a food pantry program, for example? If your immediate service goes to those in your local community, that is a good place to start. Meet with your development committee to brainstorm potential markets. Following, we show the list we came up with:

✔ Community foundations

✔ Local businesses

✔ Area churches

✔ Local arts organizations

✔ Individual philanthropists

✔ Direct mail appeal

When you start small, you aren't working from an established or tried-and-true plan. Begin with those closest to you — people you see often, vendors you work with, community organizations that work with you in similar causes. As your circle widens, so does your market. Although shooting for the big grant from the major foundation is a worthwhile and perhaps profitable act, your overall fundraising plan will be healthier for the long term if you build the steady support with gifts from a variety of sources — many of whom should be close to home.

Avoiding Plan-Busters Like the Plague

Throughout this chapter, we talk about things you can do to put together your fundraising plan and ensure its success. But there are several red flags that you need to watch out for along the way. Following, we list a few of the major ones:

- ✔ **Not knowing your mission:** Seems pretty basic, doesn't it? Basic, but essential. You aren't going to be able to raise any money for your organization unless you know why your agency exists and what need you're meeting. Make sure that you have a strong, clear case before you even think about fundraising.

- ✔ **Choosing the wrong leadership:** The leadership for your fundraising efforts has an enormous amount to do with the way others perceive their roles in a campaign. A positive, can-do person with a willing attitude and strong connections can make a huge difference in a leadership role.

- ✔ **Having unrealistic expectations:** If you raised $100,000 last year, you may be shooting too high to aim for $300,000 this year. Be realistic in your needs statement and in the goals you set as a result.

- ✔ **Dealing with bad timing:** If your organization has recently suffered a setback in the news — a board member resigned in anger; a legal suit is pending; a large funder just denied a gift — this may not be the best time to launch a fundraising campaign. Better to do damage control now, wait until a better moment, and try again later. Conversely, if you've just had a big win, consider getting your campaign going on the coattails of your success.

- ✔ **Doing too much at once:** Are you starting your annual campaign while running a capital campaign and planning an endowment campaign? Fight the temptation to overdo. Although all components are necessary and needed, you can burn out your donors and confuse them with mixed appeals. Better to be clear and consistent — and build your fundraising programs slowly, over time.

WARNING! Can you run an annual fund and a capital campaign at the same time? Sure you can — and many organizations do. But there could be a danger involved. People and corporations who normally give to your annual campaign may think that their capital donation takes care of that contribution as well — and as a result, your annual fund could come up short this year.

To counteract that problem, make your annual fundraising efforts clearly distinct from your capital campaign, and be willing to say to Joe Donor, "We really appreciate your donation to our capital campaign, Joe. Your contribution will help us create a beautiful atrium for patients. And by increasing your annual gift to our annual fund, you can make sure that even a greater number of patients are able to use our services and enjoy the new atrium."

See Chapter 18 to find out more about annual campaigns; for capital campaigns, see Chapter 20.

Budgeting Your Fundraising Efforts

You've no doubt heard the phrase "it takes money to make money." Fundraising dollars are spent to raise funds — that's a fact that some donors may question if your fundraising efforts seem too extravagant. You are in the business of raising money and you had better go about it in a businesslike way. To meet your goals most effectively — raising the funds your organizations need in order to meet the focus of their missions — you need to walk a fine line that includes careful planning, budgeting, and accounting for the moneys you bring in and spend.

A budget is a financial plan that shows how you intend to use your resources to pay the expenses you incur to fulfill your mission. Your budget, which is approved by your board, is an important planning instrument and a way in which you show potential funders — whether those funders are individuals,

When opportunity strikes . . .

Out of the blue, a bolt of awareness may electrify your cause. For example, take the horrendous tragedy of school shootings. This issue has stirred up (and rightfully so) discussion on issues related to teens and families, gun control, media responsibility, and more. If your agency has a mission related to any of these areas, you have experienced firsthand the current of societal awareness as it turned in your direction.

Although you cannot prepare for such occurrences when you are setting up your fundraising plan, be aware of the pulse of your environment. Identify issues that are related to you and keep your eye on them. Take advantage of stories in the news — when the link is genuine — to help potential donors understand better than ever how your organization can help battle the ill they are concerned about.

Does this sound distasteful, as though it is in some way exploiting tragedy? In a circumstance as horrendous as school shootings, with the wave of pain — both personal and cultural — that follows, a natural need for healing and action comes soon after. If your organization can be a legitimate part of that healing and can help provide some of the answers that will keep such horrors from happening again, that's not exploitation — that's a real opportunity to further your mission.

corporations, or foundations — the black-and-white detail of your fiscal responsibility.

TIP

Who drafts the budget? The budget is one of those important items that requires a team to complete it. You may do the first draft of the general budget, if you are the executive director. As a development person, you may be asked to draft the fundraising portion of the overall budget. But, similar to the case statement, be prepared to answer questions and make changes after the board review. And it's never a bad idea to fly your proposed budget past your financial officer first, just to make sure that you didn't miss anything.

Making sure you include everything in your budget

The categories in your individual budget vary depending on the type of work your organization does. There are a few givens, however. When you are planning out the expenses of your fundraising program, be sure to consider costs in all the following areas (the top four are likely to apply only to larger agencies and organizations; smaller organizations or community groups may have only one or two paid staff, if any):

- Salaries and wages
- Pension plan contributions
- Employee benefits
- Payroll taxes
- Supplies
- Telephone and Internet access
- Web site design and maintenance
- Utilities
- Postage and shipping
- Rent
- Equipment costs
- Printing and publications
- Travel

TIP

You may be familiar with Form 990 — the IRS form that nonprofits use to provide full disclosure of their activities and finances. While you are putting together your budget, think about data you need for the completion of your 990 and plan your budget categories accordingly. (You can get a copy of the Form 990 online at www.irs.gov.)

Figuring out the cost of profit

So how much money does it take to make money? Different types of vehicles require different investments, but the range runs from 10 cents on the dollar for major gifts, planned giving, and capital campaigns to 50 cents per dollar raised for special events. This range of costs is another good reason to make sure that you select the right vehicle.

Some nonprofits make it a part of their "good stewardship effort" to keep their overhead costs — in the administration and fundraising areas — as low as possible. The United Way, for example, prides itself on keeping overhead costs to less than 10 cents on the dollar. Other organizations make every effort to ensure that most of the contributions they receive are applied to their mission.

In recent years, we've seen stories in the media about charitable organizations that take huge cuts for themselves — paying exorbitant salaries and taking huge liberties — from the dollars their supporters provide. These few organizations have created a cloud of suspicion that a fundraiser must overcome — today's donors want to know where their money is going and see evidence that it is, in fact, going where you say it's going. For this reason, you need to be open and forthcoming with your financial information, and keep your fundraising and overhead costs as low as possible. This open communication is an important part of creating a solid, respectful donor-agency relationship.

Knowing when to outsource and when to hire

One big question for many smaller nonprofits is when — and if — to hire a development staff member. Can the cost be justified? Should you really be thinking about adding a salary when you are still worrying about paying the rent from month to month? Common experience seems to prove that hiring a professional to create and carry out development efforts more than pays back the expense, but still, this is a big step.

We work with a religious nonprofit that has been struggling lately with this very issue. The question was posed: "If we had the money, what would we do next: hire a development person or a part-time outreach minister?" Much debate ensued and finally it was decided to go with the development person. The thinking was that hiring a development person was the way to grow the organization, which would ultimately bring in the additional minister.

Every organization faces similar dilemmas at various stages of growth. It helps to return to your mission statement, your goals, and your objectives whenever a major planning decision comes into play.

If you aren't ready to bring a development person on staff, you have other options available. You can train a corps of volunteers, but that can be a hefty responsibility if you're thinking about doing a substantial fundraising campaign. Another option is to contract with a third-party company or consultancy. From feasibility studies to campaign strategies, from plans to event management and reporting, third-party businesses are ready, willing, and able to take over campaign leadership and planning. Think about the pros and cons to putting this work into the hands of others who may not be working from the same point of passion that you and your board are coming from. Consider a compromise solution: Hire the third party to work closely with your board to design the campaign, and then let impassioned volunteers do the actual fundraising work.

People who have a passion for your mission must do the actual execution of the fundraising plan, or you'll fall short of your goal and perhaps lose some good relationships in the process.

Observe two sides to the outsourcing issue — you'll find it to be a hot and lively debate if you climb into the middle of it. The best advice here is to think through both sides carefully.

Good reasons to outsource may be

- ✔ Your stakeholders are ready and you have the interest and ability to launch a fundraising campaign but not the necessary leadership.

- ✔ You're preparing to start your first fundraising effort and want to benefit from the expertise of an experienced consultancy.

- ✔ You have a close working relationship with the third-party agency and feel that their objectivity would help you create and run a better campaign.

Good reasons to hire a development professional into your organization instead of outsourcing may be

- ✔ You're a startup organization and want one person to coordinate the design and implement the entire fundraising system.

- ✔ You feel that having a person on staff who is in alignment with your mission is critical to successful fundraising.

- ✔ You have salary moneys available (well, this doesn't happen every day!) and you want to bring in a person to work in relationship with your board to help the entire organization take a more active role in fundraising.

Sometimes, just telling the board, "It's time to hire a development person!" is enough to get them thinking more seriously about ramping up their fundraising efforts.

Whatever you decide, be prepared to discuss the issue long and hard. Whether you choose to outsource development or hire a new staff member, finding the right person for the right job is a key ingredient in making the whole system work.

Remember that outsourcing doesn't have to be all or nothing: You may want to work with a consultant on the development of your mission statement, the planning of a specific campaign, or the training of key fundraising members of your board and staff.

Using fundraising software

Fundraising software can help you organize your fundraising plan and your donor lists and provide valuable reports and analysis of your results. Should you make the investment to not only buy the software but also to transfer all your data into it? The answer is yes, yes, yes!

First, the odds are you don't have to reinvent the wheel here. You can probably import the donor lists you now keep in a spreadsheet or word processing program into most mainstream fundraising programs. After you have your current data in such a program, here are the areas in which you can expect to reap benefits:

- ✔ Donor management, including cross-references among family members and co-workers
- ✔ Volunteer management, including scheduling and tracking of hours worked
- ✔ Membership management, including keeping track of renewal notices, membership cards, and more
- ✔ Pledge processing with cash-flow projections and delinquent notices
- ✔ Major gift management, tracking memorial gifts, and generating automatic acknowledgements
- ✔ Direct mailing and other campaigns

Yes, you may have to spend some time inputting data into the software, and yes, you may have to spend some more time training volunteers and staff to use it. But in the end, it makes your organization keep track of all the details

more efficiently, and your organization profits from keeping a rec
activities, which helps you develop and grow.

Here are some fundraising software products worth a look:

- **DonorPerfect** (www.donorperfect.com) has a lot of cool features; you can purchase the software or buy a monthly subscription online.

- **FundRaiser Software** (www.fundraisersoftware.com) is a simple-to-use fundraising software tool. The basic version is priced at only $89 (but check for current pricing!).

- **eTapestry** (www.etapestry.com) is a Web-based fundraising software, which makes it easy to update your records from anywhere, not just from a single office location. If several people work on your records from their homes, rather than a centralized office, this is a logical option.

You may also consider Internet-based member relationship management systems. You pay a monthly fee for the service that provides you with online tools for managing and tracking online campaigns. A leading example of a member-relationship management system is GetActive (www.getactive.com), which starts at $1,050 per month. A lower-cost, less-polished example is MemberClicks (www.memberclicks.com), which can be as low as $50 per month. See Chapter 17 for more about use of online fundraising techniques.

Many companies offer free trial versions of their software that you can download and try to see if it's right for you.

Part II

Finding — and Winning Over — Donors

The 5th Wave   By Rich Tennant

"We want to thank you for this generous donation, however, the board is reluctant to grant your request that the new research center be in your name. I'm sure you can understand, Mr. Hairbrane."

In this part . . .

This part focuses on the donor — the most important person in your fundraising effort. Meet your donor and find out how your agency and your donor's interests coincide. Discover how to research everything from your donor's interests to giving trends. You see how you can turn a "No" into a "Yes," and how to work with your donor to ever-growing levels of involvement.

Chapter 6

Getting the Lowdown on Your Donors

. . . .

. . . .

This chapter is all about "the who" in your fundraising plan. You find out who cares about what you do and who cares about the people you serve. In this chapter, you explore various ways to find the donors who are most likely to catch the spark of your organization and involve themselves in your cause with money, time, and other gifts.

Finding Your Stakeholders

A stakeholder is, logically, anybody who has some stake in what you do. Your work impacts them in some positive way. Your failure may have the opposite effect. These are the people you want to research as possible donors. Stakeholders may be board members, staff, volunteers, clients your agency serves, or vendors and corporate contributors to your cause.

Different agencies may have different types of stakeholders. Here's a list of people who may be invested in what you do and who may just be able to make a greater investment:

✔ **Your clients:** These are the beneficiaries of your services. Who can better understand how worthwhile your mission is than those who have experienced it firsthand? For example, the family of an Alzheimer's patient who found a daytime caregiver and developed better coping skills through your organization is a potential contributor. The patient's family members believe in your cause because they have had a personal connection with it.

✔ **Current and past donors:** Current donors are those who believe enough in what you do to donate their time, energy, talent, and money to your cause. Past donors are the people who have given to you in the past but, for whatever reason, may not be giving now. At some point, your cause inspired them to give, so it can again.

✔ **Major donors:** These are the people who give at a high level and are already aligned with your mission and your message. They have made the connection between spark and action and already support you, perhaps with their time and effort as well as their dollars. See Chapter 21 for more about major donors.

✔ **Your staff:** These are the champions of your cause. You know that your staff members believe in the work they do because they commit a significant amount of time and energy to fulfilling your mission. Staff members are in the unique position of being able to see the results of what you do and have a sense of the continuing and far-reaching possibilities of your organization. For example, staff members of a research think tank see the research being done, the people benefiting from that knowledge, and the possibilities for the future. Staff members in an arts organization see increasing support for the arts, productions of exciting programs, and strong and growing arts education programs. Your staff, believing in the mission, is a logical potential donor pool for your organization.

✔ **Your board:** These are the people who steer the course for your agency. Who should believe in the work you do more than your board members? Your board members care enough to commit their time, their effort, their vision, and often their professional and personal resources; they should also be giving financially.

Chapter 4 talks about the importance of having a board committed to the cause and the need to get everybody giving. Foundations look for 100 percent board giving as one of the criteria for funding. But beyond that, having a board that includes all-giving members is a good example for all the other stakeholders, from staff to volunteers to clients.

✔ **Neighboring organizations:** These are people or groups in your community that benefit from the services you offer. Certainly you have agencies and businesses in your area that are glad you exist. For example, perhaps you buy used vans for a meal-delivery service from a particular dealership. The dealership is probably glad to get your business and may make a good potential donor. Or, if a local community theater works in tandem with a larger theater arts agency from time to time, the agency may be a good source of donations of money, costumes, or props. Similarly, the human services agency in your area may be able to come up with a list of collaborative possibilities, such as groups you know in your agency's category and the people these groups work with and serve.

Recognizing Your Bread and Butter: Individual and Small Contributions

As we note in Chapter 1, individuals give more to charitable organizations than any other giving group. Gathering all those many small donations can really add up: In fact, they typically add up to more than any single large gift resulting from that grant, corporate sponsorship, or other large gift you've been hoping for.

The smartest nonprofit organizations don't stop with getting the $25 donation from Mr. X each year in the annual fund drive. They want to bring Mr. X along, first securing his gift for a repeat year and then upgrading it to a higher amount. Over time, Mr. X gets more involved with the organization and continues to give at a higher level. Ultimately, his involvement may lead to a high-level gift, such as a major gift, a lead gift in a capital campaign, or a bequest for your organization's endowment.

Small gifts are so valuable because they have the potential to grow into large gifts through a continuing relationship with the donor.

Understanding donor levels

Donors come in all shapes and sizes, as well as giving levels. Your organization's fundraising environment is comprised of four distinct levels of involvement:

- ✔ **Level 1:** People closest to the heart — and hopefully the passion — of your organization, including members of your board, agency managers, and major givers

- ✔ **Level 2:** People who work with or are served by your organization, including volunteers, staff, general donors, members, patrons, and clients

- ✔ **Level 3:** People who may have given to your organization in the past but are not active givers now

- ✔ **Level 4:** People in the general population you haven't reached yet who have interests compatible with your mission but who as yet don't know you exist

Figure 6-1 gives you an idea of the four levels of donor involvement in relation to one another. These four levels represent the groups and individuals in your immediate fundraising environment.

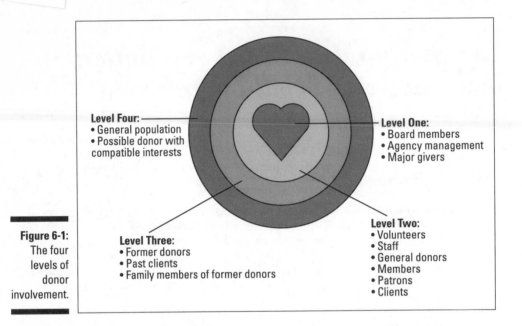

Figure 6-1:
The four
levels of
donor
involvement.

Level Four:
• General population
• Possible donor with compatible interests

Level One:
• Board members
• Agency management
• Major givers

Level Three:
• Former donors
• Past clients
• Family members of former donors

Level Two:
• Volunteers
• Staff
• General donors
• Members
• Patrons
• Clients

Capturing data on possible donors

Write down any names that come to mind in each of the top three donor levels. Later you can plug the data into your donor tracking system (see the section, "Designing an Effective Research System," later in this chapter) so you can follow up on it.

- ✔ First, identify by name those people involved with your organization at Level 1.

- ✔ Now list the Level 2 donors. If you have a small volunteer group or staff, you can list the individuals by name if you want. Make notes to remind yourself of specific people to look up, resources to use, or people to interview for fact-finding in each of these areas.

- ✔ Next, list your Level 3 prospects. Record any people you know of who have fallen off your organization's "active" list.

When people stop giving, it doesn't necessarily mean that you've fallen out of their favor. Maybe they need a reminder. Maybe they need a "we've missed you!" note. People who have given in the past are more likely to give than those who have never given to your organization. Make the most of your existing resources to help build your list and keep it active.

Doing Business with Corporate Donors

In recent years corporations have come to realize that they get a double benefit from giving to nonprofit organizations. They up their socially responsible image from a public relations standpoint, and they retain employees by supporting the causes their employees are interested in. Beyond the benefit of corporate giving, employees of these companies strengthen volunteer programs at these nonprofits and may even serve as giving board members or major donors.

Here are a few questions you can ask as you think about how and whom to approach for corporate giving:

- ✔ Which corporations give to your organization now?
- ✔ Which corporations in your area would have a link to your mission?
- ✔ Which corporations give to organizations that are similar to yours?
- ✔ Which of your board members, if any, have direct links to corporations?
- ✔ Whom do you know at any of the potential donor corporations?
- ✔ Which local corporations could you invite to participate on your board?
- ✔ What corporations might benefit from the positive publicity of being involved with your mission?

If you don't have any strong personal, peer-to-peer links to someone at a corporation in your area, subscribe to your local business journal or get the member lists published by your local Chamber of Commerce. The member list includes all kinds of companies, such as major electrical contractors, banks, real estate companies, and insurance businesses that you can approach for a corporate donor relationship.

Cause-related marketing is a popular approach for corporations that also benefits nonprofit organizations by linking them with a business. The business provides needed equipment or services for the nonprofit, and the nonprofit provides visibility in the community for the business by advertising the help it received. The business then benefits from the "good guy" image and the organization benefits from the exposure and the share of the proceeds they receive. For example, a computer company forms a link with an organization that works with kids with disabilities, or a local business may make itself a visible patron to a particular theatre or musical organization.

If your mission has national or international appeal, you aren't limited to your local area. Your research should continue on a larger scale. Start with the top corporate givers featured in the publication Giving USA (www.givingusa.org). Work through the list and see which corporate giving programs fund the type of programs you offer.

Additionally, keep on top of who's who at various corporations and keep your thumb on the pulse of the giving market. Print resources can be handy; order them online or from your local bookstore.

TIP

Note that some of these publications carry a big price tag, sometimes six hundred or more dollars. To keep your costs down consider buying a new or used copy, but don't skimp and buy an older edition. Always buy the most current edition: it's worth it.

The following publications can provide a resource for your corporate fact-finding:

- Corporate Giving Directory 2004, Taft Group, ISBN: 1569954674.
- The Chronicle of Philanthropy, `http://philanthropy.com`.
- Fistful of Dollars: Fact and Fantasy About Corporate Charitable Giving, Linda M. Zukowski, EarthWrites, ISBN: 0966131428.
- Giving by Industry: A Reference Guide to the New Corporate Philanthropy 2003, Michael Abshire (Editor), Aspen Pub., ISBN: 0834221470.
- National Directory of Corporate Giving, The Foundation Center, ISBN: 1931923051.

Most big corporations publish a brochure about their corporate giving programs. Sometimes the programs are specialized and very focused, and sometimes the programs are general and support a wide range of causes. A common thread runs through many corporate giving programs, however: they often are interested in things their employees care about or in nonprofits that serve communities where their employees live.

Different ways that corporations give

A giant multi-figure check might be the thing you'd be happiest to see, but in fact, corporations give in a variety of ways:

- The ever-popular donation
- Matching gifts, in which the corporation matches a gift made by an employee
- Encouraging volunteerism
- Donated equipment

- In-kind or pro bono services
- Donated space, such as office or warehouse space
- Partnerships, as in cause-related marketing or sponsorships for programs
- Foundation gifts
- Employee days off to volunteer as a group to an organization or a group of organizations

Finding Foundations that Care

Foundation giving can be a great boon to your organization, but getting that grant is sometimes a time-consuming and lengthy process. Do your homework, so you don't waste your time or the foundation's by submitting a grant that doesn't have a chance of succeeding. That means finding good research sources that help you understand which foundation is likely to be a good match to your mission.

The first step is to get your hands on the foundation giving guidelines to see what types of organizations they tend to fund. In addition, check out some of these resources for foundation knowledge:

- ✔ **The Foundation Center,** `http://fdncenter.org`: Find useful statistics, links, and even online orientations about becoming a successful grant seeker here.

- ✔ **Donors Forum of Chicago,** `www.donorsforum.org`: There is useful information here about the three types of foundation, independent, corporate, and operating, as well as links to various foundation directories.

- ✔ **Guidestar,** `www.guidestar.org`: This online research site allows you to post information about your organization that donors or grant makers can browse to find matches to their mission. They also have information about more than 118,000 private foundations. Guidestar's Grant Explorer product helps you look at historical information on foundation funding.

If you're scouting foundations, you can get a foundation's annual report by simply calling the foundation and requesting it. (You can order most foundations' annual reports online now.) Foundations pay out a percentage of their holdings in contributions. How much and in which different areas these foundations have given is available to the public on request.

Asking Your Board All the Right Questions

Luckily, all the work of identifying potential donors doesn't fall on your shoulders. Your board is instrumental in helping to identify the people and resources that can make your organization grow. The most important way to get your board productive in advancing funding is to get them away from the regular stuff they do and do a little dreaming about donor research and support. An off-site meeting enables board members to let go of the operating expense hassles and focus on the long-term picture.

What questions do you put to the board when you get their attention? You may have a list of your own, but as you explore areas in which you find donors to give to your cause, the two in the following sections are important:

Where did we forget to expand our donor base?

As you think through your strategic plan, you will probably discover unmet needs you want to address. And because you are now exploring a new market, these discoveries can uncover some more potential donors. This is one way to expand your general donor base.

The following questions can help you explore areas that your organization may not have thought about yet:

- Do we have new members or subscribers coming in regularly?
- Is our group growing or stagnating?
- What areas of activity could our organization be considering?
- Are any of our programs outdated or unnecessary?
- Have we identified new programs that would reach new populations?
- What is the average age of our members? Do we need to implement strategies to reach a broader group of people?

For example, a symphony that plays primarily classical and pop music wants to expand its donor base. Its members are worried that its current series isn't bringing in new patrons. The symphony needs to try something different. When the board recognizes the need ("We need to reach a new group of people"), it decides to take the symphony out into the community and change the musical selections. The idea produces several new venues, including a hugely successful program called Symphony on the Prairie, which brings the symphony out under the stars with audience members listening from their blankets or tables — complete with boxed dinners — in a natural amphitheater in the countryside. As the success of the idea grows, corporations realize the benefit of providing clients and families with a nice night out on the prairie, and as a result, the symphony gains a huge audience in the corporate market.

In the medical field, this idea of discovered need appears in the area of preventive medicine. For example, years ago, the idea of prevention appeared to work against the care that hospitals offered. Today, people realize that a focus on prevention is better for patients, families, and even hospital systems. Patients quit their sick beds and hospitals open wellness programs. And a new opportunity for giving appears. Today, people who may not want to donate money to a new burn center for the local hospital may instead be interested in helping fund the hospital's accident-prevention program — same donor, same hospital, different cause.

Who did we forget to ask?

In addition to the possibility of adding new programs that bring new donors to your door, you may be (and probably are) overlooking potentially valuable donors who are as close as your boardroom table. Remind your board members to think of friends, colleagues, and other contacts they have who may be interested in donating to the organization.

If your board is lukewarm about using its collective contacts, try a little experiment. At the next board meeting, take a set of 3 x 5 cards, and five minutes before the meeting is adjourned, say, "I am working on donor prospecting this week, and I'd appreciate it if before you left today, you'd list three peers you feel that could be potential donors to our organization. And while you're at it, put a check mark beside those you'd like to suggest that we interview as possible board members for the future."

Using Table 6-1, list the potential donors your board members come up with and add a few of your own, too. You can then find out more about the individuals by talking to the board member who recommended them or doing your own sleuthing. Write the donor's or company's name in the Potential Donor column. In the Individual/Corporate column, you can write *I* or *C* to indicate whether the donor represented is an individual or a corporation. Write the contact's name or how the potential donor is linked with your organization in the Link/Contact column. In the "Ability to Give" column, you can write *Y* or *N* to indicate whether the potential donor has the financial means to give. Finally, the column "Links to Major Donors" indicates whether the donor may be able to open the door to other people in positions of power or affluence. You can indicate *Y* or *N* in this column.

Table 6-1		**Data on Level-4 Donors**		
Potential Donor	*Individual/ Corporate*	*Link/Contact*	*Ability to Give*	*Links to Major Donors*
Jim Smith	I	Cousin uses our services	Y	Y

Your donor list is your most important fundraising asset. Everything you do, all your contacts, all your programs, is linked to the people on your donor list — those who contribute and align with your mission. Remember that your volunteers are also potential donors, and that treating them right, cultivating them well, recognizing their contributions, and inviting them to participate at ever-increasing levels is not only a smart business decision but also helps build the donor/volunteer and donor/organization relationships.

Checking Out Philanthropists

Say that your board came up with some great names of potential donors for you to follow up on. What do you do next?

Or maybe your board came up with a list of duds. Nobody has the type of resources you are looking for. Now what?

These are two very different situations, so we look at each individually.

Pursuing promising prospects

You have a great list in front of you of 15 of the top givers in your city, with links through the board members who know them personally. What do you do next? Next, you need to do more homework.

Your homework now involves finding out personal, financial, and professional information about the donor before you meet her so that you can strategize the relationship you hope will develop. Your strategy includes finding out what type of contribution the donor may be able to make to your organization, what type of investment would appeal to her based on commitments she has made to other causes, and how you will approach the prospective donor when you meet her and when you ask for her commitment.

You need to know at least the following information about high-level donors before you meet with them for the first time:

- The donor's general financial picture
- Why he may care about your organization
- What other organizations he has given to
- How much money he has given
- His pet projects and high-level interests
- His accomplishments and awards
- The people in your community that he respects

The most effective fundraising takes place between peers, which means that for the best results, the board member who identified Mrs. V. as a good prospect should be the one to call on her. He is her link to the organization, he knows her, and he can say, "You know, Gladys, I'm on the board of this organization, and I'm really proud of what's going on here. Last week when I visited the new wing we just opened, I thought of you and Robert and how we all worked together to get Mercy Hospital that state-of-the-art cancer center. I think that you'd be amazed to see what we're doing here for the kids. Would you like to come over for a tour of our facility? I'd like to show you around myself. And maybe we can have lunch together afterward, if you have the time."

You can see that Mrs. V's relationship with the board member is a key component in furthering her interest in your cause. What's simpler than a friendly tour and lunch? And what could be more likely to entice a donor into giving more toward the good work she can see being done at Mercy Hospital? See Chapter 9 for more information about "the perfect ask."

Finding the silver lining with unlikely prospects

Even if your board survey comes up dry, you still have plenty of places to start to build your donor list and look for those high-level donors.

Begin with these ideas:

- ✔ **Examine lists (public lists, that is) that similar organizations keep of their donors.** For example, an art museum looks at the patron list published by the symphony and vice versa.

- ✔ **Keep an eye on your community.** If you get the local paper, you see names of local philanthropists cropping up repeatedly in print. Likewise, keep an eye on national, international, and online news if your mission reaches farther than a local constituency. Watching, listening, and taking notes can help you discover potential resources you may miss if you don't keep your fundraising eyes open.

- ✔ **Visit the places where people go to be seen.** Certain places in your community are equated with a certain status. Perhaps one of the gathering places is a formal garden, an elegant historical inn, or an arts center. Visit these places and read the plaques on the walls; look at the named statues in the garden; pour over the portraits on the walls. This type of sleuthing can show you which families in your area have wealth — and are using it to further causes that capture their imaginations and their passions.

Researching the Internet Way

One of your best research tools today is the Internet. It provides a huge amount of information that is easily searchable. You can use it 24 hours a day and 7 days a week, where your local library or Chamber of Commerce may close its doors every evening.

Here are some of the most useful tools and approaches to use when researching online.

Browsing Web sites

There are all kinds of Web sites that could be useful to you in building a donor list. Certainly if you are researching a potential corporate giver, you should visit the corporation's Web site. But here are some other sites to look for:

- Sources that giving information, such as The Foundation Center (`fdtncenter.org`). You find data, links, and articles to help you do what you do.

- Discussion boards related to your organization's mission may give you some ideas for future programs and how you approach potential donors. By "listening in" on conversations about arts funding, for example, you may get a better picture of your potential donors' concerns and interests.

- Foundation and other giving organization sites to get annual reports and press releases, as well as their funding guidelines.

Features such as bookmarking favorite sites, history lists of sites you've visited recently, and research tools can make your browsing experience much easier.

Using search engines

Search engines abound online, and they're very useful tools. But not all search engines are created equal. The search tools each offers may vary, allowing you to search with questions rather than keywords, for example, or providing advanced search features to pinpoint your search more accurately.

Try out different search engines to see which one works best for you. Look at the help for each engine to see how they recommend that you enter search terms. For example, Google searches for sites that include all your search terms first, where Yahoo! searches for sites that include any search term. Usually sites that include all the words you enter are more appropriate to what you want.

Locating people online

Donor research means that finding out about people and the Internet provides great resources for doing that. White pages for just about every town can be browsed online. Here are other tools for finding people:

- Corporate sites often list board members or senior managers by name.

- Searching by a person's name in a search engine may get you information about the school they went to, a mention of them in a local newspaper article for a social event or corporate promotion, or some mention of their personal interests or family.

- There are people-finder services you can use to find somebody when you know her name and school attended, for example, but don't have a street address handy.

Exploring government sites

Government sites offer free information about trends in the economy that may have an impact on future giving and regulations, tax benefits of giving, and more. If you're planning your fundraising strategy, you may find government sites such as these useful:

- The IRS (www.irs.gov).

- The Catalog of Federal Domestic Assistance (www.cfda.gov).

- Combined Federal Campaign (www.opm.gov).

- The US Nonprofit Gateway (www.firstgov.gov).

Also check out specific agencies related to your mission, such as the Administration on Aging or the Administration for Children and Families.

Designing an Effective Research System

After you identify new donors, how do you keep track of all the information you accumulate? Your donor research system should be comprehensive enough to store all kinds of data from multiple meetings, because you're going to be meeting with potential high-level givers more than once or twice and will need a way to essentially track an entire relationship. Such a system requires a lot of time and planning.

Creating an effective donor research form

The following list outlines the most important categories of information you need on your donor research forms or database records:

- **Administrative Data:** The date the form or record is created, the name of the person creating it, and the way in which the donor was referred to you (board member, other donor, friend, mailing, event, other)

- **Name and Address:** The first, middle, and last name of the donor; the residential and business addresses; phone numbers and e-mail addresses; and the donor's title

- **Interests and Business Affiliations:** The donor's professional position and memberships; foundation or philanthropic interests; awards and honors; key relationships; special interests; and political, religious, and military affiliations

- **Education:** The educational background of the donor, knowledge of any continuing relationship with his/her educational institution, and social or business activities that tie him/her to education

- **Family:** The name of the donor's spouse, children, parents, and pets, including any significant or relevant information

- **Resources:** The names of the donor's bank, financial planner, tax advisor, and attorney

- **Finances:** Information on the donor's income, assets, past contributions made, and so on

- **Gift Record:** A listing of all gifts the donor has pledged and made to your organization

- **Visitation Record:** A listing of all contacts made to the donor by you or a member of your development staff or board

- **Comments:** A fill-in space for comments

These tips create a great-looking donor information form:

- Use more than one page if you need to. If you want the first page to include quick-look items, fine, but be prepared to allow for two or three pages of information for each donor.

- Make the form easy to follow and understand. Don't crowd too much on the page, and organize the categories of information in a logical fashion. You may understand the order of the items on the form, but the person who uses the form after you leave the organization may not.

- Provide a space for write-in visits.

- ✔ Include columns for totaling gifts and pledges.

- ✔ Create a good storage system of binders labeled clearly so you [...]
  which records are kept there (A-D, Corporate Donors, or whatever).

Recordkeeping with computer programs

Most organizations these days have a computer, and if you do, we strongly recommend keeping records in electronic form. They are easier to update, print, and search. Here are some tips to starting your computerized donor list:

- ✔ Use a database program such as Microsoft Access, Excel, or Symantec's ACT! to organize records.

- ✔ If you prefer, find a program specifically geared to donor tracking. Programs such as The Raiser's Edge from Blackbaud (www.blackbaud. com) or PG Calc (www.pgcalc.com) offer extra features beyond simple database record organization. There are also many Web-based programs you can use online without having to install an application on your computer.

- ✔ Make your records granular enough to be easily searchable and usable in generating form letters. For example, don't have a single field for name, but instead have a first name and last name field. Then you can use a mail merge feature to address a more personal fundraising letter to Joe, rather than to Joe Smith.

Tracking campaign related information

Besides your general donor recordkeeping, another donor system you should think about goes along with a specific fundraising effort. If you are gearing up for a capital campaign, an endowment campaign, or simply wanting to build your opportunities for major gifts, you should devise a plan that includes the following pieces of information:

- ✔ The number of prospects you want to identify for major gifts

- ✔ The characteristics you are looking for in major donors

- ✔ The definition of a major gift in your organization

- ✔ A Gift Range Chart for this campaign

- ✔ The number of calls you plan to make per week

- ✔ Your fundraising goals for this quarter (for midyear; for the year)

Evaluating your data

After you identify and contact major gift prospects, evaluate the data you've gathered so far. Ask yourself the questions in the following list to identify areas of information you still need to obtain:

- Overall, have you been targeting the right prospects?
- Do you want to revise the characteristics you are looking for?
- What is the average size of the major gifts you are receiving?
- Is there any area where your major gift campaign is doing really well? Are there areas that need improvement?
- What types of responses have you been getting from donors?
- Are you keeping up with your donor record-keeping system?
- Have you been making the calls-per-week goal you set for yourself?
- How close are you to achieving your quarterly, semiannual, and yearly fundraising goals?

Review the data periodically to fine-tune your fundraising efforts and make sure that they're on track.

Keeping Confidence: The Issues and Ethics of Handling Personal Data

Some things go without saying, but we'll say this one anyway: When you accumulate information on a person of means in your community, you have something other people want. People at dinner parties would love to hear about the net worth of Mrs. V. A con artist would be interested in knowing that you're doing research on wealthy older people in your region.

Fight the temptation to disclose what you're working on — and certainly respect the privacy of the people you are preparing to approach. The information you're gathering is meant to assist you in finding the right match — both for the donor and for your organization — nothing more. When you find the donor who shares your interest in an issue, who has the ability to give and the motivation to do so, it's an equitable, honorable relationship. You help the donor make a difference in an area she cares about and she helps you further your work. Everybody wins.

Divulging information about the person you are researching is bad business, bad fundraising, and bad news. This makes the donor nothing more than a mark you are approaching to "hit her up" for some cash. It's not about respectful relationships anymore. And you certainly won't keep that person as a donor and may get a reputation for lack of discretion that scares away many other donors, as well.

Here are a few other ethical reminders you probably won't need:

✔ Make sure that your board knows and approves your methods of donor research.

✔ Carefully consider whether a donor would consent to this type of research, or would be outraged to find that such research was being done about her.

✔ Be careful about computer security. Don't post lists on your Web site, and don't give access to your records to sharp computer hackers via the Internet; protect your computers with firewall or other security software.

✔ If you are in doubt about a research practice, check it out with your CEO or attorney.

If you leave your position at your current organization and go to work for a similar agency, where does the donor information go? Whether you're legally bound by a confidentiality or non-compete clause in your employment contract or not, information stays with your current organization — no question.

Chapter 7

Meeting Your Donor

*F*undraising is not for the fainthearted. And you'll never be more aware of that than when you sit down with your donors for the first time. What should you do? Picture them in their underwear? Imagine a successful outcome to your meeting? Be careful to present just the right image? All of the above?

Smart fundraising isn't a hit-'em-fast endeavor. It's about relationship building, which enables donors to grow continually closer to your mission and to help increasingly through their time, efforts, and gifts.

This chapter gives you insight into the motivations and potential hot buttons of the donors you meet. You won't be visiting every donor, of course. Uncle Joe, who sends you a $15 check every year for your annual fund, won't expect you to appear on his doorstep to take him to lunch. But Mrs. Benefactor, who gave a special gift to a program fund last year, would make a good prospect for your endowment campaign. As part of building a relationship with her, visits are expected and, hopefully, welcome.

Evaluating the Importance of a Visit

Attentiveness is key to building relationships in the world of donor cultivation. Mailings are fine, but you won't draw a donor closer to the mission of your agency or higher in the level of giving chart by sending her mailing after mailing.

Phone calls are more personal than mailings as long as they are not construed as telemarketing ploys — at least donors hear a warm voice and know they are getting your personal attention — but for a potentially major, long-term donor, plan to make regular visits. After all, you have a shared interest — your organization and the work that it does. Take your donor to lunch, visit her at home; bank on the fact that you are nurturing a far-reaching and, hopefully, continuously rewarding relationship.

When is the appropriate time to begin planning regular visits to a donor? Donors need special, personalized treatment at the special gifts area level of giving and above. Your goal is to secure the commitment of donors whose philanthropic goals match those of your organization. The special gifts level of giving is the first indication that the donor is willing to make a serious commitment to your organization. When the donor gives you this first hint, it's up to you to take the ball and run with it. To nurture this important relationship, you need to do more research, make a greater effort, spend more time, and create more opportunities for interaction with the donor.

Visits — and the time they take — let donors know that they are important, their contributions matter, and you want them to be happy.

Introducing Yourself to Potential Donors

There are some donors who may have been giving to your organization for several years. Some started out as volunteers helping with your big annual event; others may have served on your board for a term or two. Over the years, you may have sent them your quarterly newsletter and a few mail appeals — one for your annual fund and another for a special program fund.

You can observe several things about these donors. They:

✔ Are engaged with the mission of your organization

✔ Have had enough of a good experience to keep coming back

✔ Have increased both their giving and their involvement over the last three years

As you research prospective donors for major gift solicitation, various donors' names come up. You evaluate the donor files, educating yourself about several key points:

✔ What contacts have been made with them

✔ What donations they have given

✔ What other affiliations they have

✔ Their potential for giving (that is, what can you deduce about their financial status?)

Fully armed with a dossier of facts, you must set out to contact each of them for a meeting.

You call a number, and your prospective donor answers. You've rehearsed what you're going to say:

> *"Hi, Mrs. Donor," you say. "This is Jamie from New Beginnings. I was going over our volunteer records and I see that you've been giving both time and money to our organization for three years now."*
>
> *Mrs. Donor takes a minute to process the information.*
>
> *"Well, we're glad to help." She says. "We've really enjoyed our time there."*

As the call continues, you tell Mrs. Donor that you'd like her and her husband to be your guests at lunch, so you can thank them for their involvement and introduce them to new happenings at your agency. Mrs. Donor says that she'll talk to her husband about it and asks you to call back on Monday. When you call back as requested, the luncheon is scheduled.

Now, in order to make sure that these meetings go as smoothly as possible, you need to think about:

✔ What motivates donors to give

✔ What you offer a donor who gives to your organization

✔ How charitable giving is really a win-win proposition

The following section helps you explore each of these different issues.

Examining the Giving Relationship between the Donor and the Agency

Nonprofit organizations, or agencies, exist and thrive to help real people accomplish good works. It used to be that if someone in the community was ailing, you could rally the support right there in the neighborhood, in the church, in the family, to help the person in need. In today's world, the needs are great and complex, and spread around the globe. Nonprofit organizations exist to help people help others — through giving money, time, effort, or material goods.

And, in exchange for all that the donor gives, the nonprofit offers something in return. The relationship is not a one-sided one in which the only dynamic is that the donor gives and the nonprofit takes. Both sides have tangibles and intangibles, with the intangibles probably being the more important. These include:

✔ The donor feeling like one of a selected group that is appreciated and cultivated

✔ The organization feeling the security of being able to count on the donor's involvement and contribution year after year

An equal exchange exists, which enables the client to benefit from both the donor and the organization.

Showing donors the value of their gifts

When donors give to your organization, what do they get in return? Hopefully they see the effectiveness of their gifts — they have the assurance (and proof, through newsletters, Web sites, or other communication) that their money is going to what you said that it would go for. You show value to your donors by providing them with the following services:

✔ **Providing information:** When you help a donor find out about planned giving options, you are educating her about the various estate and tax planning opportunities. By working with her financial advisor or tax attorney, you can assist in designing the right giving plan to meet the donor's financial needs.

✔ **Evaluating options:** Your donor's time is valuable. There's a world of information out there, especially regarding nonprofit organizations. You can help your donor get informed and involved with an issue close to his heart. When you communicate, clearly and simply, the mission of your organization — in print, in person, or on the Web — you help him make informed choices about the charitable organizations he wants to support.

✔ **Interacting and corresponding regularly:** You should regularly show donors where their money is going, invite them in for a visit, and enlist their help, care, and vision in building the organization. Donors get involved, gain appreciation, and become part of a bigger system working to solve the problems of the world at large.

✔ **Being accountable:** After you receive that first fundraising gift, you owe your donor accountability — reporting on what effect the gift has had on your clients, what good has come of it, and how you plan to continue the growth in the future.

Getting more than money from the donors

What do donors offer the nonprofit? "Money!" you're thinking. But that's only partially right. And it's not even the important part. Although your donors show their involvement through financial contributions (we hope), the most important donation they are making is the donation of their belief. If donors don't believe in what you are doing and believe you are capable of carrying out what you promise and are capable of helping the populations you serve, they would not send you a check. The strength of the belief the donors have for you may vary over time and circumstances, and it's your job to keep that belief strong and the interest growing. So don't make the mistake of thinking that your donors offer you only money. Some of the many critical intangibles your donors provide are:

- **Time in voluntary services**

- **Material goods donated**

- **Donations of services and resources**

- **Goodwill in conversations with friends**

- **Visibility for your organization:** If you have a small organization and you're in the beginning stages of the process of building credibility and reputation, here's a tip on how to build that credibility: Go for the Good Fundraising Seal of Approval. In your area, you probably have certain companies and donors who are known for their philanthropic interests. When one of these groups or individuals gives to a nonprofit organization, the rest of the community thinks, "Oh, I guess that they have a pretty good thing going — otherwise Mrs. Endrow wouldn't give to them!" Look for and identify where the Good Seals are in your area, and organize your fundraising efforts to secure a donation from one of the key people.

- **Furthering of your mission:** As an organization, we receive the knowledge that others are willing to join with us in our cause, the understanding that we are doing something right, and the hope that our organization will continue to grow and to change until the issue we address is resolved.

... And sometimes there's a great, big tax benefit ...

The Charity, Aid, Recovery, and Empowerment Act (CARE) passed by Congress in 2003 enhances the value of charitable contributions to the taxpayer under law.

Under this law, taxpayers can subtract all charitable contributions from their taxable income, even if they do not itemize their taxes. The second provision, for itemized returns, gives taxpayers a tax credit rather than a tax deduction, which results in increased savings. Here's an illustration of how this works:

For example, if your taxable income is $100,000, you have no deduction for charitable contributions; you're in the 30 percent tax bracket, your tax is $30,000.

(continued)

(continued)

Now suppose that you make a $500 charitable contribution and deduct it from your gross income. Then the math looks like this:

$100,000 income for the year − $500 charitable contribution = $99,500 taxable income

$99,500 taxable income _×_ 30 percent tax bracket = $ 29,850 tax ($150 saved)

Your $500 contribution saves you $150 in taxes when taken as a deduction from taxable income in the first proposal.

Under the second instance, the tax credit, you can deduct the $500 contribution from the tax liability and save even more:

$100,000 income for the year × 30 percent tax bracket = $30,000 tax

$30,000 tax − $500 charitable deduction = $29,500 tax ($500 saved)

In effect, your donation cost you nothing!

This example saves $350 more than the first, which takes the deduction from your gross income. The second example represents a good savings that your donors will want to know more about.

Checking out what motivates giving

Why do people give? When we threw this question to a classroom full of fundraisers, they gave us these 20 whys to giving:

- ✔ Emotional response
- ✔ Tax deductions
- ✔ Belief in the cause
- ✔ Image
- ✔ Marketing
- ✔ Sense of belonging — joining something bigger than oneself
- ✔ Giving back to a cause that has helped us or someone we care about
- ✔ Getting good seats at a basketball game (personal gain)
- ✔ Peer influence
- ✔ Enjoyment
- ✔ Personal experience with the cause
- ✔ In memory of someone
- ✔ To set an example
- ✔ Pass on a legacy

✔ Honor

✔ Spiritual reasons (tithing)

✔ To have a voice in the larger discourse

✔ Empathy

✔ To make a difference

✔ Because the right person asked

We didn't list these motivations in any particular order. We just want to show that, although you may hope that people give to your organization because they believe in your mission, tax deductions, marketing, or image may sometimes be a bigger reason why a particular donor gives.

If you think about how, when, and why you give to the charities you support, you may identify with one or more of the reasons on the previous list. People have all kinds of motivations for giving — some people-serving, some self-serving. Some motivations have helping others as the goal; some motivations are no doubt grounded in the hope of social influence. As a fundraiser, you can't judge givers' motivations — the why is up to them. The what, how, when, and, hopefully, how much is within your ability to guide when your mission matches their motivation.

We asked the same fundraising class that gave us our list of giving motivations earlier why they thought that donors don't give. Their responses follow (and they're right on target, too):

✔ They weren't asked.

✔ They're unhappy with the way the organization is handling finances.

✔ Their interests and priorities have changed.

✔ Nobody said thank you the last time.

✔ They no longer have the resources to give.

✔ They didn't like the manner in which they were approached.

✔ They're insecure about the organization.

✔ The organization doesn't have long-term plans.

✔ They weren't asked for the right amount.

✔ They aren't motivated by the cause.

✔ They haven't been part of a culture of giving.

✔ They have compassion fatigue.

What is compassion fatigue? In recent years, the term *compassion fatigue* has been used to describe the situation in which the donor is bombarded and overloaded with calls for help. This month it's a hurricane; next month it's a wildfire. The food pantry needs help next, and the preschool for the developmentally disabled may close its doors if you don't help now.

Donors can be spread too thin, and when they are, they begin shutting off their charitable involvements. For this reason, we try to not paint pictures too black, needs too dire, or situations too insurmountable. Too bleak a situation can make the donor feel that the task at hand is too daunting and may not be doable for her. Instead, you want donors to feel that they are part of a winning team, working toward a thought-out effort, and supplying funds in an area that is sure to bring relief to the clients who are being served.

You may find it hard to believe that one of the major reasons donors don't give is that they are never asked. But it's true! Can you imagine visiting with a donor, having several conversations, having lunch, and then not asking them to make a donation? Rejection is a universal fear, and people everywhere try to avoid it. Fundraisers often set up the conversation to lead to asking for a major gift and then back off or chicken out. Why? Hinting for a gift is safer if you are anticipating a No. (See Chapter 9 to read about how to ask the ask directly and sidestep the whole rejection issue at the same time.)

Cultivating the Initial Relationship

As you continue to talk and get to know your potential donor, you are building trust and discovering where your shared ideals lie. If the situation is the right one, by the end of the meeting you should plant the ideas that

- ✔ You value the donor's involvement with your organization.
- ✔ You would like to involve them on a deeper level.
- ✔ You have ideas for helping them meet their estate goals and avoid excessive taxation.
- ✔ You would like to write up a few ideas and meet with them in the coming weeks.

At this point, keep the trust building. At the end of your luncheon, you want the donor leaving with a good feeling about you and her relationship with your organization. So avoid the following when you are in this initial relationship-building stage:

✔ **Making assumptions:** If the donors are in their 30s, you may assume that they aren't interested in an estate planning option — but you could be missing an opportunity. Dan's father died at 45, and he's sensitive to the issues involved with caring for one's family long term in the event of an untimely death. The key here is to listen, listen, listen to your donors, and let them lead you to the gift area that is right for them.

✔ **Being afraid to bargain down:** When you are at a point where you are ready to ask for a specific gift, don't be afraid to ask for a lesser amount if the donor rejects your initial amount. Generally, most people are flattered that you considered them part of a group that could give the amount you requested, so no harm done. If Dan says no to $10,000, don't be afraid to say, "Would you be more comfortable with $7,500, given over three years?"

✔ **Promising more than you can deliver:** Some fundraisers get focused on the goal and promise the moon to a donor in order to secure a gift. If you're one of those people, fight the temptation. Your every interaction with your donor either builds credibility or detracts from it, and making promises you can't possibly keep only hurts your organization in the long run.

✔ **Being vague about how the money's going to be used — not being specific:** Today's donor, having grown up in an age of media exposé, is somewhat leery about how nonprofit organizations spend their contributions. Be forthcoming with your information — it speaks volumes about your credibility. And remember that even if you don't want to reveal information about the sources of your income and how it is used, a ruling by the IRS makes it mandatory for you to make available to the general public IRS Form 990 whenever it is requested.

✔ **Forgetting to say thank you:** How can something so simple be overlooked? Easily — because organizations often focus on getting and not on receiving. Recognizing your donor by saying thank you, sending a card, making a phone call, or planning a luncheon needs to comprise about 20 percent of your fundraising time. Seem like a lot of time? It's not if you recognize that your primary goal is building relationships with your donors. "Thank you" are two of the best friendship-building words in our language.

One way to recognize your donors and strengthen their relationships with your organization is to get your donors together at a dinner or other social gathering. One nonprofit we worked with held cocktail parties for people who gave $5,000 or more. The receptions were a way of saying thank you — and were very popular with the donors. During the evening, donors exchanged ideas and information about the organization, such as why they gave, how they became involved, and what they liked about it, which makes everybody feel good about what they're doing. Donors also often met people they admired in the community and felt that their choices were affirmed. The internal message was, "Wow! I didn't know she supported this organization! This must be a great place!"

At such an evening for donors, the admired person's involvement serves as a kind of seal of approval for you, which translates into more passion in the hearts and minds of the donors who attend the special evening for donors.

An even better twist to a donor recognition dinner is to get a sponsor to underwrite the meal for you. You can have a box lunch or a format fete brought in, rewarding your donors and giving visibility to your sponsor — and it won't come out of your budget! Everybody wins!

Chapter 8

Cultivating Major Givers

*E*ach and every donor who has given to your organization in the past, gives today, or will give tomorrow is important to the continuation of your mission. The donor who gives substantially to your organization is one of your primary stakeholders and is close enough to care in a big way. This chapter takes a look at the special relationship you nurture with major givers and helps you make sure that you're acknowledging their gifts and commitment appropriately.

Finding the Holy Grail of Fundraising — The Major Gift

A major gift in your organization may be completely different than that in another organization. The size of the major gift is related to the size of the organization. For example, if your organization is a small charity, a gift of $5,000 would be considered a major gift. But if your organization is a major metropolitan orchestra, a gift of $5,000,000 would be considered a major gift. (Okay, that would be a major gift for any organization!)

There is no hard-and-fast rule about what constitutes a major gift. What you consider "major" depends on the average size of the gifts you receive, the size of your annual budget, and your expectations and plans for future growth.

Planning your way to major gifts

When do you get major gifts? The most logical answer is "Anytime a donor wants to give one!" But fundraisers often plan to secure major gifts when they gear up for specific fundraising campaigns. A major gift often serves as the very foundation of a campaign, ensuring the success of the campaign before the organization launches it completely. For example:

- ✔ You're planning a capital campaign where you need to determine how many major gifts you need in each of several ranges to take you to your goal. Creating a Gift Range Chart can help you determine this information. (See Chapter 5 to find out how to create a Gift Range Chart.)

- ✔ You're launching a new program and want to get major gifts from lead givers to set an example for others.

- ✔ You ask a board member to donate a major gift as a "challenge grant" to get other members to give.

- ✔ You're building an endowment fund and plan to use major gift strategies and planned giving opportunities to bring in those funds.

You have a major giving program even if you're a small organization just starting out because you need to cultivate low-level donors over time and grow them into major donors. The normal progression of fundraising is to bring the donor closer, which also means increasing the amount of giving along the way. If you haven't thought about your current giving program as leading to major gifts, explore a new and profitable area!

Chapter 21 reviews the major gift process in more detail.

Reviving your pool of current donors

Before you begin targeting major gifts you need make sure that your donor list is current and active. Your organization already has a record of who has given major gifts to your organization in the past. You need to find this information and scour it. Who has given in the past and is still active in the organization today? Has anyone who has given before disappeared? If so, you can follow up and try to find out why they are no longer active in your organization. Maybe another contact from you is just what the donor needs to get reinvolved in your organization.

After you find the information on gifts made to your organization, make a list of all the major gifts your organization has received in the last three years. Then for each gift listed, include information on what program the money was targeted for (if any), the amount given, the terms of the gift (paid in one year, over three years, and so on), and of course, the donor who gave the gift. How have these gifts been used? What activity have these donors had since they gave those gifts? These donors can still be active in your organization, with the proper attention.

Of course, unforeseen things happen and sometimes organizations fall out of favor with a donor for one reason or another. But being new to the position gives you a great excuse — when you call you can say, "Mrs. Williams, I'm the new development person at StreetReach, and I can see that you were very active in 1997 and 1998, and your involvement really helped our organization. I'm calling to introduce myself, thank you for what you did with us in the past, and invite you back!"

Targeting your major gifts

As we discuss in Chapter 5, one of the first steps in effective fundraising is to know what your dollar goal is. You may be trying to raise $30,000 or $3,000,000 this year. If you plan to renovate your building, you have to figure the renovation cost. If you need money for that music outreach program, you need to determine how much. Before you make a solid plan for the how-when-where-and-why of major gifts, you need to know the "how much" — as in how much you need to raise.

After you know your dollar goal, you can create a Gift Range Chart to help you determine the kind of major gifts you're looking for and how many of them you need.

Your fundraising plan — and the Gift Range Chart — won't include all major gifts. You will have several different major gift levels, such as $10,000, $5,000, and $2,500 and also categories for lesser gifts. Not every giver makes the same level of gift, of course, and some, given a choice and gentle encouragement, may give a much higher amount than you expected!

Major corporations are, more and more, a good source of major gifts, so much so that we dedicate an entire chapter to them. Go to Chapter 22 for detailed information about soliciting corporate gifts.

Cultivating donors who have a lot to give

After you determine how many major gifts you need to reach your fundraising goal, you need to begin thinking about which donors can help get you there. Where can you find major donors? The possibilities are endless! Here's a list of where you can begin to look:

- ✔ On your board
- ✔ On the boards of other organizations similar to your own
- ✔ In the community, making waves

- ✔ In the community, making headlines
- ✔ In the community, making money
- ✔ In the ranks of your volunteer corps
- ✔ On your donor list

What's your best tool for finding major donors? Your donor list! With that in mind, you really need an up-to-date, complete list that you use regularly. You not only find out more about your donors (and make better use of the information you already have), but also may find donors "popping out at you" that you overlooked before. Review your list regularly!

Soliciting major gifts for human services organizations can be challenging because human services are ongoing, dynamically changing services. For human service organizations, one successful area for major gifts is in the endowment area. In this case, the organization sets up an endowment fund to produce an ongoing source of funds, which guarantees that the service will continue for future generations. We cover endowments in Chapter 23.

Steps to cultivating major donors

The level closest to your organization involves those stakeholders, clients, and board members who obviously share the mission of your organization. (Read about the levels of giving in Chapter 6.) They care deeply about the cause and the furthering of your mission. Those are the people who are also going to be your highest-level donors, because their passion is in line with your own.

But most major donors don't simply start out being major donors. Often they grow closer to your organization over time, perhaps starting out by making a $25 donation to your annual fund and then gradually moving closer to the heart of your organization.

The major donor profile

If you're not sure what your major donors will be like, consider these common characteristics that we find in our daily work:

- ✔ Major donors often are involved in a number of community activities.

- ✔ Major donors have often already raised their families (50s and up).

- ✔ Major donors often have at least some college education.

- ✔ Major donors may have volunteered as a young person.

- ✔ Typically, major donors itemize their tax returns.

- ✔ Major donors are often involved in religious organizations.

The donors who give at a low level today are your major givers of tomorrow, which means that cultivation — the art of enhancing and building the donor-agency relationship — is not only good practice, it's good business. Today's $25 donor may be tomorrow's $25,000 donor.

The process of involving a donor at ever-increasing levels of giving is a logical one, as we describe in Chapter 7:

1. **Identify the donors you feel are good prospects for major gifts.**

   - Review your donor list and give records.
   - Talk to board members.
   - Research Who's Who in your area of expertise.
   - Use other research methods as needed (see Chapter 6 for more about donor research).

   Make a sublist of your main list, showing only those prospects you want to follow up on as potential major givers.

2. **Research the prospective donors.**

   As you do your homework on the individuals, verify that their interests do, in fact, support the type of work your organization does. Get a sense of their giving interests, their other philanthropic activities, likes and dislikes, preferences, and commitments.

3. **Based on what you know about the donor, design a strategy for cultivating the relationship with him or her.**

   Why type of program and/or sponsorship opportunity might the donor be interested in? Would it be best to visit in person, invite the donor out for a visit, or something else? The strategy you develop needs to be custom tailored to the needs, interests, and priorities of each individual prospect.

4. **Build, or cultivate, the relationship with the donor.**

   Depending on the prospective donor, you may meet with her several times over a period of months or contact her through a number of means, such as phone, letter, or personal visit, and schedule the true solicitation call only when you feel that she's receptive.

5. **Ask the prospect for the gift (better known as "The Ask," detailed in Chapter 9).**

   After you've cultivated the relationship with the prospect, you are in a position to ask for the major gift. Remember that you can't just jump from Step 1 to Step 5. Even if your donor gives major gifts hand over fist, the relationship building needs to come before the gift is offered and needs to continue after you receive the gift, as well.

6. **Express your thanks for the gift.**

   After you receive the major gift (we assume your solicitation is successful), expressing your thanks guarantees that you get a repeat gift at some point. If you say thank you graciously and remember — and honor — any promises you make to the donor, you will have cultivated the donor-agency relationship further. But if you neglect to express your thanks or otherwise overlook the generosity of the gift, the donor will feel unappreciated, or worse, taken advantage of. You will not see any repeat gifts from that donor in the months and years to come.

Recognize the size of the gift in a unique way appropriate to the gift. You must honor each donor, so he or she knows that the gift and the patronage are truly appreciated, especially if your donors know each other and are likely to compare your recognition efforts.

7. Account for how the gift is used.

What you do with the gift is as important to the donor as what you do to get the gift. When you secure any gift — but especially a major gift — it is vitally important that you do with it what you say that you will do. The donor needs to see where her money goes, and you need to be willing to provide that information as soon as the donor requests it, if not before, which goes a long way toward building the donor-agency relationship and may ensure that you get another gift.

Because of some of the topics in the news today, such as stories about charitable organizations using major portions of their gifts for administrative or overhead costs, many people turn a wary eye in the direction of charitable giving.

Want to really impress your donors? Don't wait for them to ask about what's happening. Go to them and say, "I wanted to show you what your gift is doing — look how happy these kids are!" Show the donor photos of the programs she has helped sponsor and let her see the fruits of her gift. Donors love to see the outcome of their philanthropy — and the sooner you can provide that information, the better.

Building a giving club

Although you may initially solicit major gifts for a program or campaign you want to fund, you eventually should incorporate a major giving program as part of your regular fundraising strategy. Colleges and universities have perfected the art of major giving programs by creating giving clubs. For example, when you give a large gift to your alma mater, your name may be affixed to the new library, to the endowed chair of a particular department, to a scholarship fund, or to any number of other long-lasting recognition opportunities.

Giving clubs actually serve a number of purposes. First, these clubs inform your donors about the benefits they receive in each of the different giving levels. Second, they help donors feel a part of something while building a sense of identity for your organization. Third, they make it easy for you to show donors how they can "upgrade" to a higher level of giving in subsequent years.

Begin a giving club by identifying the following:

More about why donors give

If you are a fundraiser, you are probably interested in what motivates people to give to causes. A good place to start observing this is with your own giving patterns. What has motivated you when you've given to an organization? Was it something in the organization's literature? Something the organization accomplished? Here are some common reasons why people give to organizations:

✔ An acquaintance of the donor asked the donor to give or volunteer (the #1 reason).

✔ She received services from the organization or knew someone personally who did.

✔ She heard a news story or read an article in the paper or online that alerted her to the organization's cause or need.

✔ She received an e-mail message from a friend about the organization.

✔ She has a friend who volunteers at the organization.

✔ The club amounts you want to create

✔ The names you want to assign to each of the clubs

✔ The benefits each of the clubs offers

Table 8-1 lists four different giving club levels for a garden club association.

Table 8-1	An Example of a Multilayer Giving Club		
Level I: **$500–$999** **The Crocus Club** **Benefits**	**Level II:** **$1,000–$2,500** **The Lilly Club** **Benefits**	**Level III:** **$2,500–$4,999** **The Iris Club** **Benefits**	**Level IV:** **$5,000 and above** **The Rose Society** **Benefits**
Garden membership	All of Crocus Club benefits, plus . . .	All of the Lily Club Benefits, plus . . .	All of Iris Club benefits, plus . . .
Tickets for two to a premier evening	Dinner with the chamber orchestra at the garden	A tour of the Arlyle Garden Home (two tickets)	Breakfast with a master gardener
Free subscription to the *GardenWalk* newsletter	Gardening classes (six) with a master gardener	An evening for two in the garden with a horse-drawn carriage ride	A special birding event for Rose Society members
		Free admission to all garden events	All-expense-paid trip for two to our sister garden in St. Louis, Missouri

Does your agency have a gift that keeps on giving? Major givers like the idea of an endowment because of the intriguing possibility of creating unlimited funding for a continuing program (it keeps going . . . and going . . . and going). People want their money to be used for something good, something that creates change for the better. For this reason, scholarship programs, research for cures, and programs that battle the recognized ills of society, like poverty, drug abuse, and illiteracy, are good candidates for major grants. Who wouldn't want to be able to say, "I gave the money that lead to a cure for multiple sclerosis?"

Stroking Major Donors' Egos

As we say repeatedly (and we can't really say it enough), giving is not just an "I-give, you-get" transaction; it's an equitable trade. What you're trading is your service to the donor for their involvement in your mission. Your organization receives something, to be sure, but you give something as well. Even those donors who "give out of the goodness of their hearts," not wanting anything in return, need to receive some benefit in order to feel good about their gifts. That benefit may be intangible, such as the good feeling that comes from helping a cause you believe in. Or it may be something like a thank-you note, call, or visit that says, "Your gift was very important to us."

Treating your donors right

What do major givers want to receive in return for their gifts? For one thing, they want personal contact with your organization. At the major giving level, personal relationships become very important. Donors want to be sure that you know who they are. They want to be recognized as higher-level participants

---

The special relationship with the high-end donor

In Chapter 7, you find out what motivates the typical donor to give to an organization. With a high-end donor, the relationship develops over time. Many conversations take place about a variety of topics, as well as about money and your organization. The fundraiser needs to provide many contacts with the donor: letters, e-mails, visits, and lunches, all in a variety of forms and over a considerable length of time. The donor grows steadily closer to what your organization does, catching more of the passion and feeling more ownership of the good work being done. The donor also begins to think about the possibility of a long-term relationship, perhaps donating to your organization in a way such that future generations may remember what the organization meant to his or her family and/or the community at large. This special relationship takes time, patience, insight, and cultivation.

than the donors who send in the $25 check once a year to your annual fund. The following list details some of the things major givers are looking for when they give a major gift:

✔ **Confidence in the board:** Your major giver is more interested in the makeup of your board than someone who gives at a lower level. If she has confidence in the leadership and fiduciary responsibility of your organization, the chairman, executive director, and other board members, she feels better about making a sizeable contribution.

✔ **The efficiency of the management:** The major giver wants not only to have confidence in the board but also some assurances that the organization is well run, efficient, and dedicated to fulfilling its mission. No one wants to donate a large sum of hard-earned money to an agency that may dry up and blow away next year.

✔ **The credibility of any advisory board:** Some organizations cultivate an honorary or advisory board. Though these individuals don't do much in the way of legwork, their names on your letterhead can be impressive.

✔ **Recognition:** Some major givers — although not all — want recognition from the organization, from the community, from their peers.

Does your organization offer named giving opportunities for major givers? If you have fountains, gardens, meeting rooms, or walkways, you can develop a program where you name the item with a displayed plaque when a donor provides the support for that item.

✔ **Personal contact:** We've already said this, but it bears saying again: Your major giver wants to hear from you. Notes, calls, and visits all say to a donor, "You're important to us and we want to keep you informed about what's going on." By giving at a high level, a major giver makes a significant commitment to you, and he or she most likely expects an equal commitment from your organization.

✔ **Financial advice:** Your major giver may want some professional assistance before the gift is complete — from her lawyer, financial planner, or a foundation executive. Have someone on your staff or board who can speak knowledgeably about planned giving instruments and tax issues, as a complement to, not a replacement for, the major giver's own financial counsel.

Some community foundations are able to give donors tax and financial advice when they consider major gifts. Check your area to find out about workshops given by your local community foundation that may help train development staff and/or your board on tax and financial issues.

✔ **More bang for the buck:** Often your major givers are business savvy and like the idea that their money goes even farther than a simple gift. For this reason, challenge grants are popular as major, or lead, gifts. Your major giver may like the idea that the money she provides "starts something" and grows into two, three, or four times her initial gift.

A *challenge grant* is a gift given to an organization that is contingent upon the organization raising a matching amount from other sources. You may approach a former board member for a major gift of $15,000, for example, as a challenge grant. If the donor agrees, the organization can go to the other board members (and to other major giver and funding sources, as well), and say, "We have a $15,000 challenge grant, and we need to raise the matching $15,000 by January 15 in order to get the grant. Would you make a donation that would take us $5,000 closer to that goal?" (For more information about challenge grants, see Chapter 21.)

✔ **Family honor:** Many families make major gifts not to secure recognition for themselves but to memorialize a family member who had an affinity for a particular group. Often these major gifts are made to endowment campaigns with the idea that the endowment then provides an investment so that the organization receives dividends to secure its existence in the future.

✔ **A worthwhile cause:** The donors of today are getting more and more involved in investigating the charities they support and giving only where they really want. This is even truer in the major gifts category. Major givers are looking carefully for the cause that aligns with their own concerns (which is another reason for you to have a well crafted, timely, and up-to-date case statement!).

✔ **Involvement in the community:** Giving a major gift may put the donor in a new social group or in a new light in a particular social group. If a family is new to an area and has an affinity for a certain cause, giving a major gift may help establish the family in that area as an advocate of the arts, human services, or some other cause.

✔ **Immortality:** If your name is attached to the new library at your local university, you don't have to worry too much about whether you've made your mark on the world. Many major givers have the desire — and the means — to do something significant, to leave the world a better place than they found it, to use their wealth to build a better future. The feeling that you have changed the world for the better by being in it is something most of us would like to experience at some point in our lives.

Peer-to-peer is the best way to approach a major giver. If Joe is the president of a local bank, prepare and send a board member, who is similar in professional and social standing, your board president, or a company CEO. How do you motivate the board member to do the soliciting? Have a board retreat that focuses on approaching major givers and helps board members get comfortable with their fundraising roles. For more on dealing with your board, see Chapter 4. For more about the nuts and bolts of asking for major gifts, see Chapter 21.

Providing donor recognition

Imagine that you are about to receive a major gift. Mr. X listened to your presentation, liked your ideas, and is receptive to your suggestion that he donate $20,000 over the next three years. You're back at your desk, soaking up your success. Enjoy the moment — for a moment. But then it's time to ask yourself, "Now what?" When you receive a major gift, or the promise of a major gift, you want to acknowledge the donor right away.

Providing recognition to your major giver is as important as all the steps you've taken leading up to the point of getting the major gift. Remember, this transaction is about relationship, and you've just agreed to accept and be accountable for Mr. X's gift — and his involvement — over the next three years. You have in effect said:

✔ "We value you — not just your money."

✔ "We'll use this donation wisely, as promised."

✔ "We'll be good stewards of this gift and be accountable to you for it."

In addition to keeping promises you make to your donor, you need to recognize your major giver in other ways, such as:

✔ Write a handwritten thank-you note on very nice stationary.

✔ Follow up by calling your donor.

✔ Make visits or have lunch with your donor periodically.

✔ Get your donor involved in high-level donor affairs, such as preview parties, soirees, grand openings, open houses, and so on.

✔ Assign the donor to a board position or committee seat.

✔ Name a program, a building, a garden, or an evening after the donor.

✔ Invite your donor to focus groups where you discuss the future of the organization.

✔ Send invitations to your donor for special events, such as seeing the birth of a baby elephant, going backstage to meet a violin virtuoso, or traveling with a select group to see a renowned speaker.

Sometimes, finding enough naming opportunities can be a challenge. One group we work with found a solution by naming items in their office area, such as the elevators, a meeting room, and so on, after particular donors. There's only one wrinkle here — what happens when the organization outgrows its current building and moves to new offices? If the office has no elevator, the development officer will have to come up with some creative alternatives to protect the agency's relationship with that donor.

Are you thinking of your organization's major givers as prospects for your planned giving program? If you aren't, you should be! Start making that list. See Chapter 21 for more about planned giving campaigns.

Chapter 9

Asking for a Major Gift

- -

In This Chapter

▶ Getting over the fear of asking for money

▶ Being aware of your attitudes about money

▶ Picking the best person to do the asking

▶ Understanding how to do "the Ask"

▶ Rating your ability to get a Yes

▶ Continuing to build that relationship

- -

Does the title of this chapter knot your stomach and raise your blood pressure?

If so, you're not alone. It's not unusual for people in fundraising, both experienced and new, to dread the moment, that oh-so-frightening one-on-one conversation with the donor, when it's time for "the Ask." When you're going after a major gift, you eventually must face this terrifying moment. The stage is set. The spotlight is on you. Your tongue feels like it's the size of Nebraska, and you hope the donor doesn't notice that your shaking hands. This chapter gives you a look at that terrifying moment and puts it in perspective with some basic management techniques for recognizing and responding to the challenges of asking for a major gift.

Keeping Focused on Your Mission

Who likes to ask for money? Nobody. It's sometimes thought of as a "necessary evil," a part of fundraising that calls for the donor to "put his money where his mouth is," and the part of the process that for the fundraiser is "The Big Show."

Sure, people are hesitant to ask for money. Why? Two reasons: because money is still one of the remaining taboo subjects (along with sex and religion) and because nobody wants to hear No. Hearing No feels like personal rejection and causes embarrassment to some people. To some, hearing No feels like a final mandate — a point of no return. To others, No can mean that they're one step closer to failure in a fundraising campaign.

We'd like to turn all those ideas on their head.

In truth, No doesn't mean any of those things. The only meaning that No has is the meaning that you give it.

Developing a fundraising system takes the work of many people for many months. By the time you get to the point where you are ready to ask a potential donor for a major gift, you will have done considerable legwork and research (see Chapter 6 for more about researching your donors).

Four tips help you stay focused on the work at hand (which is furthering the mission of your organization — not getting bucks from rich folks):

- ✔ **Remember what's real.** Money is an exchange mechanism, and you are helping this donor participate in a charitable effort he or she cares about.

- ✔ **Go for a Yes, but realize that you can live with a No.** Expect that the donor wants to make the donation, but remind yourself that Nos are not personal and have more to do with the circumstances and mindset of the donor than they do with anything you say or do.

- ✔ **Think about the other person.** It's hard to go wrong in situations where we fully devote ourselves to helping the other person. If the donor is concerned about something, help him allay those concerns. If he doesn't think that it's the right time for him to give, help him explore why and see whether other options are possible. If you focus on the "getting," you're going to feel as though you've lost something if you hear a No.

- ✔ **Remember that a No may be a Not Yet.** The donor-agency relationship doesn't end with a single No — don't even entertain that thought. This relationship is built over time and continues whether the donor makes this particular gift. Keeping this in mind can help you remember what's important about what you're doing — building the relationship and matching the "right people" with the "right causes." Timing is a major part of the whole picture.

In this chapter, you find out how to listen to Nos with a different ear and to recognize new possible outcomes of hearing a No. You also find out when to "bargain down" and when to go back to base camp and regroup. We ask you now to change your attitude that No is a word to be feared, and to consider how a No can lead to a Yes.

Life's greatest fears

What do people fear the most? Statistics show that the top three greatest fears, in order, are

✔ Death

✔ Making a public speech

✔ Asking somebody for money

Are these your greatest fears, too? If so, it's your lucky day. In this book, we help you with two of the three.

Checking Out Your Attitudes about Money

Before you can change your behavior you have to understand it. What does money mean to you? Here's a little true-or-false quiz you can take to see which of these sayings about money are floating around in your head. Some of them may be stopping you from confidently asking for major gifts before you even pick up the phone.

True or False: Money is an exchange mechanism

True. Money provides a means of exchanging one thing for another. The money exchange goes something like this: "I trade what I do for society with what other people do for society." We each have something valuable to give, and we use money as the means of exchanging that valuable something. And although alternatives to our current forms of currency have been debated for some time, it beats carrying around a load of shells!

If you believe that money is an exchange mechanism, when you visit your donor, you may find yourself thinking:

✔ "It sounds like we have just the program he'd be interested in supporting."

✔ "I'm glad we're able to help him do something good for the cause he cares about."

✔ "If he says, 'No,' I'll see whether I can find an option he's more comfortable with."

This approach helps you to see the value in what you have to offer and what your donor has to give.

True or False: Money is the root of all evil

False. Money, being simply an exchange mechanism and not good or bad in itself, can't be the root of anything. (And besides, the real quote is "The love of money is the root of all evil.") People do bad things in the pursuit and protection of riches. You can't blame money, though.

If you believe that money is the root of all evil, and you go to have that important meeting with your donor, you may be thinking:

- ✔ "I wonder how he made his money, anyway — probably in some shady business deal."
- ✔ "She's probably going to try to back me into a corner."
- ✔ "I can't wait to get out of here!"

No wonder you're afraid to ask! Time to change your attitude about money and begin to see it as a simple means of transferring things of value from one person to another, and in your case, from one person to your worthwhile cause.

True or False: Money can't buy happiness

True. Money can't buy happiness, though you may sometimes wish it could. It's a common saying, however, and one we often use when we don't have quite as much money as we'd like, and we feel that riches are just outside our grasp. "Oh well," we sigh. "Money can't buy happiness anyway." If you go to meet your donor with this on your mind, you may be more likely to hear these thoughts in your head:

- ✔ "I'm glad I'm not her — she has to give money to make people like her!"
- ✔ "This whole thing about the haves and the have-nots really bothers me. She should be giving more than she is!"
- ✔ "Why is she giving to us, anyway? Is she trying to buy her way onto the board?"

Does it matter to you why your donor gives? It shouldn't. You don't want to accept a gift you know to be unethical or illegal, of course, but because donors give from so many different reasons — desire to help, self-aggrandizement, recognition, status, and so on —it's not your job to judge the giving that goes on. Focus on the good your organization does and resist the temptation to second-guess your donors' motives.

True or False: Money talks

False. Money is an exchange mechanism. Unless you fold the check up, make a little puppet out of it, and throw your voice, it is not going to talk.

But on some level, it is true that money can make things happen. Remember the old E.F. Hutton ads? "When E.F. Hutton speaks," whispers the narrator, "people listen." The idea, of course, is that money carries with it a certain amount of power, clout, or prestige. People with money get things done. People with money have access to things that others do not. These statements are true in today's social climate.

If you support the "money talks" belief, you may find yourself thinking these kinds of thoughts during your donor visit:

✔ "I've heard that guys like this eat people like me for breakfast. What am I doing here?"

✔ "He's much more successful than I am. I can't believe I'm going to ask him for money!"

✔ "He'll probably say, 'No' — I imagine he has refusals down to a science."

As you consider your feelings and thoughts about money, we urge you to remember that money itself has no power. Individuals who have fortunes to manage may (and probably do) belong to certain clubs in town, frequent particular activities, and serve on selected boards. These people are real people — people with friends, people with problems, people with causes they care about and visions they'd like to see fulfilled. And these people, if their interests align with the mission of your organization, can be great potential donors — not because of the amount of power they wield, but because of the access and perhaps endorsement they bring to your mission.

If you bring any preconception to dealing with wealthier people, a productive one would be to guess that they respond well to businesslike reasons and sound arguments for spending their money on your cause. All the more reason to prepare well for your pitch, make it professional, and not waste their time beating around the bush.

True or False: Money creates success

False. There have been incredibly well-funded failures as well as those that have ended with the snap of their financial shoestring. What does create success — personally or professionally, in fundraising or anywhere else — is passion, vision, focus, and perseverance. And if you ever find that bottled anywhere, buy as many bottles as you can and sell them on eBay. After you make your millions, you can be the high-level donor we all come to call on.

Donors who have achieved a certain level of wealth have arrived there through any number of means. Perhaps they owned and sold successful businesses. Maybe they inherited. Maybe they won the lottery, won a lawsuit, or saved quietly all their lives. In any event, don't equate the acquisition of wealth with great success or you may be thinking the following thoughts instead of getting to know the interests of your donor:

- ✔ "He has so much money, he's going to think that our organization is pathetic."
- ✔ "I'll bet he's way too busy to come to our donor luncheon. I won't even ask him."
- ✔ "I wonder if he notices that I'm wearing shoes from Wal-Mart?"

Is the definition of money in the mind of the beholder? To some degree, yes. People attach many things to money that don't necessarily belong — power, sex, influence, and social status are all part of the affluent image. To be most effective as a fundraiser, free yourself of all definitions of money beyond that which it truly is for your organization — an exchange mechanism that helps caring people further causes they believe in.

Figuring Out Who Should Ask for Money

Long before you go on that donor visit in which you intend to solicit a donation, you should know who asks for your organization. Few things look more unprofessional than a fundraising team, standing on that proverbial doorstep, unsure about who is doing what:

"You wanna do the talking?"

"No, you go ahead."

Finding and preparing the right person to do the asking is key in securing major gifts. The right person ideally has the following characteristics:

- ✔ A peer-to-peer relationship with the prospective donor
- ✔ A giver
- ✔ Comfortable with fundraising
- ✔ Understands that the offer is something the donor wants

✔ A people person, able and willing to focus on building relationships with donors over time

✔ Forthcoming and honest, willing to help donors resolve any questions or concerns that may be keeping them from giving

✔ Confident and secure, unshaken by a "No" that could be a "Yes" down the road

Perhaps the single biggest consideration in choosing the person who makes "the Ask" is the question of peer-to-peer relationship. If you are approaching the CEO of a corporation for a major gift, have your organization's CEO or a person on your board who is a peer in terms of social, economic, and professional status make "the Ask." Another CEO doing "the Ask" makes things much easier. Similarly, if you are approaching someone who has volunteered for the organization for a long time, send another volunteer — not a paid staff member. The similarity of the roles — whether those roles are professional, social, experiential, or professional — helps build a sense of trust between the donor and the fundraiser. People in unequal positions of power — a CEO and a paid staff member, for example — often have trouble reaching the "comfort zone" that people of like means or status share.

Teaming up for dollars

Some people prefer to work in fundraising teams, which are often comprised of a paid staff member and a board member. The board member is traditionally the one doing "the Ask," and the staff member goes along for support and encouragement. The problem with the two-person approach is that some donors may feel "ganged up on" if they are put in the minority. For this reason, you need to always be explicit about your intention to visit as a team: "Diana has a brief presentation she'd like to show you about our new waterworks. Would 2:30 be a convenient time for us to come by?"

But, on the flip side, two people can be helpful in fundraising calls because

✔ They can represent two different views of your organization.

✔ They give the donor a feeling that many people support the work.

✔ It's more likely that no key points will be left out.

✔ If one person is having trouble establishing rapport with the donor, the other person may hit it off.

✔ The second person may have expertise that complements the other's.

Practice makes perfect. Even though your board members may be CEOs and top-level community members, everybody can use a brush up on fundraising skills. Before you begin an active campaign in which your board members are soliciting gifts (or accompanying you on donor visits), reserve time to do some role-playing. Have one member act as the potential donor and one member act as the fundraiser — don't make it too easy, and have fun!

In one of our role-playing sessions, the "donor" kept answering an invisible phone on his invisible desk during the meeting. The fundraiser could barely get a sentence out without an interruption. In the meeting, we laughed, watching the "donor" frazzle the fundraiser. In the real world, we knew, all kinds of interruptions and roadblocks happen in a fundraising call and the better prepared you are for them, the better the outcome will be.

What do you think of the wealthy?

Just because you're on the asking end of the fundraising equation doesn't mean that you're not wealthy yourself. In fact, peer-to-peer fundraising, as you find out later in this chapter, is the most effective means of approaching a major donor for a donation. But exploring what you think of people who have more money than you do helps you expose and weed out any negative thoughts that you have (jealous or otherwise) that may get in the way of effective asking.

You can expose your hidden wealth prejudices by finishing this statement with whatever comes to mind:

"People with a lot of money are _____ _____."

How do you fill in that blank? You may come up with any number of things:

✔ Controlling

✔ Happy

✔ In a position to help others

✔ Lucky

✔ Miserly

✔ Open-hearted

✔ Powerful

✔ Power-hungry

✔ Successful

✔ Talented

✔ Unhappy

Think about whether your responses are largely positive or negative; and if they're negative, change them. Perhaps you adopted your ideas as you were growing up (many of our money beliefs come from our early family experiences) or as you struggled over your own financial hurdles. But whatever the source of your feelings, recognize the ones that keep you from feeling strong, sure, and direct in your fundraising exchanges and get rid of them. Your fundraising abilities — and your relationships with major donors — will be better for it.

Flying solo

If you choose to go it alone on your fundraising calls, you have a number of things working in your favor:

- ✔ You are the only one responsible for doing the preparation, which means nothing (hopefully) will fall through the cracks.

- ✔ You have a good chance (assuming a peer-to-peer relationship) of reaching a comfort zone with the donor on a one-to-one basis.

- ✔ You won't feel that anyone is looking over your shoulder.

- ✔ You can go with your instincts to direct the flow of the conversation.

But, on the other hand, the amount of responsibility you carry on a solo visit may be a bit heftier:

- ✔ You have to be careful what you promise —no one checks and balances you but you.

- ✔ You can't ask an informed third party how well you did in the call.

- ✔ You are relying on your own facts and figures, with no one to back you up (so you'd better know your stuff!).

- ✔ It's possible that the donor call may not go well, and nobody can help you out of it but you.

One of the cardinal rules of fundraising is: You must be a giver yourself if you're going to ask for major gifts for your organization. Before awarding grants, foundations want to know that the board is a 100-percent giving board. This carries a lot of weight, and even if donors never know whether you give or not (few people actually ask), you will know that you are asking another person to do something you are willing to do yourself.

And your giving doesn't have to be on the same level as the gift you're asking for, although it helps enormously with major gifts. If one CEO approaches another and says, "I'd like you to join me in being a member of the Chamber Society," the message is that the asking CEO already gives at that high level, and the other CEO is being asked to donate at the same level. This comparison serves as a kind of endorsement for the prospective donor, and if the peer-to-peer relationship is such that the donor respects the asker, a natural "Yes" is set up.

Getting Down the Mechanics of Asking

After you investigate some of your attitudes about money and consider who is the best person in your organization to do the asking, you are ready to get down to the nuts and bolts of "the Ask." This section takes you through the actual process and gives you the tools you need along the way.

Recognizing the equitable exchange

Picture this: You have a pair of concert tickets you are unable to use. You decide to call a few friends to see if anyone else can use the tickets. You dial the phone happily, feeling that kind of "I have something great for you!" feeling. The first two friends you call say that they have other plans for the night, but they are pleased that you thought of them; the third is thrilled and accepts the tickets gratefully. After the concert, she calls and tells you all about it (it was great, apparently), and wants to take you to lunch to thank you for thinking of her. You didn't get to go to the concert, but you did get to be part of an exchange that made another person happy. That can be a pretty good feeling.

Why does your role in fundraising have to be any different than that? Granted, you are not giving away concert tickets (unless, of course, you work for a symphony and are giving them to your high-level donors), but what you are offering your donor is as important and as valued as a nice gift.

Fundraising isn't just about getting money from people who have a surplus of it. It's about matching caring people with the organizations that support the areas they care about, whether that's music, art, human services, education, civic affairs, or health.

Using the tools of the trade

Your fundraising starts with a toolkit. What do you need?

- ✔ Your mission and case statement
- ✔ Your donor tracking information
- ✔ Your budget and/or Gift Range Chart
- ✔ Materials for your presentation
- ✔ Pledge cards

If you still don't have materials with your mission and case statement printed on them, you're not going to get much farther until you get those in hand. You may be able to build a donor base through some word-of-mouth contacts, volunteers, a Web site, and a newsletter, but you're not going to get the kind of high-level donors you want until you have something solid in print to show (and leave with) the donor when you visit. Go to Chapter 10 for more about creating fundraising printed materials.

Knowing thy donor

Do your homework! (This statement should go without saying, but well, we said it in case you need the reminder.) Know the donor — well — before you approach him. Consider the answers to the following questions as part of the preparation for your donor visit:

- How long has this donor been giving to your organization?
- Why does he care about your cause?
- How much has he given in the past?
- How did his past donations help the clients who receive your services?
- What are his key interests?
- Which programs do you have that are aligned with his key interests?
- Have you prepared to ask for a donation in one of those key areas?
- How much are you asking him to contribute?
- What do you expect his concerns to be?
- How will you address those concerns?

We can't say this enough: The more you know before you ask, the better experience both you and your prospect will have, and the more likely it is that your prospect will see the match between your mission and his. Check out Chapter 6 for more about getting to know your donor.

Checking out each step of "the Ask"

Every process can be distilled, at some level, to a simple step-by-step procedure. Use this procedure for "the Ask" as a general map for knowing where the safe areas for conversation and comfort-building are:

1. **Open:** 3–5 minutes

   You know about the introductions bit. As you're walking in, you mention the weather. She shows you the flowers from her garden. It's been a great year for zinnias, she says. You mention how great the irises looked outside the conservatory this spring.

   And that provides segue way into the next section of your conversation.

2. **Engage:** 5–20 minutes

   "Have you ever been out to see the gardens in full bloom?"

   "No," says the donor.

   "Oh, this year we included 14 new varieties of hybrids," you continue, which enables you to spotlight a few of the things you did with the donor's contributions to the Flower Fund last year.

   The point is to truly engage the donor, to understand where she's coming from, to find out a bit more about her specific interests right now. The engage enables you to see where her "hot buttons" are. For example, if she comments, "I'll never give to that group again if they're going to remodel their offices with my money!" — you know she's not interested in funding renovations. You also uncover any key interests that may help you see how your mission and her interests match.

   The most important three words to remember during this stage of the visit are "Ask and listen!" Know what questions you want to ask ahead of time, so you can get a good sense of what the donor wants to know more about, what her concerns may be, and how you can resolve those concerns. But most important, listen carefully. Watch her face; read her body language; wait for the signs that she's really excited about what she's talking about. When her eyebrows shoot up when you mention the possibility of bringing in a well-known horticulturist to speak to a select group at the conservatory, you know she's interested. When you talk about repaving the walks with real brick, her expressions seem to cool. From that sensitive listening, you can begin to get a sense of which type of gift would most engage the imagination and interest of the donor.

Focus group for donors: "Why do you give?"

When you prepare for a major giving campaign, consider having a donor focus group to help you discover why people give to your organization. This may be something you already know, but it is something worth revisiting from time to time.

Get some of your active donors together — perhaps over a simple lunch. Ask, "Why do you give to our organization?" and capture the answers you get. Most likely, you'll get a wide variety of reasons and you just may discover a thing or two about your organization, and the public's view of your organization, that you didn't know.

3. Tell your story: 10–15 minutes

Now you're in the groove. You've set the stage, found out about her primary interests, and discovered the angle that gives you the best chance of appealing to her philanthropic interests. You now explain the program or campaign you are here to talk about. You talk compellingly about the need (which the donor should empathize with), and explain how your program or organization serves that need in such a way that gets the donor interested in being involved. During this time, you rely on the information in your mission and case statement, perhaps handing her brochures as you talk or showing her pictures of the possibilities or programs you are discussing.

During this period, don't do all the talking; it's important to stay alert to clues from your donor that she has concerns or questions. Stop and answer any questions she has. Be forthcoming and consider each answer you give as a step toward bringing the donor into a better understanding of your organization.

4. Ask for involvement: 5–?? minutes

In sales terms, this last stage is called "the close." Often, fundraisers are reluctant to use sales terminology (this is not a sales job, after all); but the result is the same: You need to ask the donor for a donation. Sooner or later, it comes down to that all-important question.

You move right from your presentation to the close. "I can see that you're interested in our visiting horticulturist program — I must admit that I thought that you'd be one of the people most excited about this idea. We were hoping you would make a lead gift of $15,000 to start out this new program. And, with your permission, we would like to name the program after you and your husband, Joe, for all the important contributions you've made to the Garden and to the community in the last 40 years. Is this amount something you are comfortable with?"

You've brought it to a Yes or No response. If you get a No, don't panic — you still have some things to do (see "Moving Beyond 'No'," later in this chapter.) If you get a Yes, hand the donor an elegant pen with which to make out her check (or bring out that pledge card!).

As hard as it may be to remember, this donor visit isn't about you or your organization. It's about your donor and how you can provide her the service of contributing to a cause she cares about, which means that you need to fight the temptation to monopolize the conversation, but instead sit back and listen attentively. What is she really saying? What are her interests? How can you best serve her? You best represent your organization when you truly have the donor's best interests at heart.

Moving Beyond "No"

Suppose that the worst happens and the donor says, "No." Chances are you're not going to get a "No! And get out!" but rather something a little more gentle, such as:

- ✔ "Not right now."
- ✔ "I'll think about it."
- ✔ "I'll have to think about it for a while."
- ✔ "I don't think that's something I'm prepared to do right now."

The most important thing to remember at this point is that in fundraising you're going to get all kinds of Nos and partial Nos. You should not give up at this point and say, "Oh, okay. Well, thanks for your time."

Instead, do a little investigating to discover the "why" behind the "No." Here are some questions you can ask:

- ✔ **"Is there something that concerns you about whether this would be a good use of your money?"** Perhaps the donor still has some unresolved concerns about your organization that you can clear up.

- ✔ **"We were hoping you'd feel comfortable giving in the $10,000 to $15,000 range, but it's most important that you give a gift you're happy with. Would you like to divide that over three years, or make a smaller gift? We'd be grateful to receive anything you are interested in donating to our organization."** Maybe the amount is too large for the donor to give in one gift. Don't be afraid to "bargain down."

- ✔ **"Is there another time that would be better?"** Perhaps this is the wrong time for the donor to give. If the donor offers a time that would be better for her, be sure to pencil in a time to meet again.

- ✔ **"What can I do to help you say, 'Yes'?"** Whether you should ask this question depends on the personality and mindset of the donor. Some who don't shy away from saying No directly may say with a wry smile, "Nothing today — sorry." But others who are more hesitant to slam the door in your face may suggest something like, "Well, if I could be sure that the funds were going to go to. . . ." If a donor gives you that kind of response, you have something to work with in terms of furthering the relationship and getting closer to the point where she feels comfortable giving to your organization.

Is it ethical to mention other people in this donor's social group who have given to your organization? It may be ethical, but whether or not it's a smart thing to do depends on the donor. Some people are put off by what they hear as "name dropping." Others are encouraged when they hear that people they respect have given to your programs. Those people serve as a kind of

Dealing with the less-than-perfect call

Not all your calls will go the way you want them to. You will have an occasional meeting when somebody is put off by what you're doing. Remember one important rule: "Don't worry about it!" Then move on to your other prospects. With the number of people you're going to see and the calls you're going to make, a few of the calls may not go well.

If you remember the big picture — what your goals are — and know that a certain percentage of calls aren't going to be perfect, you can deal with the ups and downs that come with the territory.

endorsement for your organization. Test the waters by dropping a name or two and observing how the listener responds. A cool reception means that names don't mean a thing to this person; an interested raising of the eyebrows (or other body language) may mean that names could close the deal.

Rating Your Yes-Ability

If you do have a partner for your fundraising call, you have a built-in evaluator. After you leave the donor, ask your partner, "How do you think that we did?" Hopefully your partner will feel comfortable talking about the good — and not-so-good — parts of the visit. You can find out valuable information from the insights of another person who is at least partially objective. You may want to ask this partner the following questions:

- ✔ "Did we seem well prepared?"
- ✔ "Do you think that we handled the question about last year's shortage the right way?"
- ✔ "Do you think that the donor felt comfortable with spreading the gift over three years?"
- ✔ "Did you notice anything you think that we should work on?"
- ✔ "What aspect of the visit do you think that we did best?"

After you complete the call, you need to document the information in the donor's file. Write down the answers to the previous questions, as well as pertinent facts you need for fundraising calls in the future. Even if you received the Big Gift, this relationship continues, as you see in the following section.

If the meeting didn't go as planned, consider sending somebody else to call on the person in a few months. You don't want to leave a bad taste in the donor's mouth about you or your organization if you want to maintain a long-term relationship. Maybe another person would simply be a better fit with the donor's personality, or find the timing better down the road.

Following Up after "the Ask"

Finally, the call is over. You are driving back to your office with the nice feeling of having a $15,000 check for your organization in your briefcase. Mrs. Donor was very gracious and pleased that you approached her to give the lead gift for your new program. She likes the idea of the program being named after her family, and she wants to serve on the committee to help organize the kickoff event.

What are your responsibilities toward Mrs. Donor now that she's given her gift? This is an ethical question you will be faced with over and over again in fundraising.

Donors are not just money sources. They are people with interests and passions and troubles and fears. It's not unusual to meet a major donor late in his or her life who has lost a spouse, and he or she may want to spend time talking, remembering, and visiting. When that donor writes you a major check, you have an obligation to show the donor that your relationship is not just about money. What kinds of things do you need to do to follow up after the gift? Here are just a few ideas:

- ✔ The all-important thank-you note
- ✔ A follow-up phone call
- ✔ Information on the new program as it develops
- ✔ The newsletter or e-newsletter
- ✔ Invitations to all high-level social events
- ✔ Occasional lunches or visits
- ✔ Invitations to participate in focus groups and/or special engagements
- ✔ Invitations to get involved in other organizational events the donor may be interested in

As we say repeatedly in this chapter, "the Ask" doesn't have to be a panic-inducing event. Even if you don't get the answer you want, you can make this a positive contribution to building the relationship between you and the donor — which may lead to a "Yes" down the road.

Part III
Assembling Your Fundraising Toolkit

The 5th Wave   By Rich Tennant

"Tell the Community Recycling Initiative that I've received their fundraising letter."

In this part . . .

You have at your disposal dozens of ways in which you can get — and keep — attention for your agency, whether by generating printed materials, writing winning proposals, working with the media, or heading to the phones. You can also consider whether selling something to raise funds may work for you. Use the information in this part to take advantage of those resources and put them to work for you.

Chapter 10

Printing for Profits: Direct Mail, Annual Reports, and More

. . . .

In This Chapter

▶ Putting your organization's info in print

▶ Using what you have to update your printed materials

▶ Deciding which print pieces you need

▶ Getting the direct mail basics down

▶ Creating effective print pieces

▶ Putting together a printed materials plan

. . . .

*W*hich pieces catch your eye and your imagination as you glance quickly through the mailings you receive? Which ones do you throw away? In this chapter, I show you how to perfect your printed materials — both those you mail and those you hand deliver — so that you can make sure that they are worth the cost of the paper you print them on, build your organization's identity, and draw the donor closer to your mission.

Using Print Pieces to Further Your Cause

Print pieces give your organization credibility and continue to speak for you long after your meeting is over. Think about it: You go to visit a donor to talk to her about a gift for your capital campaign. You walk in empty handed, and sit and play with your hands while you talk. No matter how convincing your presentation, without leaving something to show for it, the word pictures you paint fade quickly from your donor's mind. If you take a folder with the annual report, the current newsletter, and a program brochure or two, your donor has something to review — and remember — after you've left.

But printed pieces can also:

- ✔ Be mailed to donors you can't visit face to face
- ✔ Keep donors informed and involved with your programs
- ✔ Reach new donors
- ✔ Build your organization's identity when distributed in the community
- ✔ Be included in your corporate and foundation grant-proposal packages
- ✔ Reinforce the stability and credibility of your organization

Having printed materials also helps smooth an uncomfortable face-to-face visit: When you show the donor interesting things in your annual report, you shift her attention from you to the good work being done.

Updating Printed Materials

Chances are you won't be creating all your printed pieces from scratch. Even the smallest nonprofits have some kind of printed literature, though it may only be a fact sheet or a case statement. Before you think about printing new and/or improved materials, gather up what you already have. Taking a look at what your current pieces say — and how they say it — can help you make educated choices about what pieces you print this time around.

Use these questions to evaluate the materials you currently have and determine whether it's time to make some changes:

- ✔ What kinds of pieces do you have?
- ✔ Which pieces do you use most?
- ✔ Does the printed information accurately convey your mission statement?
- ✔ Is the program information current?
- ✔ Are board member names up to date?
- ✔ Have you had any feedback from people outside the organization regarding your publications? If so, take this into account as you plan revisions.
- ✔ Do you have a large stock of existing publications? How long do you expect your current stock to last?
- ✔ What is your print materials budget? Do you need to make do for a while and slowly add new materials as you can afford them?

Knowing what you have in stock and the quality of your publications can help you plan when you need to reprint brochures, or give you a target date to have a revision ready.

Consider updating your printed materials for use on your Web site. That way you leverage all the effort that went into the printed piece to easily provide fresh content for your site.

Selecting the Right Print Pieces

Some organizations think that professionally printed pieces are luxuries — something they can add after they have the basic fundraising system in place. Although many on-a-shoestring nonprofits put off printing costly annual reports, color brochures, and fancy engraved letterhead, you can still publish less costly print pieces now, and save printing the "good stuff" until a time when you can afford it more easily.

Saving money on printing

Here are some ideas on how you can save money on your printing:

- **Decide what you really need.** Perhaps a simple, conversational, direct mail letter is what you want. Then you may not need a full-color brochure. With strong content and good design, you can start with a simple black-and-white piece. (The section, "Assembling the basics," later in this chapter, lists different types of pieces you may need.)

- **Use a full-service copy shop.** You can print at a full-service copy shop rather than a print shop to start and still have nice print pieces.

- **Do it yourself.** Computers, graphic design software, and laser printers have made print pieces easier and less costly than ever to produce in small volume right in your own office.

- **Try to get your printing donated.** For example, can one of your board members who is a business owner help? You may be able to align with another organization, such as a local library, that can do your printing as an in-kind contribution. Ask around, and be creative. Many large organizations and companies in your area have their own printing resources and may be willing to share their resources to help your cause.

How "nice" do we want to look?

Publishing documents that look too nice — that is, with slick, four-color photos, stitched-in pockets, and glossy covers — may be a bit too fancy for a small startup nonprofit that deals with issues of homelessness. The overall impression should say to your donor, "We want you to see how your gifts are making a difference, but we don't want to use too much money to show you that!"

Assembling the basics

As your organization grows and changes, you may want to consider creating one or more of these printed materials, listed in general order of affordability:

- ✔ **Direct mail letters** enable you to reach out to new donors, renew existing donors, and focus on specific donor groups for targeted fundraising programs. You might also use a one-page newsletter format as your direct mail letter.

  Have you caught the Internet craze? Direct e-mail and e-newsletters are a new hot topic for fundraisers on the Web. We explore those ideas in Chapter 16.

- ✔ **Brochures** help you get the word out about your organization, your programs, and your needs. You might have a general information brochure, a membership brochure, an endowment brochure, a programs brochure, and a planned giving brochure, among others. As a general rule, brochures using standard paper sizes and traditional folds with only one color ink are the least costly and can start you off well. If you plan to mail the brochures, make sure to use a size that will fit in standard envelopes or work as self-mailers to avoid adding costs.

- ✔ **Pledge cards** enable your donors to respond to your direct mail piece or personal appeal by promising a specific donation, perhaps over a period of time. You can easily have a set of pledge cards printed that fit in your direct mail pieces, 'tipped' into your brochures (just like those annoying cards that fall out of every magazine you buy), and folded in your newsletters.

- ✔ **Booklets** can help you focus on a specific area of your programming. Perhaps you are creating a history booklet, or a booklet of recipes from your volunteer community, or a resource handbook for welfare-to-work moms in your area. Booklets, printed with your logo, mission statement, and contact information, help you spread the story about your organization and introduce others to your cause. Again, you can create booklets that are as simple or as fancy as you need and can afford.

- ✔ **Newsletters** are great tools for showing donors how their gifts are helping you meet the goals of your organization and making your needs known. This print piece also gives you a way to announce your upcoming events. Best of all, you can recognize individual donors for their special contributions of time, effort, or money and thus encourage others to donate as well.

- ✔ **Invitations** to stakeholders need to be printed for any special event, be it a chili cook-off or a black-tie affair. Invitations can be simple, including only the event, date, time, and reply information, along with a simple envelope showing your logo and return address.

Although simple invitations work fine (and are most cost-effective) for most events, for that special white-tie event that everyone looks forward to during the year, don't be afraid to pull out all the stops (if your budget allows). Consult a printer in your area to get some ideas on how to make your invitations memorable while staying within your price range. The consultation is also an ideal opportunity to seek an in-kind contribution from the printer, who may be willing to print your invitations at a reduced rate or charge you only for the paper.

One other publication can be helpful in spreading your mission and encouraging support: The annual report, covered in the next section. Sometimes, the annual report can be handled as a direct mail letter. The important point is to account to your stakeholders by providing an overview of your year's activities.

Technology affords several cost-saving opportunities for print materials. Buy invitation or brochure stock at your local office supply store with preprinted graphic elements, and then print on that stock, using your laser printer. Use document templates in software products such as Microsoft Word or Publisher to easily generate self-mailing flyers or brochures, or business cards.

Showing yearly progress with an annual report

Everybody from Fortune 500 corporations to the tiniest nonprofit has them: annual reports serve five very distinct purposes; they:

- ✔ Inform donors (and the community at large) about what you've been doing with the money you've received (referred to as accountability).
- ✔ Connect leaders of the organization with the public through letters or articles included in the report.
- ✔ Review the accomplishments of the past year.
- ✔ Thank the people who helped you reach your yearly goals.
- ✔ Announce goals for next year to tell donors your plans for using their donated dollars in the year to come.

No hard-and-fast rule exists indicating what you must include in an annual report. But your stakeholders expect to see:

- ✔ A letter from the board president
- ✔ Articles focusing on successes during the year

     ✔ Your mission statement

     ✔ Financial information

     ✔ A list of donors by amount or giving group

     ✔ A list of goals for the next year

A carefully timed year-end annual report should help remind donors of all the good they did in the current year and encourage them to build on their gifts in the coming year.

Discovering Direct Mail Basics

Direct mail has long been one of the most popular means of keeping donors in touch with the happenings at organizations. With a simple piece of mail, you can invite new donors to join your organization, tell existing donors what a difference their gifts are making, provide important information about the fiscal responsibility of your agency, and persuade donors to participate in giving clubs, planned giving programs, or endowment campaigns.

Direct mail is only one means of nurturing the overall donor-agency relationship — and a fairly distanced option, at that — but, done effectively, it can help you achieve a number of objectives. Direct mail may help you

     ✔ Acquire new donors

     ✔ Inform existing donors and other stakeholders

     ✔ Alert your constituency and allied organizations

     ✔ Educate your stakeholders

     ✔ Tell a story or anecdote about someone who benefits from your work

     ✔ Renew existing donors

     ✔ Upgrade donors to a higher giving level

     ✔ Discover planned giving prospects

     ✔ Bring in donations for your annual fund

Donor renewal refers to the process of contacting existing donors — they were members of your museum last year, and it is time to renew their membership. These kinds of direct mail pieces are effective because

     ✔ The donors know what they are getting (they were members this past year).

     ✔ They are in alignment with your mission.

     ✔ They already have a relationship with your organization.

When you offer a donor the convenience of renewing her membership through the mail, if she has had a positive experience with your organization, she is likely to renew. You also look businesslike and efficient, something donors like to see in an organization that they're investing their hard-earned dollars in.

Debunking direct mail myths

Many people have misconceptions about what direct mail can and can't do. In this section, we separate the facts from the fallacies.

Truth: Direct mail reaches a lot of people.

Depending on the size of your donor list (either the one you've been growing yourself or one you've purchased from a list vendor), you can send out thousands of appeals to a very wide audience. We don't recommend this, however; carefully selected, targeted mailings to prequalified donors (those donors who are already giving or are highly likely to give to your organization because they've demonstrated an interest in your cause or similar causes) are the best use of direct mail dollars.

Fallacy: Direct mail is a great way to get a lot of new donors.

Although we often send direct mail to that group of donors and potential donors who are "out there en masse," don't expect to get a great number of new donors through a blind direct mail piece sent to large populations. (You'll most likely get a less than two percent response on "cold" direct mail letters.) The most effective mailing is the one in which (1) you have a reason to believe that the donor is or will be interested in your cause; (2) you know that the donor has given in the past; (3) you are fairly certain the donor has the ability to give.

Direct mail returns are higher if the person receiving the letter knows the person who signs the letter. Why? Because somewhere in the recesses of your donors' upbringing, they were taught that it's rude not to reply to people they know.

Truth: Direct mail, done right, can keep your donors engaged.

A good direct mail letter lets your readers know what's going on in your organization, directly communicates a need (or better yet, an exciting new program), and invites them to participate.

Fallacy: You can cut down on the number of personal calls you need to make by using direct mail.

Direct mail will never replace a personal fundraising visit. First, direct mail is used to reach those donors with whom you have not yet established or are still developing a basic relationship. Second, a higher-level donor (a person who has some history with your organization who you might call on personally or take to lunch) could very well be insulted by receiving a blanket direct mail piece you send out to what might be perceived as "ordinary" donors.

Truth: Direct mail is an important fundraising tool.

Depending on the nature of your organization, direct mail can be a helpful part of your annual fundraising drive. If you have membership possibilities, sell season tickets to the theater or the symphony, or host an annual conference, you can use direct mail to remind last year's donors that it's time to make that annual commitment. If you are part of a human services organization, your direct mail pieces may ask for funds to help feed the hungry or house the homeless. No matter what your cause, direct mail reaches out to donors — past, present, and future — to let them know in a succinct but passionate way how they can best help your organization solve the problems it addresses.

Fallacy: Only national organizations need direct mail campaigns.

Even if you are a small local organization, direct mail can be an effective means of reaching a target audience that you feel would be sympathetic to your cause. If you are a child advocacy group, you can do a direct mailing to your city's family therapists, for example. Planned mailings can be effective in any locale if they are going to the right people at the right time for the right reason.

Truth: Direct mail can be costly.

Direct mail ranges from a simple self-mailing letter to a letter-and-envelope to all kinds of fancy folders or color brochures. If you add the cost of purchased (or rented) mailing lists, you may add several hundred dollars to the printing and production costs. Direct mail can be costly, but it doesn't need to be. If you keep the piece and printing of it simple, use your own list, have volunteers produce and stuff the mailing, and keep the postage down, you can do a mailing that helps you reach your goals without breaking your budget.

Fallacy: The first thing you need to do in a fundraising plan is start with direct mail.

Unless you are a new organization with a really novel approach, a unique mission, and a sure constituency, starting off your fundraising efforts with a direct mail campaign is like shooting buckshot at a wall when you only want to flip the light switch. First things first. As you develop a fundraising plan for your new organization, begin with your board as we note in Chapter 4 and go from there — working from those closest to the heart of your organization outward.

That way, you can build your donor list as you go along, which helps you focus your mailings to prequalified donors by the time you're ready to do a direct mail campaign.

Direct mail often uses the name of someone well known — such as former President Jimmy Carter and his wife who write direct mail appeals for Habitat for Humanity. If you have a high-profile spokesperson, make the most of that; even if you don't, think of people in your area who would enhance the credibility of the pieces you send out.

Using direct mail to strengthen the client-donor relationship

As we note in the preceding section, "Debunking direct mail myths," direct mail will never replace face-to-face contact with your major givers. Direct mail is a tool that casts a big net and can bring in an abundance of relatively small gifts. In contrast, the personal appeal — particularly a peer-to-peer request — can bring in a large amount with a single contact.

Your overall goal with direct mail should be to draw donors closer toward the heart of your organization, with the end goal of continually upgrading them in their giving patterns until they reach the level of a major giver, when possible. This takes time, and continual contact, of which direct mail is only the beginning. Figure 10-1 illustrates the cast-a-big-net theory — that you reach 70 percent of your donors through direct mail, 20 percent through personalized correspondence, and 10 percent through face-to-face contact.

E-mail — both personalized and bulk e-mail — is also making up an ever-growing segment of donor-agency contacts. In fact, post 9-11 fears of anthrax in regular mail drove many donors to online giving in a big way. When you consider the minimum 80 cent cost of postage for direct mail versus 0 cent cost for sending an e-mail, you can realize big savings and be nearly as effective.

Don't forget the value of personal correspondence. A personal letter is something you write directly to a specific donor, with him or her in mind, which is very different from a direct mail piece. Personal correspondence can thank the donor for his involvement, introduce the donor to a new program, and invite him to be one of the first people to help you offer your new services. Personal correspondence enables the donor to feel valued for being the high-level giver he is and encourages him to continue building his relationship with your organization.

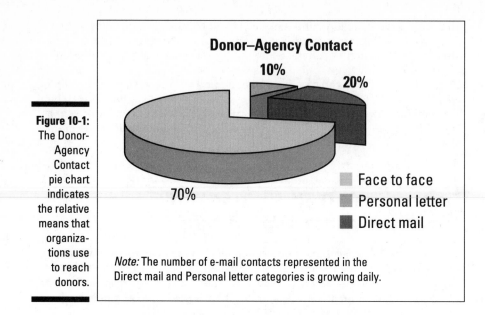

Figure 10-1:
The Donor-
Agency
Contact
pie chart
indicates
the relative
means that
organiza-
tions use
to reach
donors.

Understanding what direct mail can and can't do

So what do you want to accomplish with your direct mail program? You probably have both far-reaching and piece-specific goals.

Far-reaching goals may be to

✔ Meet your annual fund goals

✔ Renew and upgrade existing donors

✔ Gather information to update your mailing lists

Use your direct mail appeal to update your mailing lists by including a checkbox asking, "Has your contact information changed?" Provide a few lines, so donors can write in their new information, and then update the information as soon as you receive the response. This helps you keep your list current, which makes for a happier donor down the road.

As you plan your direct mail piece, it's important to do a budget that determines how much each piece is going to cost you. Know how much you need in donations in order to make the direct mail piece profitable. Where's your break-even point?

Specific goals for the direct mail piece may include

- ✔ Getting the direct mail piece into the hands of the right people (people who are likely to give)
- ✔ Getting the donor to open the envelope
- ✔ Catching the donor's attention, so she reads the piece all the way through
- ✔ Motivating her to respond to your appeal

If you're a large group, the best way you can boost the response rate to your direct mail pieces is to use intelligent lists. How can you target your mailings to a specific group? If you are introducing a new program that teaches nutrition to pregnant teens, for example, you may want to sort your list to find donors who are female, have children, work in a specific field, make a certain amount of money, and live in a certain area. Anything you can do to increase the likelihood of response by finding out more about your stakeholders helps you to both save money on your mailings and bring in more for your efforts.

TIP

The list! The list! The list!

Throughout this book, you hear us harp repeatedly on the importance of your donor list. Having a current donor list — that includes all kinds of different data, from city/state to marital status to civic associations — gives you the means by which to identify groupings for your direct mail campaigns. Following we list a few examples of subgroups you may want to target:

- ✔ Volunteers who helped with the Halloween Ball last year
- ✔ Directors of nonprofit organizations
- ✔ Donors who give through a specific corporate giving program
- ✔ Consultants in a particular area
- ✔ Divorced fathers making over $50,000 a year
- ✔ All donors interested in pets
- ✔ Working moms who also volunteer

What happens when you do a particularly successful mailing and one of your sister organizations wants to use your list? Is it ethical? Will your donors be unhappy?

The best situation is one in which you have asked your donors whether you have permission to provide their data to other agencies you feel that they may be interested in. If a donor says, "No," you mark that item on their donor card. If a donor says, "Yes," it allows you to add them to the so-called opt-in subgroup of people who have given permission for their contact information to be shared.

Stuffing the direct mail packet

When you're ready to put your direct mail piece together, what should you include? Let's start from the outside and work our way in:

- ✔ **The envelope:** Use a good-quality envelope, part of your organization's stationery, if available. Don't use window envelopes! Your donors may feel that you are sending them a bill. If you use labels, make sure that they are high quality labels — some really sophisticated labeling techniques can produce nice-looking labels that don't give the impersonal feeling that misaligned, badly printed labels can.

Some organizations hand address special invitations and personal correspondence. For special donors, this can be a nice touch, and if you have the people power to hand address any mailing (just hand the stack of envelopes around the office and get everybody to pitch in), your open rate will soar.

- ✔ **The letter:** Write the letter in a friendly and earnest tone — telling specific stories of people your mission has helped. Some additional tips for the letter:

    - Many people read only the opening sentence and the P.S. Make them count!

    - Think carefully about who is going to sign the letter. Someone well known or high up in the organization brings the most credibility.

    - Think in terms of emotional appeal, but provide facts, too. A reader may turn off if you hit him with too much emotion too quickly. Tell the story of the need by giving the facts on how his donation can help your organization meet that need.

    - Keep the letter brief, to one page if possible. Use attachments if you need to supply more details.

    - Call for action in the letter, giving the donor a specific amount to respond to ("Your gift of $75 will help feed a family of four for three months!").

- ✔ **The pledge form:** The pledge form is the actual response form the donor fills out and returns to your organization along with her pledge or donation. Be sure to include room for the donor to correct changed contact information. Remember to include your organization's name and bulk mail number on the pledge cards if you want donors to send them to you via return mail. To save money on the return postage you can get a bulk mail permit by going to your local post office, requesting a bulk mail application, and paying a small fee.

✔ **The return envelope:** Enclose a business reply envelope, marked with your bulk mail designation (or prestamped), so the donor can respond easily.

A number of nonprofits that rely heavily on direct mail techniques use their bulk mail permit on the envelope but add a note, saying something like, "Your first-class stamp here will help us feed another family!" (if the organization raises funds to feed families). This can save the organization mailing costs and give the donor yet another easy way to make a difference.

Many nonprofit organizations use the services of mailing houses to carry out their direct mail campaigns. You can find a third-party vendor to write, design, produce, and mail the pieces you want your donors to receive. Is this a good idea? That depends on (1) the nature of your organization; (2) the quality of your vendor; and (3) the limitations of your budget. Going out-of-house for production and mailing can result in a pretty hefty per-piece cost. But today you can find more self-employed contractors offering desktop publishing services that make it possible to get a professional look for a relatively low cost.

Mailing services can also be contracted out, but be sure to ask for and check the references of any mailing house you consider. A botched mailing can result in more than money lost — unhappy donors require extra doses of reassurance after a bad experience with your organization.

Testing your direct mail piece

Test your direct mail piece before you send it. As you are developing the piece — first at the idea stage, and then when you have a draft, and finally, when the design is set and you are ready to print the piece — test the idea with coworkers, your board, and focus groups of donors and volunteers. Ask questions like these to get the ideas flowing:

✔ Would you open this envelope if it arrived in your mail today?

✔ Does the tone of the letter capture and hold your interest?

✔ Do you get a clear sense of the organization's mission from this letter? Is the case compelling?

✔ If you didn't know anything about our organization, would you want to know more after reading this piece?

✔ After reading this piece, how do you feel? Interested? Encouraged? Discouraged? Motivated to do something?

✔ What do you think of the design of the piece? Is the letter easy to read and inviting? Was the envelope easy to open?

✔ Does the piece look too expensive? Too cheap?

✔ Do you have any suggestions for ways to make this piece better?

The best response you can get from a direct mail piece is the one sent to donors you know from a person they know. If you have each of the volunteers, staff members, and board members you have review the piece and each take ten letters to send to friends (with their own personalized letter in the envelope), you can dramatically improve your return (and also build additional credibility for your organization with the contacted donors).

In general, people are impressed when you don't overdo the number of mailings. By coordinating to save mailing costs, using a single mailing to send more than one communication, you show good stewardship of the donations you receive. Of course, the trick is to be able to include several ideas in the same mailing without diffusing the focus of your appeal.

Getting Tips for Effective Print Pieces

No matter what type of materials you create, there are a number of things you can do to help capture and hold your readers' attention. Follow these tips to help create your support print pieces:

✔ **Easy-to-read works.** Your stakeholders are busy people — they want to be able to see what you're asking of them at a glance. Make everything you produce easy to read and navigate. Use bold headlines that say what you mean; leave plenty of space between sections, so the reader's eye is drawn naturally to the beginnings of sections. Add photos or graphics, where applicable, to help give the reader's eye a rest. And use bullet points — those great line-by-line symbols that say, "Look at this!" — to help readers move quickly among the most important pieces of information.

✔ **State your mission.** Your mission statement should be on everything, from your membership flyer to your newsletter to your annual report. A person new to your organization should be able to see quickly what you're all about. The best mission statements are short and to the point, 30 words or less, and clear enough that stakeholders can remember your mission after they move on to other things.

✔ **Honesty is the *only* policy.** Do your current direct mail letters exaggerate? Do your readers get your letters and say, "Oh no, not again!" Remember to represent the work you do, the people you serve, and the need you have as honestly as possible. Passion sells, but facts endure. You want your donors to give because they care, but not simply about your current crisis. You want to encourage donors to enter into a relationship with you — which means giving over time — and a crisis appeal that works today may only annoy the same donor tomorrow.

Crisis letters do work — the idea is to tie a time factor in with the request for donations. But donors will turn off to a crisis appeal that comes time after time. A better use of your publishing budget is to mix crisis appeals with thank-you letters telling donors about the good that has been done with their donations.

✔ **Strive for quirky, creative mailings.** Doing something differently may get your mail, newsletter, or annual report looked at. Try a new color, a new folding system, or a unique approach. One direct mail piece we recently received had a picture of the Statue of Liberty with a sign hung around her neck, saying "Will work for food!" We opened the thing just to find out what the rest of the piece was about.

✔ **Tell your donors where their money goes.** Today's donor is a smart, educated donor, and she wants to know that the bulk of the donation she gives you isn't going right back into your printed materials plan — or your donor lunches — or any other administrative cost. Include on your mailings a note that explains what percentage of fundraising proceeds actually goes to the cause.

An even better idea is to add a small chart on your materials that shows donors at a glance how their donations are spent.

✔ **Plan the flow of printed pieces.** Think carefully about your plan and the donors you mail to when you decide how many mailings you want to send out each year. Will you send a mailing for the annual campaign and the capital campaign? Will you also publish an annual report and four quarterly newsletters? And when will the personal correspondence go out to your high-level donors? You don't want to inundate your donors with information, but you do want to keep your organization in front of them. You don't want to send a direct mail appeal every month to the same donors — that may leave the donor feeling that her donation isn't doing any good and may, over time, burn out her interest. Think carefully about who your donors are and how often they would be receptive to receiving mail or publications from your organization. You may want to do a focus group on this, as well.

✔ **Remember "the ask."** The basic fundraising letter describes the need, explains the solution, and asks the reader — in a direct fashion — to give a donation to help make the solution happen. Even in a newsletter, you can include an ask by including a Wish List for in-kind donations, a Sign Up! section, or a stapled-in envelope that enables donors to send gifts as soon as they finish reading your piece. Timely asks, for example at the end of the year when people are looking for deductions for their income tax, bring in a healthy return.

✔ **Enclose a return envelope and a pledge card.** This goes along with the idea that you want to make everything as easy as possible for the donor. If you include a prestamped, preaddressed envelope and pledge or gift card, all the donor needs to do is write the check, seal the envelope, and mail it. Note that if you use a preprinted bulk mailing permit insignia you don't get charged unless the person returns the envelope.

✔ **Keep it simple and elegant.** Simplicity is a style that appeals to a broad range of people. Think simple elegance when you are designing your letterhead, your brochures, and your pledge cards. Don't make the design busier than it needs to be — donors may not understand what you want from them.

By *simple,* we mean choose one or two typefaces and stick to them throughout the document — fight the impulse to litter your newsletter with all the cool type fonts from your computer. Elegant includes anything from the typeface itself to the headline style to the use of space and the type of paper. When in doubt about the design and style of your piece, ask a number of people to review your preliminary designs, and ask them what they like and don't like about the current look.

Of course, what "simple and elegant" means to you needs to be based on your donor base. If you are a young organization that appeals to people in their 20s and 30s, you may want a more contemporary, active look than if you are creating a piece for a chamber orchestra with an average donor age of around 50.

✔ **Say, "Thank You!"** Your newsletter and direct mail appeal (to repeat donors) gives you a great opportunity to spotlight what is already being done with the donations you receive — you can identify individual donors and say a big in-print THANK YOU. People generally love to see their names in print and get the added benefit of knowing other people in their volunteer, peer, or donor group see it as well.

✔ **Donor Honor Rolls.** These listings can be found in the back of theater programs and are helpful in donor recognition, but having a special mention in a newsletter or on a Web site can really make a donor feel special.

Even with the explosion of the Internet age and the importance of face-to-face contact, printed pieces still have a place in your fundraising plan. Although the words you write will never replace the words you say in person, printed materials, done well, can be the next best thing to being there.

Consider providing a link to PDF (Adobe Acrobat) versions of print pieces on your Web site. People can read and print these out themselves, saving your organization the cost of printing.

Creating a Print Pieces Plan

If you are gearing up to do print pieces and direct mail for the first time, begin your plan with the following tasks:

✔ **Determine a budget for print pieces.** You may already know that you want to produce a brochure, for example, or you may simply be putting money aside to develop some print pieces. Depending on your budget, you may want to put the following bullet first. If you intend these for direct mail, be sure to account for the mailing costs.

✔ **Decide which types of pieces you want to produce.** Consider the uses of the various types of materials described earlier in this chapter (see, "Assembling the basics," earlier in this chapter) and determine what you need to accomplish through your print piece. The point is to let your need drive your decision making.

✔ **Decide when in the year you want to produce pieces.** For example, you may want to start off the year with an annual report, giving details, inspiration, and success stories from the year before, and then follow this mailing (or use it in tandem with) your annual campaign appeal, which you can do as a direct mail letter, asking existing donors to renew their commitments (and hopefully give more). You may then want to produce the first of your quarterly newsletters. And as you near your organization's big spring gala, you want to send out invitations, and then soon after, it will be time for the next newsletter issue. You get the idea.

We find it helpful to design a printed materials calendar at the beginning of the year (along with bid amounts from the contractors who will be doing the design and production). A publishing plan for one year may look something like Table 10-1.

Getting donation boxes out there

One print product you might get a great deal of response to is a donation box. You see them at the cash register in the hardware store and drugstore. These little boxes sport your logo and tell people at a glance what they are giving to. Quarters pile up and the boxes cost very little.

The trick here is to get local stores to participate and volunteers to clean out the boxes on a regular basis. If you can also place a stack of brochures somewhere near the box to tell your story more fully, all the better.

Table 10-1	Sample Annual Publishing Plan		
Quarter 1	*Quarter 2*	*Quarter 3*	*Quarter 4*
January	**April**	**July**	**October**
Qtr 1: Newsletter	Qtr 2: Newsletter	Qtr 3: Newsletter	Qtr 4: Newsletter
Draft Annual Report		Annual Fund Mailing #1	
February	**May**	**August**	**November**
Mail Annual Report		Annual Fund Mailing #2	Holiday Gala Invitations
March	**June**	**September**	**December**
Spring Gala Invitations	New Membership brochure		Year-End Direct Mail Piece
Summer Schedule printed for inclusion in Qtr 2 newsletter			

When is the best time for direct mail? We have only one answer: Know your audience. For all practical purposes, avoid the holiday rush, unless you have a mission that's tied to that holiday. Otherwise, consider when your piece is most likely to inspire your donors.

Chapter 11

Writing Winning Grant Proposals

Suppose that your project is about helping teens master new technologies. You can find a grant out there somewhere with your name on it. Want to expand the capacity of your shelter for homeless women? A foundation is out there, right now, just waiting for you to ask for the money you need.

The world is an abundant place. Locating sources of funding is not the main problem. Finding the right funder is.

From the federal government to small family foundations, awards are given to every cause imaginable — from education to arts to human services to health and beyond.

This chapter tells you how to find and approach the people with the money by writing and submitting grant proposals. And although the overall process may sound simple ("They have the money, and we need it!"), every step of the way requires careful thinking, planning, and writing. If you haven't yet thought through every bell and whistle your program offers — and how you plan to pay for those bells and whistles — you find out here that you have the opportunity to fill in all the blanks as you prepare your grant proposal.

This chapter also gives you both a broad-brush and a fine-point approach to grant research and proposal writing. As you can see, we have much to say about grant proposal writing and even more is out there for you to discover.

Some grant-related definitions

Have you seen the ads for courses in grant writing? Somebody needs to tell these people (okay, we'll do it) that the person who applies for the grant writes the grant proposal, not the grant itself. The correct phrase is "writing the grant proposal," not "writing the grant." Nobody really writes the grant; the granting agency usually just writes a check.

A *foundation* is an institution founded through an endowment and supported into the future with that endowment. Foundations are tax free and can award tax-free grants for specific philanthropic purposes, should they choose to.

The *grantor* is the person/foundation/corporation who is awarding the grant.

The *grantee* or *grant recipient* is your organization, if you are being awarded the grant.

A *challenge grant* is a grant award offered by a person or foundation that is contingent on a specified amount of money being raised from other sources.

A *block grant* is a grant award usually given to local or state governments to be divided among agencies in a specific category.

A *consortium grant* is a grant award given to a group of affiliated organizations for a collaborative project.

The best way to master grant proposal writing is to practice. Each time you write one you'll get a little better, a little clearer, a little more targeted. And, we hope, you'll get more than a little money as well.

Getting a Grip on What a Grant Is

At its most basic level, a *grant* is an award of money given to a charity or an individual. If you look it up in the dictionary, you find one of the definitions to be "a gift . . . for a particular purpose." Nonprofit organizations receive grants for a variety of purposes: to start or run programs, to build buildings, and to build strategies. Grants have a common theme: generally, a grant is freely given; you don't have to repay it. One exception to the free grant theme comes in the form of *program-related investments,* which are grants made by foundations specifically for use in starting programs that fit the foundation's philanthropic agenda. You are required to repay these grants.

Locating the Grant Givers

Grants can come from any number of sources. When you create your grant-seeking program, think about which of these sources may be most likely to "catch the spark" of your organization's mission:

- **Government agencies** comprise a large percentage of the sources available for grant seekers.

- **Private foundations** award grants that are consistent with their own mission and interests. A great source for private foundations is *Foundation Reporter 2005* (available for a pricey $590 through the Taft Group [www.galegroup.com] or on the shelf at your local philanthropic library).

  Foundation Center libraries exist in each of the following major cities: Atlanta, Cleveland, New York, San Francisco, and Washington, D.C. Cooperating collections that can obtain publications on loan are available in just about every state. If you do not have one of these libraries near you, check out http://fdncenter.org/collections/index.html to find a list of cooperating Foundation Center collections in your state, or use the online subscription service to enable you to search a library online from the comfort of your office or home.

- **Corporate foundations** give grant awards to charitable organizations that seek funds in their areas of focus. The corporate foundation is often driven by employee interest and focuses on funding programs in areas where the corporation has a presence.

- **Family foundations** are foundations organized and managed by family members, a board of director, or a trustee. Grants are made in accordance with the mission of the family foundation.

- **Community foundations**, which make up the fastest growing group of foundations, are local foundations set up to make grants for community-serving programs and projects.

Finding the Right Project to Get Funded

What kinds of projects *can* you get funded? Part of the answer to that question depends on the funder you approach. Different grant makers are open to different types of programs, which is another reason you need to research your potential donors carefully before making that first contact. Following we list some general categories for which grant makers award grants.

Seed money

Everybody loves a great idea, and because of that, getting *seed money* — that startup funding you need in order to launch that new program, extend your adult day-care program, or host this year's job fair — is the easiest of grant types to get funded.

As you begin to research and approach foundations, you may grow accustomed to seeing the phrase *no operating support,* which means don't even try approaching the foundation for funds to continue the good work you are doing. Although foundations provide seed money and capital grants with a fairly open hand, only 19 percent of all foundations were willing to give to operating expenses in 2002, according to *Foundation News and Commentary,* the magazine of the Council on Foundations (www.cof.org). This was actually a four percent increase over the 1997 survey, but still doesn't represent a majority of giving by any means.

Why are foundations unwilling to support the good work they are willing to fund at startup? We have a number of possible responses to that question, but the predominant thought is that foundations like to "see" the good they do. For example, if you have a new program that the funding enables, or if you create a new computer lab in your school with the grant award, the foundation can see where its money went and get a positive sense of carrying out its own mission.

Program funds

Program funding may be slightly different from seed money in that you can often get a grant award to continue an existing program if you are trying new things. Mother's Helper, for example, is a small nonprofit organization that helps teen mothers continue their education while learning about basic parenting skills. Mother's Helper is planning to add a mentoring component to the program that will require additional volunteer solicitation and training, marketing costs, and so on. The development person who writes the grant proposal at Mother's Helper will address this new component in her proposal.

Foundations favor the possibility of replication, which means that if a foundation funds your program, it wants to know if your program can be repeated in other areas as well. If it can fund one program and watch the good spread to many places, it is more likely to show an interest in your program and the possibilities it presents.

Grants: Just one piece of the fundraising puzzle

The hallmark of your fundraising program is its staying power. Although your good ideas may touch many lives and improve conditions for your community, if you don't address the economic factors that enable the organization to sustain itself over time, your mission will always be dependent on that One Big Grant to keep it alive another year.

Staying power is one of the best reasons to see your various fundraising efforts as an interrelated whole. If your donor base is strong, your list is up-to-date, and you are continually cultivating major donors; and if you run a successful annual campaign every year, use your resources, and build relationships with individuals, corporations, and foundations; then you can reap the income you need for operating expenses from the results of your healthy fundraising system. Grant awards, then, can give you the working capital you need to be creative, to launch new programs, to try new things, to build on the solid foundation of your other mission-related activities.

Capital campaigns

Capital campaigns fund new buildings. Capital funding is another area that enables funders to see the good that's being done in a concrete way (pun intended). Capital campaigns enable funders (and donors, and your board) to create something from nothing. From an idea, to a plan, to a model, to a reality, the capital campaign gives funders the opportunity to participate in a big way, creating the future of the organization and perhaps realizing an important naming opportunity for themselves.

It's tough to raise money for a building that's already built. Recently, a museum erected a new structure. The building is exquisite; the city was pleased. But when the organization began raising money to help pay for the already-built building, the general response was, "Well, you obviously didn't need our money to get it built!" Better to let people in on the opportunity to help when the building is still a dream — then everyone can share in the excitement as the plans progress. You can attract a lot more investment — financial and otherwise — if you allow your donors to participate in the process as it unfolds than if you go to them after the fact and ask them to pay for this really great thing that already happened without them. (For more info on capital campaigns, see Chapter 20.)

Laying the Groundwork for Grant Seeking

If you have never prepared a grant proposal, you have a wide-open — and exciting — field before you. If you (or your organization) have been applying for and receiving grants, you have a track record you can review, revise, and reuse.

As you prepare to build a grant-seeking program, you need to consider several key ideas:

✔ Is your board ready to begin a grant-seeking program?

✔ Do you have leadership in place for your grant-seeking program?

✔ Have you developed a strategy for grant submissions?

✔ Are you set up to administer grants monies and report back to the grantor on their use?

Although it is possible — and sometimes by a fluke profitable — to apply for grants haphazardly, your efforts pay off better when you develop a strategy for your grant seeking. You find out how to strategize in the section, "Developing a grant proposal writing strategy," later in this chapter.

Getting your board primed

In all facets of fundraising, board readiness is important. In Chapter 4, the board carries the banner, safeguards the mission, and addresses the legal and governance issues. The board may also give you many of your best leads for high-level donors, contacts, and yes, even foundations.

If your board has been participating in the other aspects of fundraising, from brainstorming potential contacts to going on important donor calls, working on grant seeking will be a natural next step. How can your board help with your grant program? The board can

✔ Help you test the viability of your case statement

✔ Plan your grant-seeking strategy

✔ Identify areas and/or programs that are candidates for grant funding

✔ Name foundations where they have a personal relationship or contact

Ideally, your board has a development committee that manages all the fundraising efforts you maintain throughout the year. The chairperson of this committee should be a creative, outgoing, always-thinking individual — the one in the room with a million ideas and no time to act on them. The person leading your grant-seeking program also needs to be able to make associations and enjoy a good puzzle, because that's what finding the right funder at the right time and approaching the funder in the right way with the right proposal is all about — fitting pieces of a puzzle together in a way that can be extremely rewarding.

Putting leadership into place

Should your development committee chairperson lead your grant-seeking program? Not necessarily.

Depending on the number of fundraising efforts you maintain at any one time, the chairperson's time and talents may be better spent overseeing all the fundraising functions, which means that, on a six-person development committee, you might have

- One person overseeing the annual fund
- Another person on the capital campaign
- One person looking into starting an endowment campaign
- Another person taking care of special events
- Someone else watching over the donor list and Web site
- You yourself in charge of designing and implementing the grant-seeking program

Do you need a staff? Some nonprofits have huge boards with multiple sub-committees, a full development staff, and an army of volunteers; other non-profits have a small board, no paid staff, and few volunteers. If you are a one-person development shop (and you are paid or unpaid), you need to push your board to provide good leadership for your grant-seeking program (and your other fundraising functions as well).

Even if you have few resources, your board leadership should be willing to help you (1) identify grant possibilities; (2) gather the information you need; (3) locate potential funders, opening doors when necessary; and (4) provide the input you need to complete the grant application and submit the pro-posal. And having good leadership for your grant-seeking program is impor-tant for another reason, too: Any foundation thinking about funding your good work wants to see evidence that you have strong leadership from the board before it writes the check.

Developing a grant proposal writing strategy

What should your grant-seeking strategy look like? The grant portion of your fundraising efforts needs to be a part of the strategic whole. During different portions of your year (depending also on the time and people resources you have available), you need to focus on different aspects of the search. Figure 11-1 gives you an idea of a yearlong fundraising strategy and points out just where grant seeking fits in.

The strategic plan illustrated in Figure 11-1 is just one example we developed with a small nonprofit agency that was organizing its fundraising efforts for the first time. The idea is to focus energies in multiple fundraising areas — not concentrate on one at the exclusion of the others. In Figure 11-1, the nonprofit organization plans to focus on foundation donors from November to February and on corporate donors from March to June.

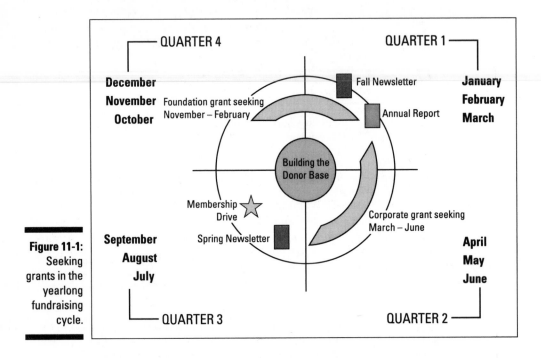

Figure 11-1:
Seeking grants in the yearlong fundraising cycle.

Notice in the figure that "Building the Donor Base" appears in the center of the figure because it's central to all fundraising activities. You must continue to contact and cultivate donors throughout the year, no matter how many other fundraising activities are going on. Remember, the donor-agency relationship is central to the health of your organization and the fulfillment of your mission. Although earning grants is an important part of fundraising, it can never replace face-to-face visits and donor contact.

As you begin to plan your grant-seeking strategy, keep the following things in mind:

> ✔ **Get help.** You can get help researching and even writing grant proposals. Your board members, your volunteers, or independent consultants and grant proposal writers can all help find prospects, draft the proposal, and assemble the necessary documents. For this reason, you may want to consider doing your grant research at a time when you have plenty of help available.

As you begin to research funders, realize that many of them have deadlines once or twice a year. As you identify the funders in your particular categories, discover the best times to apply to those funders and plan your grant strategies accordingly.

✔ **Get training.** A class can provide the instant how-to a new grant proposal writer needs. Grant proposal writing classes are often available through local community foundations, donor's groups, colleges, and online. You may want to find a class for your grant proposal writer to attend just before your grant-seeking phase begins in your fundraising calendar; then any work done in class can actually form the basis of a draft of your real grant proposal.

✔ **Get a database.** No matter how much data you uncover, you need to do something effective with it, or it won't take you closer to your goal. Make sure that your donor list is in good shape and that you set up a database in which to record foundation information. Enter the names of contacts, accurate deadlines, application procedures, and so on.

✔ **Get a case.** In Chapter 3, we discuss about the importance of your case statement — the document you create that helps your donor catch the spark of your mission. Nowhere in fundraising is the case more important than in your grant proposals. The case needs to be clear, well written, and current.

If you wrote the case statement five years ago and you simply repackage it for this year's grant proposals, maybe it's time to get a new case statement. We recommend writing a new case statement each time you do a new grant proposal — not from scratch, certainly, but with enough new material that the proposal reads like a fresh story with interest and impact.

The grant-seeking strategy you create is just a kind of ballpark road map for your fundraising plan. Throughout the year, you may hear about new grants being offered by ABC or XYZ Foundation, and you're not going to skip applying just because it doesn't fall into the grant-seeking time you scheduled! You need to take advantage of any grant possibilities that come to your attention — especially if they look like a good fit. As a general rule, though, planning time to focus on building your grant program helps you concentrate your energies where they are most effective. And even though your grant-seeking program may, in reality, look much different from the ideal one you draft at the start, having a plan gives you something to get the ball rolling.

Looking at the grant process, step by step

Your board is ready to apply for grants, and you have the leadership and strategy in place. What's next? To answer that, you need to understand the basic process of applying for a grant, which works like this:

1. **Identify a need for which you want grant funding.**

2. **Begin to develop the idea into grant proposal form.**

3. **Research grantors to see which ones support the type of issue that you are addressing.** (See, "Doing Your Homework," later is this chapter.)

4. **Get current application guidelines from the grantor.**

5. **Write the grant proposal following the guidelines and assemble all support materials.**

6. **Submit the grant.**

7. **Respond to any further requirements the grantor may have.**

8. **Get the grant award!**

9. **Submit any follow-up reports required by the foundation explaining how the monies were spent.**

Okay, so hopefully the grant process works like that. We may as well say it now: not every one of your proposals will be funded. That doesn't mean that (1) the funder is mean; (2) your proposal was bad; or (3) your cause isn't worthy. Often it means that the proposal isn't the right fit for the funder's current focus. Or it's too late in the year. Or the proposal didn't get to the right person . . . or any number of other things. What do you do when you don't get the grant? (We cover the "Nos" later, in the section, "Putting a Positive Spin on 'No.'")

Doing Your Homework

Where do you find all these foundations that are willing to fund your great program? You look for them at the store, online, at the library, at the theatre, and in the coffee shop.

Sound implausible? It's not.

Starting your search

As you become aware of who funds what, you start to see names everywhere. The John D. and Catherine T. MacArthur Foundation funds a number of public television programs. All you have to do is watch a local PBS station to hear the name of the foundation mentioned. Likewise, you hear about United Way agencies and the Bill & Melinda Gates Foundation as well. When you go to the zoo, you can see names of high-level donors, including some foundations, etched on plaques, drinking fountains, and benches. When you go to the store, you may see Target or Wal-Mart on information placards by the register touting their corporate giving program. As you begin to think about where to start your foundation research, remember the following:

- ✔ **Keep your eyes open.** You can see names of local and national foundations on all kinds of things from special event to raffle tickets.

- ✔ **Go to the library.** If you can get to your local Foundation Center library, great! The *Foundation Reporter 2005* is a terrific resource for information on foundations near and far.

- ✔ **Check out your local donor's alliance group.** Every state has a donor's alliance group of some sort. Contact your local chamber of commerce to find out the name and number of the donor's group nearest you.

- ✔ **Research your sister organizations.** Who else does what you do? What kind of grant funding do they receive, and from whom?

The best place to start looking is right at your own desk, carefully reading a copy of the newspaper and, especially, your local business journal, as well as visiting fundraising Web sites. You can pick up on which local foundations are making grants and what types of projects they are funding. And don't just check these sources now and then — you need to keep your eyes on the changing nonprofit environment every day. By reading your local business journal or visiting your chamber of commerce's Web site, you find out a lot about the exchange of money and influence in your city or town.

Zooming in on your fundraising category

Suppose that you're on the game show *Jeopardy:*

> *"Categories for $100, Alex!"*

> *". . . Where one would look for grants for a local theatre."*

> *"What is, Arts & Humanities?"*

> *"You got it!"*

When you begin using foundation and corporation reference books, you quickly realize that grants are awarded in different categories. This categorization helps foundations control the types of grant proposals they receive and helps you determine how likely it is that a given foundation will fund your particular proposal. You will see the following nonprofit categories on grant application literature and foundation references:

- ✔ Arts & Humanities
- ✔ Civic & Public Affairs

- ✔ Education
- ✔ Health
- ✔ Religion
- ✔ Environment
- ✔ Science
- ✔ Social Services
- ✔ International

After you identify which category your organization belongs to (and you may be able to be creative about fitting into more than one), you can search for the funders who grant awards in your category.

The preceding list isn't the only way of categorizing organizations. The National Taxonomy of Exempt Entities (NTEE) has devised a categorization system that includes 26 different groups under 10 broad categories. You can find this taxonomy on the Urban Institute's National Center for Charitable Statistics Web site at `http://nccs.urban.org/ntee-cc/`.

Consider a few examples to see how a little creative thinking can help you target your search for the right grantor:

Example #1: The Private School

Christ the King is a Catholic elementary school with students in grades kindergarten through eight. The school is currently putting together a grant proposal to enable them to rewire the electricity in the school so that they can add the necessary equipment for Internet capability and telecommunications.

Sue is the mother of a third-grader and the volunteer in charge of grant research. As she begins her search, she considers

- ✔ The local parish
- ✔ The archdiocese
- ✔ The parents' group
- ✔ Local foundations
- ✔ Corporations near the school that support education
- ✔ Private foundations

As she researches foundations, she looks for funders who award grants in

- ✔ Education
- ✔ Religion

Example #2: The Local Theater Group

The Phoenix Theatre prides itself on doing "cutting-edge" theater with a social conscience, often bringing in plays that stimulate discussion on a variety of challenging issues. As part of a play's normal run, the Phoenix hosts a symposium with the playwright and any agencies in the area that serve a need that the play illustrates. One play last year, for example, dealt with the issue of domestic violence, and the symposium included volunteers from the human services community that could speak professionally about those issues.

As Brenda, the development person, begins her search for funding of these symposia, she tries

✔ The local arts council

✔ Business groups and professional associations

✔ Community foundations

✔ Local foundations

✔ Corporations near the theater that support the arts

✔ The state arts commission

✔ Private foundations

✔ The National Endowment for the Arts

The categories her programs fit into include

✔ Arts & Humanities

✔ Social Services

✔ Other categories, depending on the program and focus of the funding. For example, in a symposium on the importance of family support for hospice care, the Phoenix might approach a funder with a history for supporting Wellness programs in the Health category.

Using local sources first

Although grant sources abound all over the globe — and they do — your best bet is to start with those closest to home. Sources right in your area are likely to fund you simply because you're local. How do you find the ones closest to your neck of the woods?

Start with the following local sources:

✔ Community foundations

✔ Local private foundations

✔ Organizations associated with the services you provide

✔ Local corporations and corporate foundations, especially those near the site where you provide service

A little bit of sleuthing can go a long way. Prepare to spend as much or more time educating yourself about your local funders as you do researching and writing your proposal. A good fit is half the battle: You can have the best-written, most exciting proposal in the world; but if you miss the deadline or submit to a foundation that doesn't support your type of mission, you are going to come away empty handed.

Remember the importance of face-to-face meetings with major givers. Personal meetings can make a difference with foundations, as well. When you have researched a foundation and found a local funder that's a good possibility for your program, find out whether the director is open to an in-person meeting. (Often, the funder publishes in its grant guidelines or in the foundation reference books whether it accepts personal meetings as an inquiry method.) Relationship building is at the base of successful fundraising, and if you're willing to build that relationship with your local funder, it can enhance your chances of getting that grant — if not today, then in the future.

Don't feel that you need to hang out at your local newsstand or spend entire days at the library doing your research for local possibilities: Check the Web first. Many community foundations, business journals, and corporate foundations are available online. Some even have grant applications and guidelines you can download on the spot.

Working your way away from home

What happens when you exhaust your local fundraising options? Suppose that you received a grant for $10,000 from the XYZ Foundation to provide seed money for a job-training program your organization is starting for teens. Congratulations! After you celebrate, you realize that you're $15,000 short of your goal. What's the next step in your grant-seeking plan?

Use the XYZ grant to leverage other grants. Getting any grant at all — regardless of the size or the source — is a seal of approval for other funders. The fact that you have secured funding is an encouraging sign to those who may consider funding you in the future. Getting funded means that somebody thought that your organization was worth investing in.

The next step is to research foundations not found locally and corporations that are similar in mission to the XYZ Foundation. Review your proposal, and revise it to mention the money you're getting from the XYZ grant. Then make that trip to your nearest Foundation Center library. Get your hands on one of the foundation reference books (see the list in the sidebar, "Resources for grant research") and begin your search for foundations that are a good match for the program or project you seek to fund.

Resources for grant research

Use this short list of helpful funding references as you begin your search. But don't stop here — you can find many more out there!

Look at publications by the Taft Group (Rockville, Maryland; www.galegroup.com), including:

✔ *Foundation Reporter 2005*

✔ *Corporate Giving Directory*

✔ *World Guide to Foundations*

Look up Foundation Center (New York, New York; www.fdncenter.org) references, including:

✔ *The Foundation Directory (online or CD)*

✔ *The Foundation 1000*

✔ *National Directory of Corporate Giving*

✔ *Foundation Fundamentals: A Guide for Grant-seekers*

✔ *Guide to U.S. Foundations, Their Trustees, Officers and Donors*

On the Foundation Center Web site you can use the Foundation Finder searchable database to find good foundation matches. You pay a small subscription fee, but the ease of searching the information online is well worth it.

Surfing the Net for grant opportunities

Most grant makers have Web sites. In many cases, you can find not only the mission of the foundation online, but you can also print or download the application guidelines and maybe even the application as well. You can find all kinds of information to help you — including recent grant awards, grant categories, the foundation's grant-making strategies, and so on.

Figure 11-2 shows the Grants.gov Web site that provides information about all federal grant programs. Notice that, toward the top right of the Web page, you see a link to apply for grants. Here you can download complete guidelines and application materials for a variety of grants.

Why use the Internet? It's fast, and even better, it's current. Consider the Case of the Outdated Guidelines. Last year, a foundation's proposal deadline was October 30, but this year it's September 30, but the change happened before they could print new guidelines. How can you find this out? Check the Web site to make sure that you have the most current copy of their grant guidelines. More and more, funders are beginning to provide that information on the Web: it saves them time and trouble (and postage), and makes accessing the information that much easier for you. See Chapter 6 for more on using the Internet to research funders.

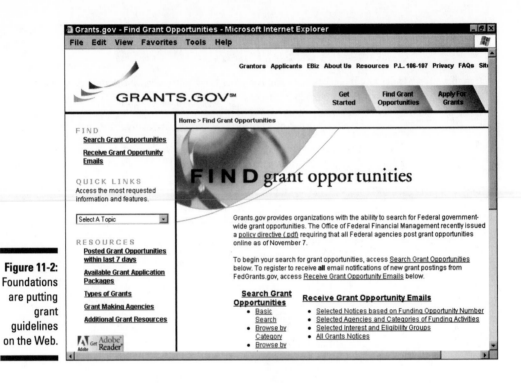

Figure 11-2:
Foundations
are putting
grant
guidelines
on the Web.

Digging deeper to find the right grantor

The foundation and corporation reference books and Web sites provide a wealth of information about the grant makers you want to investigate. Which pieces of information are important? What data is most helpful? Find the following data for each corporation or foundation:

✔ **The areas the corporation or foundation funds.** Many foundations support a wide range of areas in varying degrees. For example, in 2004–2005, the Pew Charitable Trusts Foundation awarded 128 grants totaling $99 million. Sixty percent of the grants went to Public Policy related causes (which is great news for you if you're part of a public policy activist group), but only 20 percent went to improvement of Civic Life. You can use this information to help you determine which candidates are most likely to fund your particular project and which ones are the long shots.

✔ **What the amount of the average grant is.** The reference books list both a grant range (from smallest to largest) and an average grant amount. If you are seeking $120,000, you know that you're way off base if you're considering approaching a foundation with a $35,000 average award.

✔ **How many grants the foundation or corporation awarded last year.** Obviously, the greater the number of grants awarded, the better it looks for you. Numbers can be deceiving in this regard; however, the foundation probably also receives a greater number of proposals than smaller foundations. More important is how closely your program fits its mission and how clearly you make that connection.

✔ **At what time of year, or by what date, the organization accepts proposals.** Different foundations have different proposal timeframes, usually connected to when the board of directors gets together to discuss grant possibilities. Send your proposal in plenty of time to hit the deadline.

There's an age-old debate about whether it's better to come in at the wire, with the latest possible proposal, and grab a lion's share of the attention, or to get your proposal in early so the reviewers have time to think about it and grow to love it. The most important thing, in our opinion, is to have a well-researched, well-targeted proposal that fits the interests and abilities of the funder and doesn't oversell the real good that can be done.

✔ **The submission process the foundation or corporation wants you to follow.** How important is this? Very! Some funders want letters of inquiry; others want full proposals; still others invite visits. Some funders won't accept unsolicited proposals at all, so read the listings carefully! If you don't do what they ask you to, even if it's just attaching some supporting document, you may lose on a technicality.

Inquiring Minds Want to Know: Letters of Inquiry and Guidelines

Some funders want you to submit a letter of inquiry before they send you the grant application guidelines. What is a letter of inquiry, and what should you put in it?

A *letter of inquiry* is a letter (okay, that part was obvious!) you write to the foundation giving them an overview of your project and requesting the grant application and guidelines.

The funder is looking for a way to quickly determine whether your proposal is in line with their funding goals. They want a brief summary of your project or program, a sense of the grant amount you are seeking, and an understanding of the principal people in your organization, and a summary of how the programs runs. Read the listing carefully to determine just what the funder wants to see and then do your best to deliver it in a timely and professional manner.

And what about grant guidelines? These essentially tell you how to prepare a grant proposal just the way the funder likes it, which is important information to have. What types of specifics do grant guidelines provide?

✔ The mission and focus of the foundation. (This typically includes the categories in which the foundation awards funding, such as Arts & Humanities, Education, and Health & Welfare.)

✔ Eligibility requirements for grant seekers

✔ How the foundation evaluates proposals

✔ What types of projects are funded and what types are not

✔ Questions the funders want answered in your proposal

✔ Deadlines for proposal submission; the schedule for grant awards

✔ Contact and proposal submission information

✔ What types of supporting materials are required and in what format

Grant guidelines are an important road map for the grant proposal you are preparing. Some grant guidelines are available on the Web; others you call or write for. No matter how you get them, be sure to take them seriously.

Many organizations today accept, or in some cases require, online submission of grant applications. Check the foundation's Web site to see if they do. This can sometimes be a lifesaver when you're up against a tight deadline.

Sitting Down and Writing the Proposal

After you do your research and identify one or many potential funders, the next step is to write the grant proposal. Before you start groaning, think of it this way: grant proposal writing is the art of passing the "spark" of your mission on to those funders who may be willing and able to help in a big way.

As you create each piece of the grant proposal, use the most compelling information from your case statement so that the proposal helps the funder understand the following things:

✔ Your organization has an effective solution to a real need the funder cares about.

✔ You have thought through the program carefully.

✔ You have planned out the process to implement it.

✔ You have selected strong leadership for the program.

✔ You have been (and will continue to be) financially responsible with the program.

✔ You have a track record of accountability and will keep the funder informed of the program's progress.

Although the proposals you write may vary depending on what the funder wants to see, a complete grant proposal usually includes the following elements:

- ✔ Cover letter
- ✔ Executive summary (also called the *abstract*)
- ✔ Introduction
- ✔ Program need/program statement
- ✔ Program goals, objectives, and evaluation
- ✔ Program budget and budget narrative
- ✔ Leadership, staffing, and location
- ✔ History of the organization
- ✔ Addendums such as your 501(c)(3) letter and financial statements

How long should a grant proposal be? Only as long as it takes to convey the problem, the solution, and the facts the funders need to make their decision. Let the grant guidelines give you an idea of what length the funder expects. Some foundations ask for brief (even one page!) proposals. Others leave the length open ended. Because you want to keep the funder reading, keep the proposal streamlined and interesting. Don't restate on page 4 something you said on page 2. Tighten your prose and lead the reviewer to the conclusion that you are describing a program she'd like to fund.

In the following sections, we look at the elements of a grant proposal one by one.

Creating a successful cover letter

Your cover letter introduces your organization and explains to the funder what is in the proposal package. The cover letter also includes any and all contact information you can provide for your organization, including e-mail addresses and a Web page, if you have one.

Executing a stylish executive summary

The executive summary has been called the single most important section in your proposal. It should be short — one to two paragraphs — but complete. The executive summary should give a complete overview of your proposal, telling the funder who you are, about the need, how your organization plans to respond to the need, how the funder can help you affect that response, and how much money you need to do that. Because of the volume of proposals foundations receive, they are often divided among board members to review, and the executive summaries are the sections that speak to the over-worked, time-crunched executive. Make your case clearly, compellingly, and concisely in your executive summary.

Ask a number of people both inside and outside your organization to read over your executive summary after you finish it. How could it be better? Does it get to the point quickly enough? Does it say what you want to say? Use the reactions of your peers to streamline the summary so that it's as effective as possible.

Introducing yourself

The introduction should also be brief, explaining a little more specifically what's to come in the grant proposal. You can include a table of contents if you choose, although in shorter proposals, this is unnecessary.

Stating the program need in a program statement

Your program need should paint the picture of the cause that your organization exists to support. This and the program statement can come right out of your case statement, if that document is up-to-date. You may want to tweak the information a bit, including specific examples of people who have been helped by your organization or situations that need your help, which can help the funder "connect the dots" between the need you are describing and the real people you serve as well as what you're proposing and potential funder's funding criteria. The more you can connect what you need with the funder's mission, the more chance you have of obtaining that grant.

Outlining program goals, objectives, and evaluation

This section shows the funder that you have thought through, step-by-step, the goals you want to achieve through this program. You may have a number of different measurable goals, such as:

Goal 1: Increase teen participation by 15 percent.

Goal 2: Open the youth center on weekends from October to May.

Goal 3: Implement teen leadership program by June 1.

Objectives are the smaller, measurable increments that detail the specific steps you want to take to reach your goal. Objectives tend to measure either a process step or an outcome. An example of objectives for Goal 1 might be:

Objective 1-1: Host a Web design workshop for teens where they upgrade our site.

Objective 1-2: Meet with school counselors and caseworkers to identify new candidates.

Objective 1-3: Increase awareness through PSAs, posters, and media outlets.

Objective 1-4: Use volunteers to increase awareness.

Evaluations inform the funder of your timeline for when and how you will reach the objectives you list. Be sure that your evaluations are measurable. For example, for Objective 1-1, a measurable evaluation would be "Workshop will be scheduled before March 15 and will include a participants' sign-in sheet." This timeline and plan for the sign-in sheet helps you be sure that you are actually working, with provable data, toward both your objective and your goal.

Detailing the program budget and budget narrative

As you might expect, any funder thinking about giving you money is going to want to know specifically what you plan to do with it. Your budget needs to show that you've thought it all out, that you've tried other sources (or plan to), and that you are willing to make investments yourself in order to make the program happen. Most foundations, corporate or private, want to know that you have a "100 percent giving board" before they award a grant to your organization. They also want to know that you have sought creative ways to have services and goods provided as in-kind donations. (See Chapter 4 to find out more about giving boards and Chapter 5 for more about in-kind contributions.)

The budget narrative explains your budget numbers in broad but accurate terms. You don't need to walk the reviewer through every nickel and dime (nor should you include every nickel and dime in your balance sheet — rounding to dollars will do). But you do need to explain where your major expenditures will be, how you've planned for them, who you've approached, and what results you anticipate. Be as clear and forthcoming as you can, but expect questions.

Foundations often ask for clarification on various points in your proposal. Instead of being alarmed when you get the call, be excited: It means that the funder is interested enough in your idea to pursue it further.

Online resources for grant proposal writing

Check out the following Web sites for guidance as you prepare to write your grant proposal:

✔ The Foundation Center: `http://fdncenter.org/`

✔ Grants.gov: `www.grants.gov`

✔ Grant Station: `www.grantstation.com`

✔ On Philanthropy: `www.onphilanthropy.com`

Leadership, staffing, and location

You need to tell the foundation about the leadership you're selecting to run the program or project. This information is very important to the funder because having good leadership is as important as having a well-thought-out plan, and the funder wants to know that you have the people to put your program into action. Include biographies and resumes of the key people involved with the program, and be prepared to have them sit in on a site visit if the funder asks to meet with you face to face.

The location of the program or project gives the funder a good idea of what type of facility you have, which ties to the practicality and the "thought-through-ness" of your idea. If you plan to increase teen participation by 15 percent but you're already up against the fire marshal's limit for your small bungalow, the funder may question your plan. If you have a nice facility with room to grow, the site will work to your advantage. Having an appropriate facility assures the funder that your program — and ultimately its money — makes a real impact on the need you so eloquently communicate.

Running down your history

Some grant proposal books may tell you to lead with the history of your organization, and you certainly can do that if you believe that your organization's history plays heavily to what you're trying to communicate in your proposal. In most cases, however, the reader skips over what you did yesterday to find out what you're doing today. History is important, but in a grant proposal, it's probably not the most important thing you want to communicate. Because you have only a few minutes of the reviewer's time, it's better to lead with the strong stuff and include the history at the end.

Your organization's history may include a long list of accomplishments and famous people who have aligned themselves with your mission, or it may be the simple story of a need and the people who address it. Examples of your accomplishments should illustrate your ability to make a difference. Whatever your story is, remember to tell it with heart and spark.

The rest of the story

At the end of your proposal, you need to attach a copy of your 501(c)(3) letter from the IRS, at least one year of financial statements (certain funders may request more), and your organization's budget for the current year (not just the program or project budget that you included in the proposal). Check the guidelines for any additional materials that might be required, such as sample marketing materials.

Following Up on Your Proposal

How long do you wait after you submit a proposal before you follow up? Until your fingernails are gone? Until you can't stand it anymore?

Most funders will give you an idea in their grant guidelines what to expect in terms of review time. If you are uncertain, call and ask how long you should wait before checking back. You may get a "don't-call-us, we'll-call-you" response, but in most cases the administrative assistant will give you a workable timeframe. A brief call or letter after that day comes and goes will suffice for contact, but stay current with your contacts, documenting your calls and the responses. Most funders respond in a reasonable amount of time, and you'll most likely be contacted with questions and/or visit possibilities if they are actively interested.

And besides, who has time to sit around and worry about a submitted proposal? You have to start researching those corporations!

How goals, objectives, and evaluations differ

A goal answers the question, "What do we want to accomplish?"

An objective answers the question, "How will we accomplish that goal?"

An evaluation answers the question, "How will we know that we've accomplished it?"

Handling a site visit

Before giving a major grant, foundation representatives want to come see what you do. The experience of seeing the need and the work firsthand is very telling — and often inspiring.

What should you do when the foundation contacts you and wants to make arrangements for a site visit?

✔ **Relax.** The foundation isn't coming here to "check up" on you or debunk your great proposal. Instead, the grantors are interested in seeing with their own eyes how the work you do fits with their mission and goals.

✔ **Plan.** Think about what the representatives can participate in that would give them a taste for your mission. Think "hands-on," as opposed to "presentation." Meeting your clients, hanging out with your teens, and hearing your patrons talk about the difference your organization has made can have a bigger impact than charts and figures over coffee.

Putting a Positive Spin on "No"

What does a "No" mean? It could mean any number of things:

✔ The funder has already funded many programs similar to yours this year.

✔ The funder has other priorities right now. For example, you may have submitted a grant for your arts organization, and the funder is currently focusing on educational issues.

✔ The funder didn't understand what you were asking for.

✔ The timing isn't right, and the funder may want to wait until you're further along in the development of your program.

✔ The funder doesn't feel that your organization is at the right point in its growth to tackle the proposed undertaking.

✔ The funder isn't the right one for your organization.

"No" is not the end of the world. Review your proposal to make sure that it's as strong as you can make it, and try the next candidate on your list.

Chapter 12

Projecting Your Image by Using the Media

. . . .

In This Chapter

▶ Using radio, TV, print, and the Internet to get your news out

▶ Getting along with the media

▶ Dealing with damage control on media disasters

. . . .

*Y*ou're not camera shy, are you? Don't worry — many people are, at first. But being willing and able to pursue media exposure for your organization is not only smart for your fundraising program; but also it's advantageous for building the overall credibility of your cause. Arming yourself with some basic how-tos for handling, and even enjoying, media relations can give you the confidence you need to see media for what it is: a golden microphone to address masses of people.

Although working with media takes a little time and some careful and creative thought, your use of the media can go a long way toward building the awareness and reputation of your organization. Having an outgoing personality helps, but it's not a prerequisite. All you have to do is master a few media basics and you can communicate your cause clearly and with passion.

In this chapter, we take you through a number of media channels, helping you investigate ways to get positive attention for your nonprofit organization through radio, television, print media, and the Internet.

Getting Out There and Getting Media Exposure

Many fundraisers work day in and day out without giving a lot of thought to media coverage. If media attention happens, great (assuming it's positive!), but who has time to go looking for it? When you consider the amount of time you spend researching donors, narrowing your list, and educating people about your mission and your programs, however, you realize that spending just a little time planning some media exposure can pay back many times over in terms of public awareness and interest.

How can you use media exposure to help your organization?

- You can create a radio spot, advertising your upcoming gala.
- You can do a television interview, talking about a new survey on teens, released by your organization.
- Your organization can be the subject of a feature article in your newspaper or local magazine that ties in to concerns in your community.
- You can participate in an online chat in a Web site that deals with issues in your organization's area of work.

Think of media exposure as simply education. When you run the 30-second radio spot, you are telling the listeners:

- Who you are
- What you do
- Why they should care
- How they can help

In the television interview, perhaps on your area's News at Noon, you can

- Show viewers what your organization is about. (This visual may be the name and phone number of your agency or your organization logo displayed on the television screen, or a video of a recent event at your facility.)
- Allow viewers to put a face with a name.
- Inform viewers about your organization, perhaps for the first time.
- Interest viewers in your organization's current happenings or upcoming events.

In a print article in your local paper, you can

- Relate how your organization is currently addressing real needs in your community.
- Convey a sense of the spark of your mission.

✔ Educate readers about various programs.

✔ Include contact information encouraging readers to donate time, goods, or money.

For many nonprofits, the road to media exposure begins with a simple press release, which can be mailed or faxed, promoting the accomplishment or the need. Be sure to include the name of someone who can be contacted about the information. You can follow up with a phone call, if you want. This approach is likely to work better if you have taken the time to develop good relationships with media leaders in your community. Human-interest stories — stories of people's successes, challenges, and needs that draw empathy and sympathy — are widely used in all media, and most nonprofits have these stories by the dozens.

Just as you do with donors and grantors, find out what interests your local media and how you can help your needs and theirs come together. These people get inundated with press releases and bids for inclusion on their pages. Give them interesting information in a professional format and you'll get into their good graces.

A time for us

One of the challenges in getting media exposure is that you have very little time in which to say some really important things. Take a look at these comparisons:

Radio: A typical PSA (public service announcement) gives you only 30 to 60 seconds of airtime.

Television: Even a lengthy news interview may be only two minutes of actual airtime; when you clip out newscaster lead-ins and voice-overs, you may have only one minute of real footage from your organization or your interview. More typically, you have less than 30 seconds.

Online: If you are leading a chat, you have a longer period of time (up to an hour, in some cases); but the medium requires tight control — a group chat can be like carrying on 20 individual conversations at once. Moderated discussion forums and your own Web site allow you to post information and leave it there indefinitely for people to see. An online broadcast or "Webcast" can give you greater flexibility, but viewers tend to watch only the first few minutes of live or pre-recorded content.

Print: Print is a medium in which the time allotted is virtually unlimited. You may have an hour interview with a reporter, which translates into a (hopefully) good story that the reader can read again and again if she chooses. If the article appears on the newspaper's Web site, you can link to it from yours for even greater exposure. Keep copies of print articles to make available in your fundraising packets, as well.

Working in Sound Bytes: Public Service Announcements (PSAs)

If you aren't using any media at all right now, you may be pleased to find out that you have one completely free media avenue open to you right this very minute — PSAs. PSAs are radio, television, and sometimes print stories that enable you to get the news out about what your nonprofit organization is doing. Are you hosting a chili cook-off next month? You can record a PSA about it. Are you preparing to release your latest community development report? You can let your city know through a PSA.

Government regulations of the public's airwaves require that TV and radio offer free public service announcements to local nonprofit organizations. Although many newspapers offer such announcements as part of their civic responsibility, no federal regulation requires that they do so.

When you talk to the folks at the radio station, request that your PSA be aired during prime listening time (6:00 a.m. to 7:00 p.m.). Often PSAs get pushed to the off-peak hours (7:00 p.m. to 6:00 a.m.) because the paying clients fill the commercial air slots, but it's worth asking for prime time. Also, don't hesitate to ask if they offer special deals for nonprofits buying airtime; many do.

Most stations allow nonprofit organizations to come into their studios and tape the spot with their equipment. You don't have to spend the money to have the segment professionally produced at a recording studio. Many do have requirements about how much advance notice that you need to give them. Check with the station's community affairs director to get the local rules. Alternately, use your computer sound recording program (Windows has this feature built into Windows Media Player, for example) with an attached microphone to record the spot and submit it in electronic format on a CD or even via e-mail.

What should you include in a PSA?

- ✔ Your organization's name
- ✔ Your nonprofit status (if you are a 501(c)(3), the IRS designation of a nonprofit, say so)
- ✔ Your mission
- ✔ Who you serve
- ✔ Important information about the event or project you are announcing
- ✔ A way to contact you for more information (include your phone number and Web site or e-mail address, if it's easy to remember)

Consider this example of a 30-second PSA for a small nonprofit:

> Blankets for Emma is a nonprofit organization in the Toledo area organized to provide support, education, and warmth to those caring for HIV-positive infants. This February 23, Blankets for Emma will host its first annual Knit-A-Thon at the Cathedral High School gymnasium from 1:00 p.m. to 8:00 p.m. For more information on how to participate in the Knit-a-Thon or to sponsor our knitting volunteers, call Dorene Wilson at 555-555-5555.

If you are recording for radio for the first time, here's a tip: smile. When you smile as you read, the sound of your smile carries in your voice — no kidding! Listeners will find your voice more pleasant and personable and may just end up smiling, too.

Looking Good on Video

Come on; tell the truth — you have always wanted to be on television, right? With the seemingly endless range of cable channels, the ever-lengthening morning and nightly news, and the dozens of talk shows (stay away from the ones that tend to have fistfights), television presents you with a great opportunity for wide exposure.

Getting on the small screen

Getting on television can be a major deal for the small nonprofit. For larger organizations, television may be ho-hum, just part of a day's work. The big-city symphony hires professionals who know how to work with television: from "Meet the Conductor" interviews to "Saturday Sonatas" breaks between cartoons on Saturday mornings; these symphony leaders know how to use the airwaves to reach out to their constituents — and their constituents' children. For the small nonprofit, however, you frequently may be on your own.

Here are a few examples of ways you can get television coverage:

✔ Promote a special, black-tie event where a prominent personality is appearing.

✔ Suggest a feel-good story for the nightly news about a success you were involved with.

✔ Work on a televised fundraising campaign for your public television station. (Hey, don't laugh — you could sit there for an hour answering the phone with your nametag and organization name in front of you. The message to viewers is "we help other organizations, too," and that says a lot about the character of your agency.)

✔ Do one of those PSAs we cover in the preceding section "Working in Sound Bytes: PSAs."

✔ Do a how-to segment on a locally produced show. For example, in Indianapolis, you can produce a segment for the local public-television show *Across Indiana* on the restoration of the historic gardens at Garfield Park.

✔ Pay for advertising time, instead of only using what's free.

✔ Use your own local public access cable station to televise your own telethon fundraiser, getting people to come in and perform while your volunteers pick up the phones and collect dollars.

Not all TV minutes have to be donated. The United Way is now paying for some airtime, which is a big change from using only donated airtime as they did in the past. United Way found that by paying for the time, it could choose the prime time spots it wanted, rather than having to accept the time spots given for free. Because PSAs frequently run in time slots unattractive to advertisers, the shift to buying airtime means that the United Way is more likely to reach its target audience and increase awareness in the areas they most want to affect. To help the cost of the purchased airtime go as far as possible, the United Way was able to get participating stations to match the amount of time purchased as an in-kind donation.

Handling television interviews

Suppose that your idea has captured the attention of a local TV news producer. She'd like to send a reporter out to talk to you about the ranch you run for at-risk teens. Now what?

First, say, "Sure! Come on out!" in the most confident voice you can muster. Next, you need to prepare for the interview. Use the following list to help you prepare:

✔ Who is the best person to talk to the reporter? Whether it's the founder, the board president, the executive director, or you, make sure that the person who does the talking is (1) personable; (2) articulate; and (3) passionate about your organization's mission and the work you are currently doing.

✔ You only have a very few minutes on tape. What do you want to say most? Get clear in your mind what you most want to say and then, even if the reporter asks questions that take you in a different direction, steer the conversation back around to what you really intended to say about your organization. (See *Public Speaking For Dummies,* 2nd Edition, by Malcolm Kushner [Wiley] to get ideas on how to make a flawless presentation!)

✔ What do you want viewers to see? Think through the eyes of the camera. What does the place look like? Where should the interview be shot? How can you help viewers get a sense of your mission? The best impact is the picture of work actually being done, not people talking about the work that is done somewhere off-camera. If you have footage of your people at work, provide it to the producer to cut away to during your interview.

✔ Think success stories. Although the temptation to focus on the need may be great, remember that you want to show viewers that good things are happening at your organization and inspire them to want to be part of the good that's going on.

You don't have anyone who is media-savvy? Check again. Every volunteer list has somebody who has done some public relations (PR) work in the past. (If you haven't asked your volunteers to fill out time and talent sheets, check out Chapter 4.) Contact that volunteer and ask him or her to help you prepare for your television interview. If you search the list and come up empty, contact a local PR firm and ask them to donate 30 minutes of their time as an in-kind donation to review some TV basics with you. Or get a good book on public and media relations from your local library or bookstore.

Of course, if you're a big outfit (and sometimes even if you're not), it's not unthinkable to partner with a local station to do a 30-minute documentary on your organization, its mission, its history, and its future. As you would expect, though, this requires establishing a good relationship with your local media, which takes time, talent, and persistence to pay off.

Taking Advantage of Print Opportunities

Suppose that getting into print is your objective. Depending on your background and the type of organization you are working with, this may be easier than getting a slice of that coveted airtime you need for a television interview. What kind of print opportunities do you have in your area?

Your local media may include

✔ A daily or weekly newspaper (morning and afternoon in some cities)

✔ County newspaper

✔ Chamber of Commerce publications

✔ Local business journal

✔ Locally produced magazines

✔ Community newsletters

✔ Corporate newsletters that sometimes spotlight employee volunteer activities

And what are they all looking for? Something quotable (see "Making yourself quotable," later in this chapter) — things that people will talk about and repeat today and tomorrow and come back for more.

A key to making good use of print coverage is to use every bit of news as another reason to get in print. If you run a playwriting competition, announce that you're accepting entries, and you've selected judges; publicize the pending final deadline for entries, the judges' choices, the awards ceremony, and so on. Build excitement about longer programs and keep the public engaged.

Making yourself quotable

Editors love a good quote, and there's nothing wrong with writing a few favorites up beforehand. After you have identified what you want to say, you can write a few statements that relate to that idea. For example, if you are going to be interviewed about the upcoming Knit-a-Thon for Blankets for Emma, you may want to mention the 60 families you served last year through this event. Possible quotable remarks may be:

> "Helping 60 families warms a lot of people."

> "We want to be the warm embrace that helps families face the cold shock of HIV."

> "Blankets for Emma was born out of a basic human need for comfort in a time of crisis."

> "Helping makes me feel good," said one 7-year-old volunteer.

> "One smile on one face can make my day."

What makes a good quote? To make a good quote, your statement must

✔ Sound right

✔ Be short enough to remember

✔ Tug at the heartstrings, the intellect, or both

✔ Include either a direct or indirect call to action

In other words, your quote should almost burst with meaning and impact.

Fixing mistakes in print

What happens when the reporter gets it wrong? He forgets to add that you are a 501(c)(3), and he publishes your fundraising goal for your new campaign as one million when it's really only $250,000. Worst of all, he misspells the name of your biggest donor, the one who recently gave you a donation large enough to purchase art supplies for your kids for the next three years. What do you do when the article is just plain wrong?

First, keep your cool. Next, write down the errors in the article and call the reporter on the telephone. Go over the items with him (calmly), and ask him to print a correction in the same spot in the next issue. He probably needs to talk it over with his managing editor (in fact, you may need to talk it over with his managing editor, as well), but most newspapers are willing to correct errors that you call to their attention. And the correction gets your name in print again.

Choose your battles wisely. Don't be ready to duke it out over every misspelling or the erroneous reporting of an upcoming event. If the article compromises your mission, tarnishes your reputation, or in some other way creates a negative public awareness, by all means take your case to the editor. You want to maintain a long-term relationship with the publication, but be willing to contest false or misleading statements in print.

Leveraging Online Coverage

The newest media on the block is on the Internet. Nonprofit organizations are getting more and more active online because in most cases it's free exposure to a huge audience. Most have their own Web sites. Chapters 15, 16, and 17 deal in-depth with a number of Web issues, but in this chapter we look at media exposure online.

Your first step is to get "Net savvy." If you're not an experienced Web researcher, it's time to get busy. Use the search engines that we suggest in Chapter 11 to look for sites that talk about the topics philanthropy, charitable giving, fundraising, and nonprofit organizations. Search for sites that relate to your mission: If you help homeless teens, search with terms such as "teens," "homeless," and "runaways." Check out the promising sites and find out

- ✔ What they have to offer in terms of information or resources
- ✔ Whether they allow nonprofits to put their own links on the site
- ✔ Who you can contact if you want to contribute an article idea or story

Posting your story everywhere

You can also approach the editors of online versions of print publications about possibilities for features articles. Sites such as MSNBC (www.msnbc.com), USA Today (www.usatoday.com), or your local newspaper may be open to your ideas. Visit them and review their policies on article submissions.

Though the Web has global reach, for your purposes you're most likely to get interest in your cause right in your own community. Your area (city, county, region) may already have a Web site dedicated to local nonprofits. Or, if you don't find a site that's completely dedicated to NPOs, you probably can find a community site that lists events and happenings in your area. Our hometown of Indianapolis has www.indy.com and http://community.circlecity.com/, which, among other things, give nonprofits free exposure on the Web. The information the nonprofits provide on these sites is nothing fancy, of course; but you can add your organization's name and mission to a page along with a link to your organization's own Web site. (You do have a Web site, don't you? If you don't, you may want to seek some grant funding to develop one.) Figure 12-1 shows a simple listing of youth and family organizations on http://community.circlecity.com.

When you list your organization on a community Web page, be sure to include a link to your own site; then when visitors click the link, they can get more information, and perhaps even make a donation, from your Web site.

A *banner ad* is an advertisement on a Web page that stretches, like a banner, across the displayed page. Banner ads often use animation to attempt to grab the visitor's attention while they are reading the content of the page.

Figure 12-1: The cheapest and easiest Web exposure is a free listing on a community site.

Hopping on news feeds

A lot of sites don't have time to write all their own content. They use something called news feeds or RSS (really simple syndication) to pull stories from other sources and display them, or links to them, on their site. The Christian Science Monitor and CNN are just two sites that offer news feeds. Some news feeds aggregate stories from many sources. The point is that getting your story placed on a site that provides news feeds of its stories to others multiplies your exposure.

One other hot source of online information is blogs (short for Web log). A blog is simply a collection of frequently updated stories, comments, and links. Individuals who simply want a soapbox run some blogs. Major media publishers or special interest groups run others. Search online for "blog directories" to find lists of all kinds of blogs with all kinds of focuses, and then try to get your information included on the ones most directly related to your cause.

Making Friends with the Media

Does your local feature reporter yawn when he sees you coming? Have the radio stations stopped running your PSAs? How do you get your media contacts to wake up and take notice of the good things that are going on at your organization?

The following list provides a few ideas on how to come up with stories and other media ideas that the media will want to run:

- ✔ **Plan an event that links with another story currently in the news.** For example, if a measles outbreak has occurred in your area, your Vaccines-for-Every-Child program fits right into the media hoopla. Or, if you run a literacy program, you could plan a Read-A-Thon to occur just before school starts to fund your new reading program, and plan a Graduate Celebration at year's end to reward clients who have achieved their goals through your program. These success stories make a nice topper to the sometimes hard-to-take evening news.

- ✔ **Look for happy media opportunities.** Suppose that someone's favorite feline climbed to the top of the tallest tree at your recent Humane Society pet show, and your board president, who also just happens to be the fire chief, climbed a ladder and got her down. Grab your camera, or better yet, alert the media, if they are close. You just might get to be the "good news" at the end of the show. (Of course, don't create such opportunities where none exist — experienced news people can smell a plant-the-cat-in-the-tree hoax a mile away, and it can damage your relationship and your credibility with the press. Besides, you don't want to endanger a pussycat or your board president for your 15 seconds of fame.)

✔ **Don't wait for the media to call you.** If you have a good idea, be willing to talk about it. Don't alienate your media contacts by barraging them with inane ideas, but when you have an interesting idea that lends itself to a good radio, television, or print story, knock on the necessary doors.

✔ **Stay tuned to the media in your area, and in your area of service.** Know which topics are hot now and which are yesterday's oatmeal. Don't approach a television producer with a story on a clown rodeo that your ranch is hosting the same week that a clown is arrested for drunk driving.

✔ **Refresh your content.** If you've been describing your organization the same way for two years in every press release, or if the paragraph at the end of your releases describing the history your group has read the same for five years, rewrite it to jazz it up.

Be sensitive to the timing, the ideas, and the amount of work your ideas create for the reporter and producer. The more you can do yourself, the more attractive your idea will be.

Remembering on-air cues

When you're sitting in the hot seat and feel that the big open eye of the camera is on you (or the oversized microphones hanging above your head), keep your wits about you and remember these things:

✔ **This is FUN!** Relaxing is the name of the game, and if you practice what you want to say most until you know it inside and out, you can relax and be yourself and say what you came to say. Don't think that we're advocating reciting a script, however — we're not! Instead, know your thoughts well enough that you can relax and say them naturally, as you would say them to a friend. You're representing good work. That belief in itself, and not your performance, is what carries the day.

✔ **Practice, practice, practice.** Before you go on the air, try a mock interview with a friend or colleague, especially if you know somebody with public speaking or media experience.

✔ **Keep it short.** Whether you are being interviewed or contributing to a panel discussion, keep your comments brief and packed with meaning. We all roll our eyes at the puffed-up experts who hog the camera and drag out to five minutes what could have been said in one. Say what you want to say, say it smart, say it fast, and be as clear as possible. Your viewers and listeners (and interviewers) will thank you for it.

✔ **Give them something to remember.** When we are interviewed, we try to leave viewers or listeners with something concrete they can try, a new idea to consider, or a new tool to use, whether they are in our industry or just listening casually out there in Audience-land. For example, if you work for Blankets for Emma, encourage viewers or listeners to be sensitive to families in need and provide the name and address of a Web site or national clearinghouse for HIV statistics. Or, if you work in a literacy program, list three things parents can do to help their children love reading. Whatever your area of service, find something that will help viewers and listeners be glad that they tuned in.

✔ **Make a good first impression.** Start your interview smiling, whether you are on camera or sitting in a recording studio. Relax as much as you can, and keep a positive frame of mind, even if you think that you may be asked some tough questions and inside are quivering a bit. When the camera's red light blinks on, don't do a Fred Flintstone and stare blank-eyed and slack-jawed into the lens. As the producer counts down, take a deep breath and release it, sending with your exhale any negative thoughts and tensions about the interview. Then smile and answer the questions one at a time, as they come, in the best way you know how. That is good enough. (For more on how to do a great interview and get control of your nerves, see *Public Speaking For Dummies,* 2nd Edition, by Malcolm Kushner.)

✔ **Dress for success.** On video, which is what most media use these days to record, busy patterns in your clothing can actually cause distracting patterns. Avoid patterns and stripes, or bright white clothing. Your best bet is something simple and subdued. And here's a little tip: blues work great on video.

✔ **Don't just tell them; show them.** If you have control over any part of the story — for example, if the television crew is sending a cameraperson out to your facility to film the interviews on-premises — use every opportunity to show viewers what you do instead of simply telling them. You can always talk about your programs (the editor can put it in as a voice-over), but let the video show your enthusiastic volunteers working with the people you serve. That, done well, carries a powerful message words cannot convey.

People are people are people, and even in an interview, you aren't talking to a camera, you're talking to a person. Even when it's a call-in show, there are real people at the other end. Remember that the person you are talking to is the most important person in the world at that time. This great advice came to us early on from a person experienced in dealing with the media. What hangs us up in interviews is often the intimidation of it all — a new area, something outside our normal comfort zone, with so much seeming to ride on our individual performance.

Give each person your undivided attention and focus carefully on the subject at hand. The media feeling just falls away and it becomes part of what you're so good at: that relationship-building skill that is so much a part of the fabric of fundraising.

Controlling the damage of media disasters

Not to end this chapter on a somber note, but we thought that we'd better give a few tips on what to do when the perfect interview doesn't materialize. If you follow the suggestions throughout this chapter, of course, you shouldn't have any big media blunders right there on the air. But sometimes things happen outside your control: a board member gets investigated for something, a volunteer feud breaks out, and an inebriated MC hosts a special event. There may be times when you get exposure that you don't want.

Getting the crisis under control fast

When a disaster does happen and the media comes running, you need to think quickly on your feet about what to say to protect the reputation of your organization, and to protect the trust you've built with your community. Here we give you some ideas that will help you to quickly handle such a situation:

- ✔ **Don't be defensive.** Denial is not only pointless; it can be downright dangerous when you're talking about reputations, as the current political environment in the United States has shown. Instead of defending your organization, shifting the blame, or claiming innocence, evaluate the situation as quickly as possible and then face the issue head-on. (It's okay to tell the media, "We don't know yet, but we're finding out," until you know what happened.)

- ✔ **If you goofed, admit it.** You may think that this is a logical outcome of not being defensive, but admission is something else again. Did you drop the ball and apply $10,000 in restricted funds to your scholarship program? Admit it. Whether it's a public or private gaff, be determined to tell the truth about it. Of course, if it's a private issue, there's no reason to go seeking media exposure to reveal your mess. That's not the kind of exposure that you want!

- ✔ **Do something about it.** If somebody has been hurt or harmed, or maybe just annoyed, and the media picks up the story, start by saying, "Our organization doesn't exist to create situations like this. We're here to help at-risk teens master the skills they need to be successful in life. We're not yet sure how this happened, but we are going to make very sure that this doesn't happen again. Now, here's what we're going to do about it . . . " And then be sure to provide specifics on how you will approach this situation in the future. The bad press turns into an awareness-building story that can help people find out about your organization and how it responds to a problem.

- ✔ **Don't ignore the situation.** Be sure to address continuing questions about the problem with an honest face and straight talk. This reaction is important, both for the continuing pride of your organization (seeing how you and your board weather this storm gives added strength to your staff and volunteers) and for the rebuilding of your relationship with the community.

When trust has been broken, a quick fix and a claim of redemption doesn't guarantee anyone's belief; be prepared to use this situation as a positive building block — and a significant learning experience — for the organization you want to be in the future.

Drafting a media disaster plan

Although nobody wants to anticipate media disasters and consider ways to limit the damage done as a result, having a disaster control plan is a good idea — both for you, as the fundraiser, and your board, as the protectors of the organization. In one of your board meetings, put "Media Crisis" on your agenda and get the board talking about the following things:

✔ What kinds of disasters could happen in our area of service?

✔ What's the worst that could happen?

   You may want to role play a few of these uncomfortable scenarios. Or perhaps simply write out a few examples that would be realistic for your organization.

✔ How would we react if the worst happened?

   Come up with a specific series of steps that detail who takes charge, how you investigate, what team contacts the media outlets in your area, and what recovery mechanisms you use to begin rebuilding your reputation.

After you have drafted a plan, write it up and make sure that each board member has a copy. Make it part of your board packet and future board trainings. It's not something you like to think about, but the potential's there; and, as they say, better safe than sorry.

Chapter 13

Working the Phones (You Don't Have to Be Hated)

In This Chapter
▶ Being successful with phone campaigns
▶ Getting your telephone campaign organized
▶ Using the seven principles for phone calling

*I*f telephone solicitation gets such a bad rap (deservedly or not), why do so many people do it? The short answer is because it works. A number of good things can be said about a successful phone program, one of which is that it's one of the least expensive means of getting to a lot of people in a short period of time. A well-organized phone program enables you to

✔ Identify and contact new donors.

✔ Upgrade your donors.

✔ Piggyback on other campaigns. (For example, you may run a phone program to work in tandem with your annual fund drive.)

✔ Target funds for a specific program or campaign.

✔ Update your donor list.

✔ Say thank you!

But telemarketing doesn't have to taint the noble effort of fundraising. In this chapter, we show you how to plan carefully and to carry out phone programs in the best way so your phone programs can be productive, effective, and fun as well as help build your relationships with the public, your donors, and your volunteers. We also show you how to let people know that you're not trying to "get something" from them, but rather, are giving them an opportunity to participate in good work.

Just, please, don't call during dinner.

Making Phone Solicitation Successful

Phones, like direct mail and Internet opportunities, provide you, as a fundraiser, with a channel for reaching potential donors. And even though you may have a number of good reasons for developing a phone program (if your organization doesn't already have one), many of us still have that bad taste in our mouths when we think about turning telephone solicitors loose on our donor list. However, armed with a few good tips and some careful planning, your callers can make your campaign effective.

Making your callers the good guys

When you decide to organize a phone program for your organization, make each call an opportunity by

- ✔ Respecting people's privacy and calling before or after traditional dinnertime
- ✔ Calling only those individuals you know are interested in your mission and are likely to want to help
- ✔ Being attentive to people's responses and engage them without being pushy
- ✔ Caring about issues people raise and attempt to address those issues or refer the call to someone in your organization who can

If you plan on making a significant splash in the world of telephone soliciting, you may be interested to know that the high-end telephone industry is merging audio and data capabilities like you wouldn't believe. In some places, when you make a call, a computer logs your phone number; then instantly, before the operator even says, "Hello," all the pertinent data about your account is displayed on the screen: where you live, how much you've given, where you work, and what your dog's name is. (Okay, maybe not the dog's name.) If you plan to do a considerable amount of telephoning over a long term, look into purchasing (or getting donated) sophisticated phone and data systems to help you capture, use, and maintain all the data that is available through your donor list and telephone system.

When you use your phone program to update your donor list, ask people's opinion about a new program you're thinking of launching, or simply say, "Thanks" to a significant donor, you go a long way toward building that donor-agency relationship. It's a "no-strings-attached" call that says, "We value you for more than just your money."

Knowing your no-call responsibilities

The last several years have seen much legislation and discussion about tele-marketing. It's a good idea to check the latest regulations before you start a telephone campaign, but here's the current scoop.

The FCC maintains a National Do Not Call Registry; however, you may not realize that it doesn't cover all types of calls. Only calls made to sell goods or services through interstate phone calls are prohibited. The National Do Not Call Registry does not prohibit calls from political organizations, charities, or telephone surveyors.

What if you sell products to raise funds? You may still be able to call if you have done business with the person in the last 18 months. This is considered an existing business relationship, where, presumably, the callee has shown an interest in your products by buying them in the past. However, if some-body asks you not to call, even if you have an existing business relationship, that's it: You must not call that person again.

One final note: beyond your legal obligations, in the interest of your donor relationship, if you get the message that somebody does not want to receive calls, take them off your call list and find another way to communicate with them, for example by letter or with an e-newsletter.

It's actually illegal to telemarket to cellphones. FCC regulations prohibit tele-marketers from calling cellphone numbers with automated dialers.

Organizing Your Telephone Campaign

How much time will you invest in getting your telephone act together? In gen-eral, plan to spend more time preparing for your phone program than you spend running it. The effort you put into planning will help you set realistic goals, develop your budget, identify your prospects, train your callers, strate-gize your calls, and evaluate your results.

Short-term phone programs can be a very cost-effective way of reaching a large number of people quickly. Your costs may be minimal, consisting only of printing materials for the callers, renting the phones and tables (if neces-sary), renting a site (if you're doing a large phone bank and don't have the space at your facility), and perhaps providing free pizza for your volunteers or a thank-you dinner afterward.

Be careful about charges for calls. Sometimes the next town over, where a lot of your donors live, may be a toll call in today's complex telecommunications infrastructure. Be sure to budget in those costs.

Weekend gig or long-term program?

Is it better to run an ongoing telephone solicitation program or a short-term, program-related phone campaign? The answer depends in large part on your mission, your donors, and the breadth of the audience you want to reach. If you are a local organization soliciting locally, your range of prequalified prospects will be exhausted quickly if you plan to run a year-round phone solicitation program. Likewise, if you use volunteers to make the calls, their dialing fingers will be worn out if you expect too much from them for too long.

If you are part of a huge national organization, running a phone bank on an ongoing basis may be part of your fundraising strategy. In this case, you will most likely hire paid staff to do the calling for you, or contract the telemarketing piece out to a full-time telemarketing organization. Most folks, even if they run year-round phone campaigns, take care not to overlap calls to the same area within a specified period of time. Getting interrupted during dinner is annoying enough when it happens once; but if your prospects get calls from your fundraisers two or three times in the same month, they're going to strike your organization from their giving list. Why? Because the organization isn't handling its data effectively (or its callers wouldn't be calling multiple times). And if an organization can't handle its own data, how will it handle a donor's money?

Setting your goals

You need to know specifically what you want to accomplish with your phone program, both in terms of tangible and intangible benefits. An example of a phone program goal is to run a weekend membership drive where you sign up 200 new members, upgrade 300 existing members, and raise $40,000. Write your goals, and post them on the wall (in big, happy letters) where your callers can see them.

The goals you write need to be straightforward, positive statements that everyone involved can remember easily. Print the goals at the top of the first page of the materials you give to callers during their orientation.

Budgeting your costs

Figure your costs for the following items as you budget for your phone program (assuming, of course, that you've already followed up on every in-kind possibility you can think of):

- ✔ **Materials.** Be sure to include photocopies of your mission statement, the telephone script, a question-and-answer page, a page with contact numbers, pledge forms, and a page listing the various membership levels of your organization. You also need paper and pencils for volunteers to log the numbers they call and to take notes that fundraising staff members may need to follow up on.

✔ **Phone rentals and charges.** If you are setting up a formal phone bank, you need to plan for the equipment you need. Talk to your local phone company and find out costs for things such as hard-wired phones and cell phone rentals. Factor in any nonlocal access charges.

Consider using a Voiceover Internet Protocol (VoIP) provider for phone calls to avoid long distance charges if you are calling beyond your local area. Essentially this is a way to place calls by using your Internet connection, circumventing your phone company entirely. Also, consider whether you need callers to be sitting at computers to record updates to donor data records as they solicit donations.

✔ **Facility rental.** If you need to find a location where you can run your phone-a-thon, investigate many places before you decide. You may be able to use a church basement, a meeting room at the library, a school classroom, or a community center, if the facility has an adequate number of phone lines or you have permission to get temporary lines installed. If you plan to televise your phone-a-thon, however (such as on your community cable station), you need a place that presents the image you want to present, which may rule out some places.

✔ **Food and support items.** If you have a staff of 12 volunteers working four-hour shifts, you need to sustain them with some refreshments. Free soda, bottled water, and treats (fruit, candy, and cookies) are in order. Boxed lunches or an end-of-the-day dinner is a good thank you. Budget this recognition of phone-a-thon volunteers in with the overall program because, even as you are approaching new donors or upgrading existing ones through your phone program, you are building an increasing level of involvement with the volunteers who are helping out.

As you plan and budget the cost of your phone program, think about asking for in-kind as well as monetary contributions. Who could donate some boxed lunches? Who could donate the facility or tables you need? Make a list of all the items you need and some possible suppliers who could donate these items, and then start calling potential suppliers early in the program. No sense in paying out of pocket for things companies would be glad to donate.

Targeting your prospects

Planning is important. Preparing your callers is important (you hear more about this later in this chapter). But nothing is as important to a successful phone campaign as carefully selecting the people you plan to call. Spend time talking about your prospect list with your development committee and with the group in charge of putting the phone campaign together. Answering these questions can help you get a great list together:

- ✔ Where can you find your prospects? Will you buy a list, trade a list with a sister organization, or use the list you already have? Do you have another avenue that you can explore?

- ✔ Who in your existing list has the interest and ability to respond to the phone program?

- ✔ Who in your community would be a good source of information on additional prospects?

- ✔ How do you alert new prospects about the upcoming phone-a-thon? Consider mailing out postcards, letters, or a sample newsletter with the headline, "Phone-a-thon begins March 14!" printed in the most visible place.

It's okay to get help in identifying prospects. But this job shouldn't be for one person alone. Get your development committee together, and give each member a blank sheet of paper; set a timer for ten minutes, and ask the committee to brainstorm all the people they can think of who would be likely to respond favorably to a phone campaign. Then compile a master list of those names or ask each person to be responsible for contacting those people during the phone-a-thon (and collect the lists afterward). Either way, you have a personal link ("Diane Wilson gave me your name — she thought that you would be interested in hearing about our new program at Blankets for Emma").

And yes, you can start at the top of your donor list, and just go down the list, one by one, calling each person. However, selecting a subgroup that you are fairly certain will give is a much better use of your time.

An impromptu phone bank

The new play was a smash hit. The review hit the streets at 7:00 a.m., and by 7:30, Ingrid had faxed copies to 12 of her strongest volunteers. She put a note on the cover sheet: "We received a GREAT review for our latest show! But this weekend is the last full weekend of performances, so we need to act quickly. Will each of you please sit down right now, read this review, and then call five friends to tell them about the show? We're offering a ten percent discount to people who buy their tickets by responding to our phone campaign. Please make sure that you make all your calls by Wednesday evening at 9:00 p.m., and call me at home (555-5555) to let me know how you all did! Thanks very much! Good luck!"

The response was terrific — 55 of the 72 people called purchased two or more tickets. This tactic was an effective use of a grass-roots phone bank: People received calls from people they knew and trusted, and the added incentive of the discount helped sway them in the organization's favor.

Gathering your materials

When you're pulling together materials for your telemarketers, think "training," and think "simplicity." Most likely, your callers will not be experienced in phone solicitation. You want to provide clear, focused training that keeps them motivated and optimistic and gives them answers to their questions.

Your orientation and training packet of materials for your callers needs to include

- **Your mission statement** (preferably on the first page, in plain view)
- **The goals of your phone program.** Knowing the goals of the phone program helps callers keep focused on why they are calling. For example, your goal may be to raise funds for that new delivery van; to help move your program into third-world countries; or to send a semi-load of groceries and housewares to the victims of the latest hurricane. Include with each goal the target amount you plan to raise, as well as any other important objectives, such as the number of people you want to reach.
- **A question-and-answer sheet** for common questions callers may run into
- **A volunteer schedule** telling callers when to come in and how long to stay
- **Positive reminders** for the callers to help them make the best possible presentation
- **Pledge cards** for the prospect's response
- **Report forms** to list the donor's response and any items you need to follow up on after the call
- **A small notebook and a pencil** for questions and notes that need follow-up
- **The donor information data sheet** needed at the phone-a-thon

Give your callers sheets that contain only the numbers they are assigned to call. Agree on a method for marking (1) calls made; (2) calls not made; (3) out-of-service numbers so others don't duplicate their efforts later.

- **The script you want them to work with**

Even though you want your callers to be natural on the phone, you need to provide a script to remind them of key points and keep your message consistent and avoid confusion.

Of course, the script is the single most important material you supply your callers. In the section that follows, we provide some tips for writing a great script.

Writing the all-important phone script

Of course, each script for every organization is different (or it should be!). But in general, your script needs to tell the listener:

- ✔ The name of the organization

- ✔ A very brief statement of the mission

- ✔ The fact that the caller is participating in a campaign to raise funds for a specific program, and then describe what the program is

- ✔ An example sentence for the caller to use to ask the renewing member (or current member) if she would like to upgrade her gift

  For example, "We really appreciated your $25 gift last year and are hoping that this year you'll consider increasing that amount to $35."

After you draft the script, which should be no more than five or six sentences, read it aloud a number of times to check its effectiveness. Have your committee review it and also read it aloud. Be determined to edit the script until no one stumbles, it sounds as natural as possible, and the ideas are clear and simple to grasp. When you're finished drafting and polishing the script, you're ready to give it to your callers.

Some people write their scripts with alternative phrases built in, enabling the caller to personalize the discussion and take the conversation in the appropriate direction. For example, you may have the caller ask, "Have you heard that last month our organization was awarded the Caring Hands Award for Bartholomew County?" If the donor says, "Yes," the caller goes on to the next part of the script, which builds on that idea. If the donor says, "No," the caller takes an alternative route and gives a little history of the award and the program that brought it about. Using alternative phrases gives your caller some flexibility so he or she can tailor the situation to address questions the listener may want to know more about.

Questions in a script are tricky. Don't include questions in your script unless you also provide the caller with a response for any possible answers. For example, if your script asks, "Of course you care about underprivileged kids, right?" and the person being called says, "No, I don't," your caller will be at a loss as to how to proceed. Either don't phrase this as a question, or provide suggestions of how you caller should respond to each possible answer.

One wise step to take is to read your script out loud to as many people as you can before you hand it to volunteers to ensure that it is as natural sounding as possible. Many volunteers don't feel comfortable straying from the script, so it's helpful to give them something to read that doesn't sound like they're reading.

Preparing donor materials

You need to prepare a different set of materials to mail out to your prospective donors in advance of your phone-a-thon. Publish a postcard, letter, or newsletter that lets your prospects know they will receive a call (this turns a cold call into an expected call).

You need pledge cards, envelopes, and return envelopes to mail out to interested prospects after they say, "Yes" to your request.

Additionally, have extra organizational brochures and newsletters on hand to send to donors who request additional information. Be sure that your callers have a notebook or a column on their phone log to record which prospective donors want this additional information.

Finding and training your callers

After you have a healthy list of donors and prospects, and you know what you want to say and do, where do you get the people to make the calls? Here are a few ideas:

- ✔ **Start with your board.** Anyone interested?

- ✔ **Ask your volunteer corps.** If you have a group of positive, like-minded people, you may have a swirl of interest. If you have a collection of busy professionals, you may get a lot of people looking at the ceiling. Persuade reluctant volunteers with: (1) How much good they can do for the organization, (2) How they will benefit socially by helping in a group for only a few hours on a special weekend, and (3) A promise of a reward, such as a discount on their membership renewal or an invitation to a thank-you dinner after the campaign is over.

- ✔ **Go to the people you serve.** If your nonprofit is a school or university, consider asking parents, alumni, or the students themselves to do the calling.

Hopefully, your callers will be all charged up and eager to get started. This isn't always the case. Some people are surprisingly intimidated by the phone — even more so when it comes to asking for money. For this reason, give an upbeat, team-building training session to walk your callers through the process and encourage an atmosphere of fun and challenge.

You could hold the training session the night before the phone-a-thon begins, and it need only last an hour. The training agenda may look like this:

- ✔ **Introduction:** Thank everyone for coming and tell them why the phone-a-thon is going to be a fun thing to do. Hand out the orientation/training packets the callers will be using.

✔ **Mission:** Talk briefly about your organization. Most of your callers may already know the main points. Focus on your recent successes and plans for the future, which leads up to the phone-a-thon.

✔ **Goals:** Explain the goals for the phone-a-thon and get everybody excited about achieving them. Post them on the wall as you explain them. Let the callers know the goals are also available in their packets.

✔ **Packets:** Go through the packet of materials you assembled, explaining each sheet, and practicing the script if you have willing participants. If not, you take the lead and practice with a staff member. Remember to keep the practices lighthearted, but show callers the importance of knowing the script, the helpfulness of a friendly voice, and why smiling works.

✔ **Demonstration:** If you have a phone available, or the phone bank is already set up, take the callers to the tables and show them how the phones work. Explain how make an outside call and what they need to do if they (1) need to put a call on hold; (2) get disconnected; (3) need to ask a staff member a question. Use the phone log sheet to show the callers how to enter the information they receive. Explain how to get the attention of the person who will be available to help if they run into trouble.

✔ **Schedule:** Go over the calling schedule with your volunteers so they know when to come in and how long they are scheduled to make calls.

✔ **Q&A:** Open up the floor for questions the callers may have. Be willing to role-play to illustrate. Most important, be as upbeat and positive as possible. If the phone-a-thon is fun for the callers, the sense of lightness will find its way into their calls, and your donors will hear it.

Practicing the script is important for callers. Suggest that they start by reading the script out loud in front of a mirror, working on any places in the script where they stumble. Have them tape themselves and listen to their tone of voice. Is it friendly? Is it clear? Where can they improve how they handle parts of the script? Getting callers to sound natural with your script is a big part of keeping the potential donor on the line.

If the callers have willing friends, have them practice making a few live solicitation calls. Give the friend a list of questions to answer. Did anything turn her off? Was the point communicated clearly?

Identifying the best times to call

Somebody's dad's favorite telemarketing deterrent: "Well, you're calling during dinner right now, but if you give me your home phone number, I'll call you back as soon as we're done. By the way, what time do you eat?"

Okay, so if you have to catch people after work, but you can't commit the cardinal sin of calling people while they are eating dinner, when's the best time to get them without annoying them? The answer depends to some degree on your prospects. What kind of lifestyles do they live? Are they young, with children? Or older, with (supposedly) quieter evenings?

While you are planning your phone-a-thon, discuss with your committee a range of possible timeslots. When you settle on a few, call some donors that you know personally and ask how they would feel if called during those times? (You can also ask if they would like to help serve on the phone bank.) As you select the timeslots for your phone-a-thon, be as respectful as you can of your prospects' privacy. That respect translates into more effective phoning with fewer angry responses.

Make sure that you track your data! After your phone campaign, you need to evaluate how much the phone campaign cost you and how much you made, how many Yeses and Nos you got, and the number of new donors you identified.

If the phone-a-thon lasts more than one day, choose a colored marker for each day so that if callers on subsequent days go back through the lists to pick up calls not made, you can tell which calls were made on which days. For example, if Friday is Blue, Saturday is Red, and Sunday is Green, you will be able to tell at a glance by reviewing the phone log which day your callers contacted the greatest number of people. Similarly, have a space on your log sheet where the caller can write in the time he began and finished that particular list; then you know not only which days the calls were made but also in which timeslots they were made.

Troubleshooting telephone interactions

You're bound to run into all kinds of personalities and situations when you take your mission to the phone lines and begin a solicitation program. What kinds of people will you encounter, and how can you best deal with them? Here are a few of the tough types your callers may run into and a few ideas on how to best handle them.

The big hanger-upper

You dial. He answers. "Mr. Reynolds, I'm with Blankets for Emma, a nonprofit organization — "

Click.

You sit staring at the phone. Do you assume he accidentally hit the disconnect button and call him back? That's a judgment call, but you probably already know the answer.

Next? Just move on, and don't take it personally.

The inquisitive listener

You dial. You smile. She answers. "Hi, Ms. Watkins, my name is Ruthie Mayfield and I'm with More Than Enough, a nonprofit organization that specializes in . . ." You continue with your script.

Ms. Watkins is still listening. "And what are you asking for?"

"A donation of $35 would buy a month's worth of cereal for the Franklin Children's Home," you respond.

"And how much of that actually buys cereal?" Ms. Watkins asks. There's an edge in her voice.

You reply that 90 cents of every fundraising dollar goes to the cause. You offer to send her information on your organization, which includes your budget and expenditures.

"How long have you people been around?" Ms. Watkins wants to know.

Settle in — she has a long list of questions. And although you may want to simply get her pledge, get off the phone, and get to the next person, answering these questions in a helpful, forthright manner is important. You are educating a donor — someone who could be a major donor in times to come — and that is a valuable part of your phone program, even if it's above and beyond the call of duty.

The doubter

You dial. You smile. You talk. Jim Lovejoy hesitates. "How much?" he asks again. "I don't think I have that right now," he says.

You try a different approach: "You do have the option of spreading your pledge over three months," you say, "if that would be easier for you."

Jim thinks. "I don't know — "

"Perhaps you could go ahead and make your pledge today and break it up over the three-month period, and in the meantime I'll send you our materials showing you the work we do and letting you read more about how your donation will be spent. How does that sound?"

Jim ponders. Although you can coerce a doubter, don't bulldoze him. Try to sleuth out where his hesitancy lies and answer any questions you can. And at the end of the conversation, if he's still in doubt and unable to commit, tell him you'll put him on the mailing list and send him some materials. At the very least, he may be a contributing donor in the future.

The stressed professional

On the phone, you get Madeline Outoftime, who has just rushed in from a long and harried workday with only the time to change shoes and rush out again to an association meeting. She answers the phone, already impatient.

"Hi! I'm with More Than Enough, a nonprofit organization — "

"Oh! Not now! Not now! I'm on my way to a meeting and I'm going to be late — "

You try another strategy. "Would it be okay to call you later?"

A pause. "Oh, sure. I guess. Who'd you say that you were with?"

"More Than Enough, a nonprofit organization — "

"I've heard of you," Madeline says. "Call back tomorrow evening, around 7:00."

Professionals are often skilled at making connections and establishing rapport. If you call when she asks you to — 7:00 p.m. tomorrow night — you will also succeed in building a level of credibility with her, which is just a few steps away from making her a donor.

The disenchanted listener

Dialing . . . the phone rings once, twice, three times.

"Hello?"

"Mr. Carey, I'm with More Than Enough, and this weekend we are doing a phone drive to raise funds for a new meal delivery van. We show that you were a volunteer last year, and we'd like to thank you and ask whether you'd consider making a $35 donation to help with the new van."

Mr. Carey clears his throat. "You know, I was pretty fed up with that place," he said. "It was too disorganized. People had their maps mixed up. Twice I showed up when I was scheduled, and they sent me home, saying they had too many volunteers."

"I'm sorry you had that experience," you say, "and I've heard from other people that things were a bit disorganized that first year we were in operation. I'm glad to say that now we have a new director and two full-time staff members and a corps of over 60 volunteers — people like yourself who cared about the amount of hunger in our city — unnecessary hunger — and wanted to do something about it. You know, you should come by and visit now that we're well into our second year. I think you'd be pleasantly surprised by what you see. I'd be glad to show you around myself."

From that point on, if Mr. Carey is receptive, you can talk about the growth that is causing the need for the new delivery van, and then wind back around to the solicitation. Before Mr. Carey will give, however, you have to deal with the disenchantment of a negative experience with your organization; otherwise, those feelings will stop you dead in your tracks.

Following up

After the phone campaign is over, spend time evaluating the results. But before you do that, you need to mail out what you said that you would to the prospects. If a donor made a pledge, you need to send the direct mail pledge piece. If she paid by credit card over the phone, send the receipt and thank-you note. If he requested more information, be sure that you put those items in the mail within a few days of the end of your phone program.

Expediency is important. Set a goal to send out pledge cards or receipts within days — maybe as quickly as one or two business days — from the end of the phone-a-thon. This expediency communicates your professionalism to the donor and helps build that all-important credibility. Remember to save a few volunteers in your back pocket to help with this effort.

Playing by the Rules

Calling potential prospects or existing donors isn't a tough thing. By keeping some common-sense principles in mind, your callers can have a positive phone-a-thon experience and increase both the donations and the goodwill for your organization.

#1: Respect the donor

Throughout this business of fundraising, the idea of listening to and respecting your donor is primary. As a representative of a nonprofit organization, you are not out to "sell" anybody anything. You don't want to coerce a donor to give when he doesn't really want to or can't afford to. The best fundraising situation (because fundraising is really about building relationships and joining with others to help improve our world) happens when you reach a donor who cares about what you do and offer him a chance to participate in the fulfillment of your mission — through giving money, time, services, or donated goods.

#2: Be friendly

The worst thing your callers can do is sound as though they expect the person answering the phone to hate them. While a caller is dialing, he should forget about the stigma of telephone soliciting. He needs to remember that he's different — his organization has a mission he's proud of, and he's giving the prospective donor the opportunity to become part of something really exciting. Even if the person answering the phone is less than friendly with the caller, he shouldn't take it personally. He just needs to remember that he's representing his organization, and his friendly voice and demeanor will speak well of the agency, even if the prospect says, "No."

#3: Know the script

We can't over-emphasize the importance of the script. Callers should know it by heart, sentence-by-sentence, phrase-by-phrase. They should know the meaning inside and out and be able to restate it in their own words. Ask the callers to picture themselves calling a surly prospect, a pleasant prospect, and an inquisitive prospect. How does the script fit each of these situations? Always give your callers a fallback when the script doesn't work, providing a way to refer the caller to someone else at the organization.

#4: Believe in your cause

Believing in the cause shouldn't be hard to do if your callers are willing to pick up the phone and make calls on behalf of the organization. Have callers reread the mission statement, visit the facility if they haven't been there for a while, and witness the work being done so they can bring renewed enthusiasm to the phone effort.

#5: Use your best phone "smile"

Some people who run telemarketing rooms say that callers should dress professionally so their professionalism carries through in their voices. Others say that casual attire is better because a caller who is relaxed is your best caller. Whichever side you line up on, there's one garment callers should always wear while phoning donors whether they're in a suit or jeans: a smile. When a caller smiles, her words sound different, more melodious, and the tone rings pleasantly in the listener's ear. A smile also helps callers stay more relaxed and focused on the good message they're delivering.

#6: Get the donor's name right

Just as people hate to get direct mail that has their name misspelled, if you mispronounce the person's name in a phone call, it does not carry well with the recipient. The mispronounced name tells the listener, "This person doesn't know me," and the thought that follows quickly is, "This person wants something from me." Instant resistance.

As part of your donor research, familiarize yourself with the pronunciation of all the names on your list, and make sure that your callers know the difficult ones ahead of time. If you are uncertain about the pronunciation of some names, ask someone who knows to help you. That first bit of contact, that correct pronunciation of a person's name, opens a door that is hard to pry back open after it's closed.

#7: Don't take "No" personally

How many times do you say, "Yes" to a telephone solicitor? Now put yourself in the solicitor's seat. She receives a lot of Nos. When you are working on a phone campaign, be prepared to hear, "No" a number of times. Don't take it personally. It's not your voice or your manner or your script (although, you should certainly be open to improving in any areas that may stand some improvement). More than likely, it's the simple stigma of telephone soliciting itself. It may be the wrong time. You may have reached the wrong person. Keep trying and shake off the Nos. And remember — each, "No" takes you that much closer to the eventual, "Yes."

Even when the prospect tells you, "No," you have made an impact and a personal connection for your organization. That connection helps build awareness for your agency, which may result in a donation down the road. That's why it's especially important to be friendly, professional, and accommodating. Though the person may not give, he could be impressed by your group. It's all part of your public awareness effort.

Chapter 14

Charging Ahead with Tchotchkes: Giveaways, Gifts, and Sales

. . . .

In This Chapter

▶ Thanking (and encouraging) your donors with gifts and giveaways

▶ Selling things to make money

▶ Running a raffle for dollars

. . . .

*A*t the grass-roots level of fundraising there are some tried and true methods of making money that put you in the role of exchanging something for your donors' money.

You've probably encountered these types of scenarios yourself:

✓ Your nonprofit radio station runs a campaign offering coffee mugs, DVDs of music, or a dinner for two at a local restaurant as incentives, with the gift depending on how much you give.

✓ Somebody dressed in a green dress (do Girl Scouts still do that anymore?) comes to your door selling cookies. You immediately order ten boxes for the good of the group (and you just love those peanut butter ones, right?).

✓ Your local church sells you a ticket for a chance to win a large-screen TV.

Although these approaches to raising funds can be labor intensive, what with people answering phones, walking door-to-door, or sending out little gift packages in the mail, if you have the volunteer support, they can be successful.

The approaches I describe above can be a great way to not only raise money, but also to raise recognition of your group throughout your community because they are so one-on-one.

This chapter shows you the ins and outs of using all kinds of trinkets to reward donors for their gifts, make money by selling cause-related items, and run those ever-popular raffles to raise money.

Exchanging Gifts for Donations

Giving people something for their money can be a good way to get them to give. Of course, these people know that the coffee cup they get for donating $10 to your group only costs you $1.50 and that you're keeping the profit as a donation. But for many reasons, that gift can close the donation. And as a side benefit, gifts, boldly emblazoned with your organization name and logo, provide a promotional perk.

A *tchotchke* is a Yiddish word often used for a giveaway knickknack or trinket without much value. This term is frequently used for items given away at trade shows or for gifts given for donations in fundraising campaigns.

Attracting donations with gifts

Giving a gift in return for a donation works for a few different reasons:

✔ Even though the donor public knows that the coffee mug or T-shirt isn't actually free because they are handing you a check to get it, it feels like it's free, and people love free things.

✔ Many people want to give, but don't get around to it. When they hear that they might get a DVD of music they like, it's just enough to push them over the edge to give. After all, perhaps they were going to buy that DVD anyway, or perhaps they can give it to somebody whose birthday is coming up, saving them the hassle of buying a present. Whatever their reason, getting something tangible can tip the giving scales.

✔ For some people there is prestige in having a calendar on their desk that sports the public radio logo, or a T-shirt that shows that they gave to the local homeless shelter. If these folks are going to give something, they want the world to know about it. Why not help them?

Using giveaways for maximum exposure

Keep in mind the promotional bang you can get for your incentive gift buck. Be sure to put your organization's name and logo on whatever you give away. People will notice the item sitting on a desk, ask their co-worker Charlie about your group, and if they like the little gift, perhaps even come to you to get one of their own — in exchange for a donation, of course.

Consider choosing giveaways that get the most exposure. Something that goes on a desk at work gets seen by more people than a travel clock that only gets seen by its owner in hotel rooms on business trips. A gift that can be worn or carried around, like a tote bag, is a great option for maximum promotional exposure. Gifts such as food might be tasty, but, even if chocolates can be personalized, one or two gulps, and they're gone!

If you can afford it, you might keep a small stockpile of the most popular gifts around after the campaign. Sometimes people contact you to get the same gift for a donation only to find you shipped the surplus back when the campaign ended. After all, you can always use them as door prizes at fundraising events.

Adhering to gift-giving guidelines

Does anybody really need another coffee mug with a printed logo? No. Absolutely not. So, unless you come across a very unique coffee mug, avoid these cliché gifts like the plague. Try for something unusual that is not being given away by every charity in town.

Here are some gift-giving guidelines:

- ✔ Choose items that relate to your organization's mission. If you're working on animal rights, choose an animal shaped item. Nobody gives to a group they have no interest in at all. The people who do give have some connection to your mission, so play to that connection.

- ✔ Choose the best quality you can afford. You have to set a budget, so you can actually make money off the campaign, (see the next section for more about budget) but don't skimp and offer something tacky. It won't motivate people to give, and if they do give, the tacky item will reflect badly on your group.

- ✔ Some people get the gift to hand it on. Consider who the donor might give the gift to. If your group is an organization that helps kids in some way, your potential donors probably like kids and might just like a gift that they can hand on to a child, such as a toy truck.

- ✔ If you can, offer something people can't get anywhere else, such as a cookbook from your volunteers or a framed copy of the poster for your last fundraising event.

You may offer a gift the donor never actually gets, but that furthers your cause. For example, if you're an environmentally conscious group, offer to plant a tree in exchange for a donation. If you help the homeless offer to provide five dinners to homeless people for the donation. Just remember to provide something — a button, a decal, or a bumper sticker, for example — that you can send to the donor, so he can tout what he did.

Going gift shopping

Where do you find these fundraising gifts? There are hundreds of companies that specialize in promotional gifts. Just about everyone of these companies has a Web site, so start by doing a search online for "fundraising gifts" or "fundraising incentives." Remember that you will pay less per item the more you buy, and these companies can print your name and logo on just about anything in the world.

Try these Web sites to start researching your giveaway:

- ✔ www.branders.com: The variety of categories of products on this site is impressive.

- ✔ www.justfundraising.com: Order the fundraising sample kit to get yourself started. It's free and can be ordered online.

- ✔ www.fundraisingdeals.com: Check out some of the fundraising advice and links on this site, as well as a great variety of gifts.

The quality and uniqueness of the gifts you give can have a huge impact on the success of your campaign. Take the time to choose gifts that appeal to your potential donor base.

Calculating your return on investment and giveaway budget

Gifts cost money, and that money comes out of your group's profit at the end of the day. For that reason, you should be savvy about what you give, how much it costs, and the standard ordering practices of promotional gift companies.

First, be aware that items will cost you less the more you order, and many companies require a minimum order. These facts can lure you into buying 3,000 glow-in-the-dark Christmas ornaments to get a great price, only to find yourself stuck with 2,000 of them (and 2,000 glow-in-the-dark things could light a small city).

Don't be afraid to try to cut a deal with a promotional item vendor or manufacturer. If you're making a bigger buy use the same "sales" skills you bring to selling your donor on making a gift to get a better deal on promotional items. With smaller vendors you might also be able to offer to spread their name around the community to get them more business as a way to earn a discount.

Budgeting a giveaway is a logical process, if you follow these steps:

1. Set a goal for what you want to raise.

2. Determine giving ranges and set a logical formula for profitability. For example, for a $25 donation the most you might want to spend out of pocket for a gift is $5. If you hope to get 300 donations of $25 each, or $7,500, this would give you a net amount raised of $6,000.

3. Don't forget costs beyond the gift: shipping of the gifts to you, postage to mail out the gifts, promotion of the campaign, and other items can all add to what you have to spend to get each donation dollar.

4. Consider the timing. If you have to pay a lot of money upfront for gifts and it will take you months to run your campaign, you may have to lower the quantity of your initial order. Just make sure that you find a vendor who will do a reorder promptly if you find you're running out in the middle of your promotion.

5. Be sure that the amount you're spending on a gift and the amount that you're asking people to give for a donation match the giving ability of your community. Don't offer a $25 car breakdown kit for a $100 donation if most people in your potential donor base can't afford a $100 donation, and don't have a car.

Some companies accept purchase orders, which gives you a little time to pay. But this policy may be limited to certain types of organizations, such as schools. Also, some Web sites offer free shipping, which can save you a lot of money in the end. Check the vendor's payment and shipping policies before placing the order.

Selling Cookies (or Candy, or Whatever)!

Selling things to make a profit that goes into your groups' coffers is a time-honored method popular with schools, community clubs, and other local groups. Selling offers a very different dynamic than asking for a donation with or without a gift in return. It puts you and your volunteers on one side of a commercial transaction, which has its pros and cons.

Here are some things you should consider when looking at launching a fundraising sales campaign.

Today there are some pretty exotic items to sell for fundraising, so get creative. For example, Gourmetfundraising.com offers specialty foods such as popcorn, pasta, and dessert mixes; and Itsmyartwork.com offers products such as jigsaw puzzles and greeting cards based on children's artwork that you provide.

Getting fat on selling door to door

You probably won't raise a quarter of a million dollars with door-to-door selling, for a few reasons. First, it's limited by the number of volunteers you can assemble, and by the logistics of moving around the geography of your local community. However, if you have a small initiative, say a piece of equipment you have to buy or a trip you have to fund, selling can be a good way to go that gets lots of people involved.

The main ingredient in selling items to raise funds is to consider whether you have a strong foundation of volunteers who will do the selling for you. Beyond the number of volunteers, make sure that these are people who are comfortable with selling and that you give them something to sell that they can believe in and that people will find attractive.

You may find that many people, kids and adults included, are comfortable going to their family or immediate neighbors to sell, but beyond that, they are hesitant to approach the house or apartment of a complete stranger. Set your estimated sales figures accordingly.

In this day and age, sad to say, you have to be cautious about sending kids or anybody else around to the door of complete strangers to sell things. Consider asking a local store for space on their front counter or outside their place of business to offer your goods for sale. Everybody you have working the booth in front of the store is well protected from the dangers of walking into a stranger's house alone.

Organizing your sales effort

When organizing a fundraising sales campaign, there are certain key things to keep in mind:

- ✔ **Set personal goals.** Everybody who is out there selling should have a personal goal to motivate them and help you understand what your final sales might look like.

- ✔ **Create a list of prospects** based on neighborhood area, specific prospect names, or groups of people such as downtown businesses. Provide your volunteer sales force with these leads and this guidance. If you don't, people may get hit up again and again by your volunteers, growing weary of your cause instead of embracing it.

- ✔ **Encourage everybody to sell first to the people they know.** You'd be surprised how many people a single family comes in contact with socially, at work, and in various settings such as the local gym or school clubs.

- ✔ **Suggest that sellers keep their sales material with them at all times.** You never know when they will encounter somebody who might buy.

✔ **Provide some basic sales training.** It's not fair to send a 14-year-old out into the world to sell without explaining some of the basics, such as being personable and polite, and how to ask for the sale. Cute will only get her so far.

✔ **Do everything you can to make the sales process easy for buyers.** Provide order pads, receipts, catalogues, and anything else your sellers need to make the sales transaction smooth. This includes providing identification and credentials to your sellers so their customers know that they are associated with a legitimate organization and selling effort.

Handling the money

You can order products upfront, but before you do you should have a pretty good idea of what quantities you will need. Especially with perishable food products, overordering can leave you with a ton of stale cookies (or chocolate, fruit, or whatever).

One way around this is to use a *presale brochure fundraiser* technique to avoid a lot of upfront costs. In this scenario you order brochures from a vendor for your volunteers to take around to get orders. Give each customer a receipt for his order, so he has a proof of purchase. When you have your buyers' cash in hand, you place the orders. Be sure to advise your customers of how long it will take to get the items they ordered, so they don't get annoyed at the process.

There's little upfront cost, and you know what quantities to order, so you're not stuck with lots of leftover items. The one issue with this process is having to make two trips to every customer's home or place of business: one to order and one to deliver the order.

Check to see if the company you buy from offers a guarantee that allows you to return damaged products or products you or your customers are not satisfied with. You also need to be ready for complaints from customers, just as if you were a retail store selling a product. Ask a few volunteers to be available to field these calls or letters after the sale is over.

Be sure that you put a system in place to collect funds and make sellers accountable. The last thing you need is dozens of people coming to you claiming they plopped down money for products, when the volunteer never showed up with the goods. Try to collect money frequently, such as every few days. The quicker people turn in their funds, the less chance money or orders will get lost or misplaced. Some companies that sell fundraising products provide you with sales envelopes for accounting for sales that you can give to sellers. Remember: Your volunteers aren't professional salespeople and need all the help you can provide.

Sponsoring a Raffle

Raffles are another labor-intensive fundraising effort because people have to go door-to-door or stand in shopping malls to sell individual tickets. However, raffles can make a tidy chunk of change for your organization, especially if the big prize has been donated. All a raffle costs you in this case is shoe leather and the price of printing the raffle tickets.

Of course, you can go to a local print shop and ask to get the cost of printing the raffle tickets donated, as well. Just be sure that you plan to spend money on promoting the raffle so you can spotlight both the printer and prize donors appropriately, because that's what's in it for them.

Don't skimp on the tickets. That ticket is all that people are getting for their $5 or $10, so it should look professional and not like a piece of paper cut into strips. Always put numbers on your tickets, so people feel that there is some accountability for their donation.

Finding the prizes

Picking the right prize is the foundation of a successful raffle. It's the honey that attracts the donor bees, the lure that gets people to pull that $5 out of their wallets.

Cars, trips, and electronics are usually pretty popular. The ideal scenario is to get most prizes donated. To find prize donors, start by asking people who are already involved with your organization. You may find that one of them owns a business that may help out or has a contact that can contribute. Here are a few enticements to offer them:

✔ Think of all the great tax benefits!

✔ Piggyback onto our publicity and get your name out there.

✔ Get people thinking that the best thing in the world would be to win your [washer] [television] [vacation package] and they'll transfer their thinking to your product when it's time to buy.

Not every prize has to be a car, appliance, or vacation to Hawaii. Offer different levels of prizes so people feel that there's a better chance of winning something. Try these suggestions for lower level gifts:

✔ Approach local restaurants for gift certificates. They get free promotion in your raffle publicity, and may get somebody into their restaurant who has never been there before who could become a future customer.

✔ Get the local museum or zoo to donate two free daytime passes.

✔ Ask for a local B&B to donate an overnight stay at a time of year when they are usually hunting for visitors.

Another option is to look to your group's activities for some of your prizes. If you provide free meals to senior citizens and have some good cooks in your rosters, consider a gourmet dinner prepared in the winner's home as a prize. If you offer transportation to work for people who have no cars, make your prize a chauffeured shopping trip to a nearby city. Whatever you offer, get creative!

We don't recommend purchasing a big, costly raffle prize out of your own bank account. It can be risky, given that you don't know how many tickets you will sell. Always look for donations of prizes as the foundation of your raffle.

Understanding the legal and financial ins and outs

Raffles can involve some legal issues that vary by the state you live in. For example, in some states you have to sell a certain number of raffle tickets to give away a pricey item like a car. It's always a good idea to have some legal advice and draw up some kind of agreement with the donor of any big prize before you start selling tickets. Otherwise you could be left holding the bag.

Another important consideration is what you charge for your raffle ticket. The ticket price should relate in some way to the value of the big prize. Too much and people can't afford it. Too little and people think that the prize is cheap. You also have to think about how many tickets you can realistically sell before setting the price point.

Don't be afraid to ask people to buy more than one ticket. Their chances of winning increase, and extra tickets multiply the results you get from each and every ticket sales encounter.

Be sure to account carefully for all the income from and expenses of a raffle. In the end, though people may buy a raffle ticket to get a prize, they are also handing over their $5 to support your cause and expect most of their ticket cost to go to your constituency.

Peoplepower is key

Your raffle's success depends on the number of people who will get out there and sell tickets. Create personal goals for everybody, and give clear timelines for selling tickets. Get people excited about the prizes, so they can convey their enthusiasm. Consider offering prizes (donated, of course) to your volunteers for the most tickets sold.

Remember to maximize raffle sales by promoting and offering tickets for sale at various other organization events. If you're sponsoring a booth at a local community event, offer raffle tickets for sale there. Don't forget to promote the raffle on your Web site (though legal requirements may not allow you to sell raffle tickets online).

How much time should you allow your people to make their sales goals? You have to provide your people at least a month, and for really large prizes such as a car, you might get exposure for your raffle event for two or even three months before the buying public get restless and wants to know who won.

You won!

Don't forget to promote the event after the fact. Get more publicity mileage out of the prize awards by holding a press conference, taking a photo of the winner driving away in her brand-new car and putting it on your Web site, or placing a press release about the winners in the local paper. Don't fail to give each and every prize away, or your credibility for future raffles may be called into question.

Also, don't forget to reward the volunteers who made this low-cost, high-profit-margin venture a success. Hold a dinner, send out thank-you postcards, or give them prizes for their efforts. If you do, they'll be more inclined to help again with the next fundraising event.

Part IV
Leveraging the Internet

The 5th Wave   By Rich Tennant

"At what level membership can we put you down for—'Foliage', 'Lawn', or 'Fertilizer'?"

In this part . . .

*E*verybody expects to find you on the Internet today, so in this part, we take a look at what's involved in getting your own Web site online and working for you. You take a peek at using e-mail and e-newsletters to keep people informed, involved, and giving. Finally, discover how to use the Internet to make the public aware of who you are and what you do by e-branding yourself all over the place.

Chapter 15

Creating and Using a Web Site

. . . .

In This Chapter

▶ Getting your own Web site

▶ Keeping content current and exciting

▶ Getting people to come to your site

▶ Collecting donations online

. . . .

Almost anybody who is anybody seems to have a Web site these days. And the online exposure is more than just fashion — it can mean a whole new world of people interested in your mission and willing to help.

The Web is an exciting area for fundraisers — a new (but not the final) frontier. Each day we find out more about who our Web visitors are, what they are interested in, and how our organizations can best reach them. We are discovering (sometimes the hard way!) the perks and pitfalls of online technologies, and how to use our Web presence to the best effect.

This chapter takes you on a speed-of-light tour through various online fundraising possibilities. We show you how to find out whether you need a Web site and what kind of site you may need. We show you how to go about fundraising online. We also tell you who uses the Web for philanthropy (such as donors who want to give!), and what you need to know about them.

Don't get left behind — start thinking about how your organization may look in cyberspace, and see how you can serve your donors better, faster, and more efficiently by using the Web.

Putting Up Your Own Web Site

The Web is a relatively new phenomenon, as far as fundraising is concerned, and having a site gives you the opportunity to build the beginnings of an online community and connect with your donors in new and exciting ways. But you have to know what the purpose of your site is and how you can get the most out of it.

Deciding if you really need a Web site

If you're not already online there are two questions you need to ask before blasting onto the Web: "Do you need a Web site?" and "Can you build and maintain a Web site?" The answers will be more than a simple yes or no. Consider these questions as you weigh the possibility of creating a site for your organization:

- ✔ **Does your mission serve people in a large geographic area?** The Internet helps organizations with a widespread donor and client base to overcome geographic boundaries. Because donors anywhere in the world can access your Web site, you are not limited to the long-distance phone service, the television coverage, or the reach of the post office you may usually use to get the word out.

- ✔ **Are your donors likely to use the site?** If your donors are primarily elderly, a smaller fraction of the group may be comfortable with the technology than, say, young professionals and their families. Of course, one reason you may be thinking about putting up a site is to attract a younger constituency. And older individuals are surfing the Web in greater numbers as the technology becomes faster and easier to use. People with disabilities are finding that they can connect with others online when they can't get out of their homes.

- ✔ **Would your organization benefit from linking to other groups online?** Some organizations link successfully to larger groups with similar missions. This sharing of information is considered community building and is helpful for donors seeking information on specific topics.

- ✔ **Do you feel you need to give your donors a way to contact you?** If you are aware that a substantial percentage of your donor base uses online services, the opportunity to produce another point of contact for your donors is an attractive one. Even if you simply put up a "Here I am!" site with your e-mail address, donors may be more apt to contact you by e-mail than by picking up the phone to call you or by writing a letter.

- ✔ **Do you have a practical use for a Web site?** You may, for example, include a form that both captures visitor data and enables prospective donors to order your annual report.

- ✔ **Do you have someone to create and maintain the site for you?** If you have a Web-savvy volunteer or the money to staff a Web position, great — but if it's going to fall on your shoulders to maintain the site, or you aren't sure where the help will come from, you may want to consider waiting. If you don't have the resources to maintain your site and keep it current it may make a negative impression on potential donors.

✔ **Do you have a lot to say about your organization?** The Web is all about current information with up-to-the-minute news flashes. If you don't have a lot to say, or you can't produce new information on a consistent basis, people may visit your site once, but they won't keep coming back, except, perhaps, to get your address or phone number. Plan to build a professional-looking Web site with interesting and fresh content and then publicize it so people know how to find it.

As a representative of a donor-services organization, you have another question to ponder. If you open a Web site, how can you ensure on the Web that you are who you say you are? Your donors want to know.

Part of the excitement of the Web is also its single biggest liability — the anonymity of it. Big organizations and small organizations can all look alike. You can run a nonprofit from your living room with no overhead and nobody knows the difference. You can respond quickly and easily to donors, trends, and Inernet events. How do your donors know that you are reputable? If they donate online, can they be sure that their donation is used the way you say that it is used? For this reason, building your site while considering what your donors need to know in order to make informed decisions is a great donor service. Provide your Form 990s online. Give visitors e-mail access to staff in your organization. Respond quickly. Give history and photos, as well as a clear vision of your mission and the need it addresses.

Remember that people are somewhat cautious about online scams and their personal privacy (as they should be). Be willing to go the distance and then some, showing your online donors that you mean what you say. Down the road that will mean better-informed, more-committed constituents, and a well-developed, useful, thriving Web site.

Understanding how to use your site

If you decide that a Web site is in your organization's future, here are some ways you can use it:

✔ Have a basic site that says that we're a viable entity, and here's how to contact us.

✔ Introduce visitors to your mission.

✔ Show pictures or videos of the good work you do.

✔ Introduce your board of directors.

✔ Invite visitors to get involved.

✔ Publish an online newsletter or informational articles.

✔ Display your wish list of most-needed items.

✔ Outline how people can get involved as volunteers.

✔ Ask visitors to sign up for your print newsletter.

✔ Accept online donations.

✔ Sell cause-related products such as T-shirts or coffee mugs.

✔ Provide discussion forums and blogs, so people can engage each other and your staff on issues facing your organization and society.

✔ Connect visitors to other sites with information about your cause through links to helpful information.

For information about setting up and maintaining a Web site, find a copy of *Creating Web Pages For Dummies* by Bud Smith and Al Bebak (Wiley).

Does it matter to donors and foundations whether you have a Web site? In a word, yes. Donors and foundations want to "look you up on the Web" before they make a commitment with their time and money. We live in the age of the educated donor, and the Web is increasingly the easiest and fastest research tool around. Not to mention that having a Web site lends you credibility as a real entity.

Creating it yourself or hiring it out

Creating and publishing a Web site is getting easier than ever. You can use popular programs such as Microsoft Word or Publisher to create a Web page with pretty slick-looking templates. You can sign up with a hosting service that may provide its own Web-creation tools. You don't have to be an Internet geek to create and post a professional-looking Web page.

Whether you design your own page or not, you have to pay somebody to host it. Hosting services provide lots of useful tools to get you set up with your own Web site and the cost isn't always that high. Visit www.web-page-hosting-review.com to get an overview of some of the many services out there.

The expertise it takes to add in all the bells and whistles for a Web site isn't always in your grasp. Designing forms that collect visitor information or donations can be tricky. Adding links that don't get broken on a regular basis takes some know-how. Making sure that animations and videos play in most popular browsers without a hitch may require some experience.

Only you can decide if you have the resources to make a professional-looking Web site yourself or if you need to find a professional Web designer. Decide what you want your Web site to do, what it's worth to you, and what image you want to present first, and then do what you need to create a solid Web presence. Keep in mind that a bad Web image can do more harm than good; you may have to bite the bullet and pay somebody to set up a basic, nice-looking site and build on it slowly as your budget allows.

Ask around your volunteers: somebody is bound to be Web-design savvy. See if a local Web-design firm will do the design work pro bono or give you a break on the price for keeping a banner ad for their services displayed on your site.

Adding Content and Keeping It Fresh

Putting stuff on your Web site and letting it sit to gather dust for months on end is not a recipe for online success. Posting content that is boring and out of date will be equally deadly. Perhaps the biggest challenge to having a Web site is keeping what you put on it current and worthwhile. How do you do that? That's what the following sections explore.

Putting your contact information front and center

Don't hide your light under a basket. Many people who come to your site do so simply to look up contact information. Don't make them go through pages of content and scroll down just to find a simple phone number. Put your phone number and address on every single page. Include a "Contact Us" page that puts all your contact information in one easy-to-find place, including a way to e-mail staff members directly.

Finally, do not forget to brand your site. This simply means to put your organization logo front and center on every page to help create an awareness of your group that will surface again every time that visitor sees your logo on a brochure, in a mailing, or posted at an organizational event.

Including information that saves your volunteers' time

One of the real benefits of a Web site is that people can find things there that would otherwise cost you, either in the form of a printed brochure or a staff member's time. Put your events calendar, your facility address, your times of operation, or anything else that people ask on a frequent basis up there.

Writing content yourself

If you have the bandwidth to write fresh, new materials on a regular basis, more power to you. But writing online content just intended for online consumption is time consuming, especially when you need to refresh it almost daily.

Try to spread the work around and post articles written by you, other staff members, board members, or volunteers. Even though you may have to edit materials for quality, organize a writing effort that involves many people to keep new ideas and perspectives at the forefront.

Using existing materials

The best bet for keeping online content fresh is to find ways to use materials you already created for other purposes, perhaps slightly modified for Web style. Consider these sources:

- ✔ Grant proposals describing exciting new projects
- ✔ Brochures
- ✔ Print newsletter
- ✔ Your mission statement
- ✔ Fundraising direct mail pieces
- ✔ Case studies of people served by your group
- ✔ Press releases
- ✔ Posters for upcoming events
- ✔ Newspaper articles about your activities
- ✔ Reprinted letters of gratitude from constituents (with their permission, of course)

The point is to take advantage of other materials you've created to keep your Web site interesting. How would you modify these materials for the Web?

- ✔ Add graphical elements (photographs, animation, or video) or sound.
- ✔ Modify their format to use Web-friendly fonts and offer a printable and downloadable version.
- ✔ Keep them briefer, more to the point. People don't read lengthy documents on their computer screen, as a rule.

Pulling content from other Web sites

Another way to add interest to your Web site is by adding content from other sites. There are a few ways to do this. One option is something called a news feed (a kind of subset of this is called an RSS feed). Essentially you use code provided by another site to place a feed of their content onto your site. That way you could display, for example, headlines from a government site on funding initiatives on your own site.

You can also put links to other sites on your site. This provides a way for people to jump to another site to read their content, and then return to your site to keep browsing your content. Though they obtained the content from somebody else's site, they got to it through your site, so it psychologically expands what you have to offer them.

Attracting Visitors to Your Site

What point is there in having a Web site if nobody goes there? After you've made the choice to have a Web presence, and decided how you're going to design it, create it, and populate it with information, there's one more very important piece to the Web success puzzle. You can let people know about your site in a variety of ways.

Publicizing yourself

The most obvious way to let people know about your Web site is to note it on each and every scrap of material that leaves your office. Here are just some of the places you can note your Web address:

- ✔ Business cards
- ✔ Brochures
- ✔ Grant applications
- ✔ Banners for events
- ✔ Bumper stickers
- ✔ Direct mail solicitations
- ✔ Thank you notes
- ✔ Volunteer nametags
- ✔ Press releases

One very important way to get people to come to your site is to try to get a Web address (also called a URL) that people can easily guess. If your name is Parents for Character, an obvious address would be `www.parentsforcharacter.org`. But if that happens to be taken by somebody else, try `www.parents4character.org` or `PFC.org`. People often simply try a logical address in their browser to find you, and the more straightforward your Web address, the easier they will find you.

Getting into search engines

Search engines such as Yahoo! and Google help people find Web sites. However not all searches are equal. Many search engines regularly 'crawl' around the Web searching out new sites to include in their index. Most sites also allow you to submit your site to them, but they do not guarantee how it will be returned to users of a search. In fact, I searched Google with the keywords "search engine" and their own name was returned fourth in the list, after other search engines such as Lycos and AltaVista!

The best bet to having your information show up in searches is to pay bucks to get the search engines to return your site at the top of a results list or in a special section of premier results. But if you're like most nonprofits, you aren't likely to have such advertising dollars. So follow these steps to get the best exposure:

- ✔ Submit your URL to as many search engines as you can. Go to www. searchengineshowdown.com for a list of engines with ratings and features.

- ✔ Think carefully about the keywords that will return your name in a typical search. If you are an animal-rights group of course list yourself under animals, dogs, and cats, but also under veterinarian, pets, and cruelty.

- ✔ Try paying a submission service to submit your information to many search engines at once. Sites such as www.morevisibility.com and www.wpromote.com are examples of these services.

- ✔ Don't forget to get included in lists of nonprofits on nonprofit information sites such as www.charitywatch.org. When people search those sites for your name, it will pop up.

Adding links to others' sites

While you're working with that Web designer to design your site, don't forget to have him or her also create an easily distributable link to your site. Giving others the simple code they can place on their site so people can jump to your site can bring you lots of traffic. Some sites will post an icon or your logo for the link, others will just include a text link, your name highlighted in blue that people can click to go to your site.

Here are some ideas of people or organizations you can ask to link to your site:

- ✔ Similar causes in other regions of the country or world
- ✔ Sites that are central points for information about your type of cause

✔ Local organizations or corporations that you work with on a regular basis

✔ Media sites such as local newspapers that offer a local nonprofit links page on their site

If you modify your site address in some fashion, don't forget to redistribute new links or provide a way for them to be forwarded from the old link to your new site. Otherwise, people trying to get to your site will hit a dead end and may give up trying to find you on the spot.

Collecting Donations Online

There are three aspects to collecting money on your Web site: how will you get people to make that donation, how will the payments be processed, and how do you keep your donors' payment information secure? Here are the answers to all three questions, in brief.

Making the pitch

If you want to accept donations online, that's great. You'll be providing your donors with a convenient way to support you that they can access 24 hours a day. You provide a way for people moved by information you provide on your site to donate right then and there without having to call up anybody to make a pledge. But you have to set yourself up to promote your online giving.

Be sure to note that on all your print materials that donations are accepted online, along with the Web address. Even if you're sending a paper donation form to somebody, note your Web information on it. Some people not finding a stamp or envelope handy may decide to give, but be happy to find an alternate way to make the donation.

Make your donation form easy to fill out, navigate, and submit. Also, make the donation form you post online printable, for those who start to give online and then change their mind and decide to print the form and mail a check instead.

Note that you accept online donations on your home page. Make sure that everybody who visits the site is alerted to the feature, and knows how to use it.

Setting up the system

Essentially, setting up online payments involves designing an interactive form that users can easily fill out, and setting up a form of payment. If you already accept credit card donations, you are pretty much set up to accept credit card payments submitted online in a manual fashion. You can receive the electronic form in your office and process the payment along with any others.

If you aren't set up to accept credit cards you will have to get a merchant ID and other things in place. Sites such as WorldPay (www.worldpay.com) explain what's involved in setting yourself up to accept online credit card payments. Finally, you can use a payment service such as PayPal (www.paypal.com) to accept payments from people's bank accounts with bankcard payments.

Don't want to go through the hassle of setting up to receive online payments? Consider using a third-party charity donation site to gather online donations for you. Sites such as Network for Good (www.networkforgood.org) and Active Giving (www.active.com/activegiving/) offer a service where they handle all the donation submission and processing for you.

Keeping payments secure

How you set up to receive online payments is important because you need to make sure that your site is secure, so transactions aren't visible to every Tom, Dick, and Mary roaming around out there. You need to use a network protocol called Secure Sockets Layer for secure electronic financial transactions. Look for a Web hosting service that provides this option. It's also a good idea to post a privacy policy on your site, reassuring people that protections such as SSL are in place and that you will respect their personal and financial information and not share it with others.

A current concern of NPOs is the issue of nonprofit registration. For example, if you are planning to fundraise in the state of Illinois, you need to register your organization with the appropriate agency in that state. But what happens when you fundraise online and can reach any and all states at one time? Do you need to register in every state just in case? Some people say yes, it's better to go the cautious route; others say no. We say check with your legal advisors before beginning a fundraising campaign on the Web. Regulation and registration on the Internet are changing quickly — be sure, if you intend to collect money in cyberspace, that you have someone to turn to who can help you navigate the legal issues.

Chapter 16

Getting the Most from E-Mail and E-Newsletters

*I*n our hi-tech age, you can't ignore the potential for e-communications. Many people on the run prefer e-mail to a phone-tag marathon. They can respond at their own convenience, and it's often quicker than a phone conversation with its social niceties (So, how are you doing today? Nice weather we've been having, huh?). Also, sending information to folks via e-mail or an e-newsletter is much cheaper (and faster) than buying envelopes and sticking on stamps. In addition, you can send all kinds of things, from an audio file to a PowerPoint presentation, in the blink of an eye.

So why hasn't your organization jumped on the e-communication bandwagon? Whatever your excuses, this chapter provides the motivation and information you need to get e-mobilized.

Avoiding E-Mailing Mistakes

Just as the telephone can be used for good or evil (a call from Uncle Charlie, how nice; another telemarketer at dinner, what an annoyance!) so can e-mail. So, before you send some kind of online mass mailing, think about what you will say, whom you will contact, and how these people will perceive your communication.

Don't use e-mail to spam

Spamming is the practice of sending out a lot — and we're talking a lot, like hundreds or thousands — of unsolicited e-mails in a hit or miss approach to connect with a potential customer or donor. The people who get spam may have contributed to or communicated with your organization. They may not give a darn about your mission to save endangered Equatorial birds. You may have bought a list of e-mail addresses from somebody who swears all the people on it are interested in hearing from groups like yours, but that may or may not be true.

Folks who receive spam at the least will delete it, and at the most will determine never to do a thing to help an organization that has encroached on their privacy and inundated them with messages they never asked for.

The option to spamming is to use a well-qualified list of your own or an opt-in list, which we talk about later in this chapter in the section, "Boning up on the benefits of opt-in."

Don't be a sloppy e-mailer

E-mail may be a quick and easy way to dash off a note to a colleague, but when you use e-mail to communicate with a donor, you can't afford to make your communication sloppy or mistake ridden. Sending a badly phrased or unclear e-mail is a waste of your recipient's time. Sending e-mail full of misspellings and grammatical errors sends a message about the caliber of your organization. Never treat donor e-mail, whether to a single person or hundreds of potential donors, with any less care than you do your organization's brochure, annual report, or paper-based mass mailings.

Here are some proper e-mail tips:

- Use spell-checker; most e-mail programs have it, and it only takes a few seconds.
- Read over your e-mail, or better yet, have somebody else in your organization read it over before you send it to catch clumsy phrasing or mechanical errors.
- Keep copies of e-mail content in documents in word processor format. When you need to edit and send a modified version, just do so in your familiar word processor program, and then cut and paste it into e-mail (and you avoid the chance you'll hit Send before the thing is perfect!).

How to Use E-Mailing Campaigns

The last section told you how not to use e-mail. This section tells you how to do e-mail right. Here are a few things you should consider:

✔ Know whom to e-mail

✔ Know what to ask for

✔ Know how to structure the e-mail itself

Figuring out who to send the e-mail to

Before you start sending out e-mails willy-nilly, you have to have people to send them to. There are a few sources of e-mail addresses to consider.

Acquiring addresses of people you know

The first set of people to target with e-mail, the absolutely best-qualified list of folks to approach, is people who you know have an interest in your organization. This would include volunteers, past donors, patrons, or members. However, before you can send e-mail to these people, you have to have their e-mail addresses. That's why it's important that you start good e-mail list building practices today.

The odds are your donor files, for example, only note e-mail addresses for a few people. You will have to acquire people's e-mail addresses over time. Look for opportunities such as these:

✔ If you are a nonprofit arts group, add an e-mail address line to the form people mail in to buy tickets to your next event.

✔ When you next throw a party to thank your volunteers for their time, put out a sign-in sheet and include a request for e-mail addresses.

✔ If you run a raffle to raise money, add an e-mail address line to the raffle ticket stub.

✔ If you are chatting with a major corporate donor over lunch, ask for her business card, which will include her business e-mail address.

You know that a highly qualified potential donor address is worth hard cash to your group. It's time to put that same thinking toward the value of an e-mail address.

Boning up on the benefits of opt-in

One alternative to using a list of people you already know is to buy or build *opt-in* lists for your e-mail campaigns. Opt-in means that people have asked for information from your organization. Not only are these people a richer potential mine of donor dollars, but also they are less likely to be annoyed when you communicate with them.

Opt-in lists are created in a few ways:

- ✔ When people register on your Web site, they may indicate in the sign-up form that they are open to receiving information from you.

- ✔ You may have a relationship with another organization where their members have agreed to receive communications from related organizations and they share their addresses with you.

- ✔ You may buy an opt-in list from another group or opt-in list vendor.

However they did it, opt-in folks have somehow said that they are open to receiving communications from you.

You can use an opt-in service, such as Spam Alternative (www.spam alternative.com) to do your opt-in emailing for you. These organizations have built up opt-in lists from sites such as free e-mail providers, where people get a free service in return for agreeing to receive advertisements and promotions. They may even provide tracking services for your e-mailing, letting you know how many recipients actually opened and read the e-mail, and how many responded in some fashion.

Knowing what to say

An e-mail campaign should be as well thought out as any paper-based direct mail campaign. Though it may seem less costly to click the Send button after you have a list of people to e-mail, there is a cost associated in terms of designing the e-mail content, strategizing its purpose, and following up on the e-mailing. There can also be a cost to doing e-mail wrong.

Consider your e-mailing's purpose and desired results before clicking Send. Some organizations use e-mail to solicit donations, others to maintain their donor relationships, and still others to find and interact with volunteers. The possibilities are really endless, but whatever the reason for the mailing, understand what you want to get out of it before it goes out.

Using e-mail to get that donation

The most obvious use of email for a nonprofit organization is to try to raise money. E-mail itself is simply words, just like a solicitation letter. But the Internet harbors some cool technology that goes way beyond a paper letter.

✔ **Include a hyperlink (usually just called a link) in your e-mail.** A link is typically a graphic symbol or bit of text that people can click to go to your Web site or to an e-mail form to reply to your message. You can even include a link to a page where they can make a payment right on the spot, either through your site or a third-party payment vendor such as PayPal. Make sure that you use a secure technology such as SSL for receiving payments online and announce loud and clear in your e-mail that donating online to you is safe. Ask your Web designer about how to do this.

✔ **You can also attach a printable form that people can print out and mail in with a check.** Consider using a format such as Adobe Acrobat, which anybody using the Adobe Acrobat reader can open. Adobe Acrobat reader is free software, and you can even offer a link in your e-mail (`www.adobe.com/products/acrobat/main.html`) that people can click to download the reader on the spot.

✔ **You can set up an automated confirmation that sends an e-mail receipt to the donor instantly.** The receipt serves as a tax record, but more important, it can include an instant thank you and recognition of the donation that will make your donors feeling appreciated.

✔ **Use graphic images in your e-mail to drive your message home.** Show a picture of your new building, include an image of a group of distressed teens who you have helped with your programs, or add a graph showing improved results from your efforts over the past year.

✔ **Consider asking people to forward the donor mailing to other people they think may be interested.** E-mail is easily forwarded, and it's a free way to expand your message to other potential donors you don't even know.

Using e-mail to build your donor relationship

Beyond the way that you get names to communicate with, consider what you're communicating. Don't constantly hit people with bids for money. If every e-mail from you is a bid for dollars, eventually recipients will add your organization to their junk mail list and never read another message from you. Consider alternating fund raising messages with useful or interesting information about your group or your cause to help build your donor relationships.

Use those alternate e-mail communications in the following ways:

✔ Let them in on upcoming events or changes in your organization.

✔ Note a milestone in giving levels and thank them for helping.

✔ Provide a case study of a specific way a person or group was helped by your efforts.

✔ Share a scanned thank-you note from a child your organization saved from homelessness or abuse.

✔ Acknowledge a special gift or all the people who gave in that month.

Using e-mail to find volunteers

Don't forget your volunteers, that oft-neglected group of souls who give to you in the form of time and passion. It is relatively easy and cheap to send out an e-mail thanking them for their efforts, informing them of achievements, and singling out people for their contributions.

If you have a big initiative coming up that will need a lot of volunteer hours, you can also send a sign-up e-mail to past volunteers and those who have expressed an interest in volunteering.

Structuring an e-mail for results

So what exactly should you put in these e-mails? No matter which group you're sending to or what your message is, a well-structured e-mail typically includes:

- ✔ **A clear and concise subject line:** Many people decide whether to read e-mail by looking at the subject line. If yours is vague it may seem like spam; if it isn't inviting the e-mail may get deleted before it is ever opened. Instead of using a subject like, "Read this immediately!" try "Find out how you can save a child from abuse." Be specific, and be compelling.

- ✔ **An identifier saying who you and your organization are right up front:** People naturally want to know who is talking to them before they are receptive to the message. State your name, position, and organization right upfront.

- ✔ **A focused message:** E-mail is usually read on a computer screen, not printed out and read from a page. Reading on a computer screen isn't that easy on the eyes, so long-winded messages are an e-mail no-no. Keep your message crisp, to the point, and well organized to keep your reader reading.

- ✔ **An explanation of any attachments:** Don't bury an important part of your message in an attachment people may or may not read. Also, because people are afraid that attachments carry viruses, many may be reluctant to open one if you don't assure them that what it contains is legitimate.

One final note about how to write your e-mails: e-mail is not a formal type of communication. Busy people, who want their information fast and to the point, read it on the fly. Don't put people off by having an overly practiced or wordy style. Be sincere about your message, be to the point, and make your reader feel comfortable with your communication.

Don't forget to provide a way to track the results. Assign a campaign code of some sort to each e-mail so questions or donations coming in as a result can be attributed to a specific campaign. In that way you can identify which campaigns are most successful and improve your content for future mailings. You can buy e-mail campaign management software such as e-Campaign from

LmhSoft (`www.LmhSoft.com`) or the free download of Arial Software's Email Marketing Director (`www.arialsoftware.com`) that will help you do this. E-mail services such as Vertical Response also help you design your e-mail with templates and design tools for a monthly fee.

Using the Power of an E-Newsletter

Although a large majority of nonprofit groups have their own Web site, a small proportion use e-newsletters, which is a shame, because e-newsletters are a great way to stay in touch and build relationships for your group.

E-newsletters (also sometimes referred to as e-zines) are essentially electronic documents that you send out via e-mail to those who have subscribed. They can contain articles, advertisements, and even links to other documents or Web sites. E-newsletters are typically informational rather than promotional.

People subscribe to an e-newsletter by clicking a button on your Web site, or a link in e-mail you send announcing the e-newsletter and filling in a form with contact information.

After people subscribe to your e-newsletter, you can send it out to your list on a regular basis, such as weekly, biweekly, or monthly. You should also provide a mechanism for people to unsubscribe, if they want.

Choose the frequency of your e-newsletter mailings with one thing in mind: how often you can generate truly fresh, interesting content. If people hear the same stuff from you a few times in a row, they'll stop reading and unsubscribe. Also, keep in mind that the regularity with which you deliver your e-newsletter can help you keep your communications momentum going, so pick a realistic delivery interval and always hit your publication deadline.

Catering to donors' interests

Be sure that your e-newsletter is of interest to your donors. That means that you can provide information about your own group's activities, but also give them information on general trends in your area, information about what other groups are doing, events of interest, and so on.

For example, if you are an animal-rights group, don't just tell your subscribers again and again about your group and its mission, because that will get old. Sure, include information about your group, but also include pictures of pets available for adoption at the local animal shelter, information on the pet parade coming up at Halloween in a nearby city, grooming tips for housebound cats, and a recipe for healthy dog biscuits. Your donors' interest includes your group and its activities, but they're more likely to enjoy your newsletter if you address their broader interests, as well.

Creating your e-newsletter

E-newsletters are typically created with HTML, the programming language used for Web documents or text that you produce in a word processor. Although you can simply create a document in your word processor and save it in text or HTML format, our advice is to get a software package such as eNewsletterPro from AdComplete or use an online e-newsletter service such as Constant Contact.

These tools typically include HTML templates, such as the one shown in Figure 16-1 from eNewsBuilder, predesigned to look attractive and eye-catching to people using any Web browser. They allow you to insert graphics and your logo easily. They also include a lot of other tools for e-newsletter management.

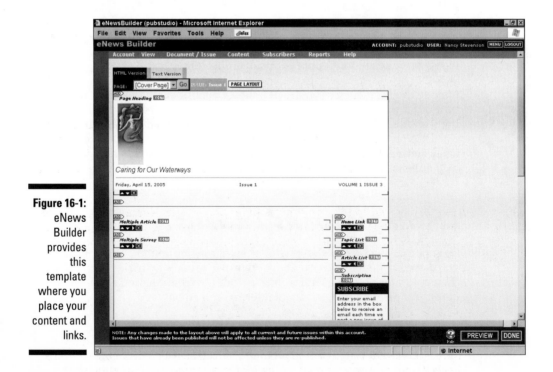

Figure 16-1:
eNews
Builder
provides
this
template
where you
place your
content and
links.

Software to the rescue

Whether you're doing e-mail or e-newsletter promotion, don't forget to check out the latest software and online programs to help you automate things. Getactive (www.getactive.com) and Memberclicks (www.memberclicks.com) are examples of Web-based systems that enable you to produce e-mail and e-newsletters, but also offer features for managing the larger context of relationship management and tracking. You can take advantage of templates, design tools, and distribution tools that make your e-mail and e-newsletter life much simpler.

Here are some design tips for an effective e-newsletter:

- ✔ Include a masthead that will have information such as the newsletter name, your organization name and logo, the date, subscription, and contact information.

- ✔ Use a typeface that is easy on the eyes. Verdana, for example, was specifically designed for use in Web documents to be read on-screen.

- ✔ Use headlines effectively. Grab the reader's attention, but also make it clear what the article is about. This saves people time, and people value their time and expect you to, as well.

- ✔ Add graphics and color for interest. Whether it's an attractive border, a photograph, or a chart, use a mix of visuals and color to make your e-newsletter more attractive and interesting.

- ✔ Provide links everywhere. Links can take people to your Web site, other Web sites, a donation payment form, or more information about the topic of the article they just read. You can save space in your newsletter and squeeze more in by putting a summary of an article with a link to a full article on your Web site that those who are interested can follow.

 An e-newsletter is still a newsletter. Rules about using a compelling lead paragraph to put the important information right upfront and answering key questions like who, what, when, where, and why apply in writing your article content just as they do in any form of journalism.

Adding multimedia pizzazz

More organizations are including links to video or are embedding video, audio, or animation content in their e-mail or e-newsletter communications. People tend to listen to or watch multimedia content with great interest because sound and images can sell where words fail to. Do you have a short video of your clients receiving help or an arts performance your group sponsors? Can you provide an animation explaining the scientific ins and outs of how your group is working to improve the ecosystem?

And, it's generally true that those who watch or listen to such messages tend to be more likely to take action or donate.

Automating e-newsletter delivery

Delivering an e-newsletter is as easy as sending e-mail. But to effectively use an e-newsletter as a promotional tool, you should get a bit more sophisticated in your delivery methods. The same software packages and online services that help you design e-newsletters also typically provide tools to set up and manage the delivery of your e-newsletter.

Features may include:

- ✔ Subscribing and unsubscribing options.
- ✔ The ability to personalize the e-newsletter. Using this kind of feature allows you to include a greeting to the recipient by name in the body of your newsletter.
- ✔ Delivery set up that may allow you to send as many as 20,000 messages an hour.
- ✔ Verification of e-mail addresses. This is useful because sometimes people subscribe with phony e-mail addresses.
- ✔ Management of e-mail lists with import and export features. If your subscriber lists are kept in Excel, for example, this allows you to import the list of contacts for generating your mailing.
- ✔ Tracking features that show how many people opened or clicked on links in your newsletter.

Some useful e-newsletter tools and services include Exact Target (www.exacttarget.com), eNewsletterPro (www.eNewsletterpro.com), and eNewsBuilder (www.enewsbuilder.com). eNewsBuilder's form for setting an e-newsletter mailing is shown in Figure 16-2.

Trying to build your subscriber list? Add a link to your newsletter subscription form at the bottom of each and every e-mail you send out.

Figure 16-2:
You create a
new issue
in eNews
Builder
for every
newsletter
you send.

Linking back to your site

One great use for your e-newsletter is to drive people back to your Web site where you may include a donation form, a volunteer sign-up form, or more detailed information on your services or activities. Always include a link to your site in your e-newsletter, or even several links to different areas of your site related to certain stories.

The first best way to get people to subscribe to your e-newsletter is to include a button to do so on your own Web site. However, for wider exposure, you can also get your e-newsletter posted in e-newsletter directories such as EzineSearch (www.ezinesearch.com) or EzineWorld (www.ezineworld.com).

Chapter 17

Extending Your Branding Online

One approach to successful fundraising is to simply get your name out there and do it in a way that gains the public's trust and admiration. The Internet is an excellent way to get some presence for your organization in people's minds, often referred to as *branding*.

Branding is a hot buzzword in business these days, and it is equally important to nonprofits. Think of the little kids dancing around the globe in the Unicef logo, or the bright red cross of (you guessed it) the Red Cross. People get to know your logo, your name, and your mission, and the next time they think of giving, they just may think of you.

But extending yourself beyond the borders of your own Web site can have other benefits. You may partner with other sites to accept donations on your behalf or sell branded merchandise and give a percentage to your cause.

In this chapter, we explore some of the great online tools you can use to jump-start your branding, promote your cause, and gather donations online.

Blogging Your Way to Funds

A recent trend in online publishing is something called a blog. (Sounds awful, doesn't it?). A *blog* is simply an abbreviated term for a Web log. Think of blogs as personal online journals where dozens or even thousands of people come to comment and debate issues or topics. A blog can contain commentary, responses, links to other sites, photos, or even a personal diary. Blogs began when journalists in war zones at the beginning of this century began to publish news or share their thoughts online. Blogs caught on with the public, and now you can find blogs on practically any topic.

As an individual fundraiser you could consider creating your own blog. You can visit sites such as www.weblogtoolscollection.com or www.ezsgblog.com to find simple tools for creating blogs. After you've created it, get your blog listed in blog directories such as www.blogcatalog.com for maximum exposure. Or spend some time visiting blogs that relate to your area of interest, and post a few of your own comments, sharing the mission and passion (and Web site!) of your organization with others.

Though blogs began as a kind of grass roots, individual form of expression, today many companies and organizations are creating their own blogs. For example the *New York Times* hosts several online blogs. Charities are not left out; visit http://donate-things.org for an example of a blog that's all about donating cars to charity (see Figure 17-1).

You might also check out a related phenomenon called RSS Feeds. This technology allows you to create a feed from a blog or other content onto your Web site. It's a great way to add fresh content to your own site. Check out *Syndicating Web Sites with RSS Feeds For Dummies,* by Ellen Finklestein (Wiley).

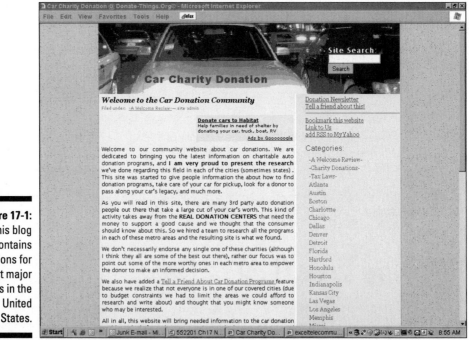

Figure 17-1:
This blog contains sections for most major cities in the United States.

What do blogs cost?

The answer is, not a whole lot, except the cost of your time to post content, monitor the blog discussion, and respond. For example, Eblogger (`www.blogger.com`), Google's blogger service, is absolutely free. It can take as little as a few minutes to set up a blog. Perhaps the greater cost is in marketing your blog. But consider that you can piggyback your blog marketing onto every other marketing vehicle you use such as brochure or your Web site, and again, it's mostly a matter of your time.

How do you write a good blog?

Writing a blog is a little different than writing your brochure or a fundraising proposal. The idea here is to keep people intrigued and participating. To that end:

- ✔ Post questions that get people thinking and contributing their own ideas.

- ✔ Offer statistics about your cause that people may not have been aware of.

- ✔ Don't get into fights with contributors of blog postings because they could be potential contributors to your cause. Do use their contrary postings as an opportunity to tell your side of the story professionally and calmly.

Using Charity Portals and Malls

You may think that soliciting donations online means setting up your own Web site with a shopping cart feature to collect the money, complete with the ability to process credit cards and send out e-mail confirmations. That can sound like a lot of work (and possibly expense) to a small group with no full-time staff. But there are alternatives to this do-it-all-yourself method of accepting online donations.

Charity portals and charity malls are gathering places for fundraising organizations that let somebody else promote you and process payments. Some of these sites provide 100 percent of any donations they collect to your group; others keep a percentage to run their sites.

One of the major changes the Web has made is that transactions are happening faster than ever. In the for-profit world, you can apply for financing for a new couch and have approval in 45 seconds. In the philanthropic community, donors want to make decisions, be presented with giving options, make their donation, and be recognized for their gifts, all within a very quick timeframe. Providing them with an efficient way to give online can really help your cause.

Going, going, gone!

Online charity auctions are a recent phenomenon. This can be a cool way to raise money for a particular cause or event. MissionFish (www.missionfish.com) is one good example. You can trade on eBay through the MissionFish site. eBay sellers select a charity to sponsor, and then a portion of any of their sales goes to that charity. Donors can go to www.missionfish.com to see a list of eBay sellers associated with giving. There is an easy to use sign up process on this site to get your nonprofit registered with MissionFish. You will need to provide information about your 501(c)(3) status, a mission statement, voided check, e-mail address, and electronic version of your logo. And best of all, registration is free.

Entering the portal

Charity portals such as Just Give (www.justgive.com) and Network for Good (www.networkforgood.com) host donation efforts and provide links to a wide variety of charities. This service provides a charity with tremendous promotional visibility for a small fee. If you pay the fee to be a featured charity, you may get a page of your own that people can find through searching the site or exploring your category of giving. If you are included on a link page, you can reap the benefit of many people jumping to your own site to hear your message direct from the source.

Many of these portals also provide information and services for nonprofits, such as donation tracking and handling of donation payments. Network for Good offers an area where you can post calls for volunteers. This site also provides tools for the people making donations to set up giving accounts where donors can track a history of their contributions and access links to favorite charities.

Shopping at the charity mall

Another online opportunity awaits you at the shopping mall. No, not your neighborhood mall, with its department stores and small specialty stores. This type of mall is a virtual mall, a Web site organized to sell products online, from a variety of vendors. When your organization is part of the mall, a percentage of sales dollars are donated to your group.

Online shopping malls are springing up daily. Before you get involved, check out the following:

✔ What percentage does the mall take?

✔ How do visitors find your organization on the mall site? Are they required to sign in to a nonprofit area? Are all nonprofits displayed on a single page, so your organization is competing with dozens of others?

✔ Do you have your own address so that visitors can return to your "storefront" any time they choose?

As you become educated about your choices, you can determine which mall arrangement, if any, best fits your mission and online fundraising objectives.

A charity mall such as `GreaterGood.com` operated by `CharityUSA.org` (see Figure 17-2) is a good example. Here people can shop for everything from clothing to cosmetics, with a portion of their purchases (often up to 30 percent) going to charity. You can also expand your branding by selling products with your logo or slogan imprinted on them through a charity mall.

If you don't want to be part of a bigger charity portal or mall, but do want to accept donations online, consider simply setting up payment services through a company such as PayPal (`www.paypal.com`). There are transaction fees for this service, but they aren't huge and it's easy to set up. People just click a button to donate and go directly to PayPal's site to pay.

Figure 17-2: Greater Good.com combines commerce with causes.

Publishing Online to Boost Your Branding and Credibility

If you've ever written a press release, you know the value of just getting your name in print. On the Internet everybody is hungry for content to keep their Web sites fresh and keep people coming back. That's why they may just welcome an article or piece of news about your group. Not only will you get exposure, but also being quoted as an expert in some arena builds credibility for you and your organization.

Another great thing about the Internet is that information seldom sits still on one site. Other sites or search engines pick up articles. People forward articles to others via e-mail. Putting an article or press release out on the Internet is like dropping a pebble in a pond: The ripples can be endless.

Getting published

To get content placed online you can follow several approaches:

- ✔ Visit sites that are somehow related to your target donor groups' interests, and send an e-mail to the Webmaster, using a link on their Contact Us page.

- ✔ Check out online versions of magazines or newspapers related to your potential donors' interests to see if they include information on how to submit stories to them somewhere on their Web sites. For example if you work for a musical performing arts organization, you might check into sites that cover musical interests, local music performances, or music schools.

- ✔ Submit questions or comments that may get published to related online publications with a letters to the editor kind of feature.

Try using content directories, such as Arcana (`www.arcanaweb.com`), How To Advice (`www.howtoadvice.com`), or Articlehub (`www.articlehub.com`) to submit online content that gets exposure on many sites. These sites also provide e-zine templates and articles about how to write online content to help you out.

Creating good online content

You're more likely to get what you submit published if you write good online content. Here are some tips for doing that:

- ✔ **Pay attention to submission guidelines.** If they say no more than 300 words, don't submit 350.

✔ **Format the article correctly.** Some sites want submissions in HTML, others in plain text. There are good reasons that they ask for these formats: A proper format saves them time and effort in making your content look presentable online.

✔ **Make the title mean something.** You have to grab attention and the title of your article may be all that appears in a link a visitor clicks to view the entire article.

✔ **Use a good text editor and check spelling and grammar.** A good editor for online articles is Ziney Pro (`www.softtechsolution.com/zineypro`).

Joining Online Communities: Discussion Groups

A *discussion group* is an online community that discusses an area of common interest. Hundreds of thousands of discussion groups are available online, with topics ranging from schnauzers to special events.

Discussion groups have been around a relatively long time in the short history of the Internet. But the power of a discussion group to connect with others and stimulate conversation about topics has not abated. These community-gathering spots where people post messages are reminiscent of bulletin boards you find in your office break room or local library. Discussion group conversations can go on for months or even years and involve hundreds of people.

You can use discussion groups to connect to the fundraising community for advice, or use them to gain exposure for your group.

Checking out nonprofit discussion groups

You can post comments on fundraising-related sites' discussion groups to receive helpful information. How does it work? When you post a message, it is available in a discussion area to both members and visitors to the site. People read your message, and may respond with a comment. When you get multiple replies you end up with what's called a discussion thread.

You can find many different discussion groups that are already out there, and more are springing up all the time. Here's a representative sampling for you to check out:

✔ **Charity Channel** is offered by `CharityChannel.com`. Click on the Forum link on this home page to access discussion groups on topics such as Annual Funds and Development.

- ✔ **AFPnet** at `www.afpnet.org` includes several discussion groups. Go to the home page and click the Discussions link to sign up and access their six active discussion topics.

- ✔ **Soc.org.nonprofit** is one of the oldest nonprofit discussion groups. There are two ways to join: Use a newsreader program to subscribe to their USENET group; or send an e-mail to `nonprofit-request@rain.org` with the word Subscribe in the subject field.

- ✔ **About** is a Web site that provides information about many topics. Go to `http://nonprofit.about.com` and click the Forums link. You'll have to sign up with a member name and password, unless you want to use the Guest option to visit and check it out first.

- ✔ **The Internet Profit Center** (`http://www.nonprofit-info.org/npofaq/`) maintains an FAQ (frequently asked questions) site where they gather postings from various nonprofit discussion groups. You can sign up to get an e-mail whenever a new FAQ is posted.

Promoting yourself through discussion groups

To get exposure for your group among the donor population, it's probably most useful to post comments on sites related to your cause rather than on fundraising sites. That's because people who give money to your type of cause look for sites related to your cause whereas other professional fundraisers visit fundraising sites. If your group deals with battered women, go to sites that provide advice or services to those people. If your organization helps to take care of rescued animals, go to large chain pet store sites, sites that advise people on what breed of puppy is right for them, or pet food company sites and see if they have a discussion area.

Discussion group etiquette

When posting to a discussion group, always make the subject of your post meaningful so others can easily figure out what your topic is. Check your post for errors and clarity. Error-ridden postings are not only hard to read, but they may also reflect badly on your group. Be careful what you say: If you are responding to a negative comment about your group, don't let your emotions take charge. Be thoughtful, informative, and gracious in your reply. Remember, your comments in discussion groups reflect on your organization as well as on you. And, an irate posting can be taken up by somebody and sent around the world via e-mail or some other vehicle. Do you really want something said in the heat of the moment to represent your cause?

When you post comments in discussion groups, it's not good etiquette to post a self-serving appeal for funds. Instead, try to provide information or respond to others' questions in a way that's useful, and simply include a quick mention of your group and your Web site address in your message. Over time, you establish a presence in these discussion groups and people recognize that your group cares enough to help others out. In turn, they may wander over to your Web site and help you out with a donation. Remember, this is community building, not advertising! Discussion group involvement can be time consuming, but it can pay off in the end.

 Instant messaging and chat groups are different from discussion groups in that the conversations are held in real time (called *synchronous* in techie circles). In a discussion group you post a message and somebody reads it, perhaps days later (called *asynchronous*). With instant messaging and chat groups you send a message to somebody who almost immediately gets it on the other end and responds.

Partnering Online through Affinity Programs

Did you ever get a call from a magazine telling you that if you bought a subscription, they'd give $1 to some worthwhile cause? Or, does your local Walmart offer a program whereby you can donate to computers in local schools? That's the basic idea of an affinity program. An *affinity program* is an arrangement with a for-profit organization that agrees to donate a certain percentage of income to your charitable cause.

Excel Telecommunications (www.exceltelecommunications.com) has an affinity program that gets some attention. This phone service provider donates a certain percentage of income to participating charities. Other affinity programs are developing daily. Some of the most recent include credit cards that pay out a percentage to the sponsored nonprofit.

Look into these online malls and affinity programs for even more information (and check out Chapter 12 for even more of these great sites):

- ✔ www.charitableway.com
- ✔ igive.com
- ✔ www.entango.com
- ✔ shop2give.com
- ✔ grassroots.org

An affiliate program is different than an affinity program. With an affiliate program you put a link to another site on your own. When people click the link to go to the other site, you get a small commission. Affiliate programs can be profitable, but be sure that the affiliate sites are of good quality and that they relate to your areas of interest. Otherwise, your constituency will click on them and be offended, or just plain bored, with the result.

Keep in mind that the affinity groups you partner with want to make money off the goodwill your name generates, but they offer you an additional fundraising venue that could be profitable. Consider the character of an affinity group carefully before getting involved with their program. You are stepping into the world of commerce with affinity programs, and you do not want a badly or shadily run business hurting your own group's image or reputation.

Affinity groups are involved in e-commerce. As a result, the income you get from involvement in them can be subject to unrelated business income tax. Check with your lawyer or accountant before signing up for an affinity program.

Connecting with People through Association and Special-Interest Sites

Just as in the nonelectronics world, people find people (and organizations) in different places online. You may find that simply placing links to your site on other sites that have visitors with common interests is a good way to go.

Here are some typical connections you may want to explore:

- ✔ If your group supports animal rights, go to the ASPCA site and People for Ethical Treatment of Animals and ask to put a link to your site there, but don't forget to also contact PetSmart, which has a charity to help homeless animals, and pet food companies.

- ✔ If you represent a health-related group, such as one that works for breast cancer research, consider any site related to health concerns, as well as sites directed toward women as a group and medical associations.

- ✔ Perhaps your organization is raising funds for the arts. Try the site for your local arts council, record or bookstore, art supply store, or library.

The point here is that the groups and sites you can partner with are limited only by your imagination. On the Internet, the rule is constant change; so go ahead and ask whether a site will add a link to your site; what can it hurt?

Part V
On the (Fundraising) Campaign Trail

The 5th Wave   By Rich Tennant

al Fundraising Dinner

"Does the check writing pen go above the dessert spoon or next to the salad fork?"

In this part . . .

Different fundraising campaigns are run for different purposes: Your annual fund supports your daily operations; a special event may purchase new research equipment; the new hospital wing is built on dollars raised for the capital campaign. This part explores these different campaigns, so you can determine which one works best for your particular needs and what to expect along the way. We also take a close look at various types of funding, including major gifts from individuals, foundations, and corporations and the possibility of making an endowment work for you.

Chapter 18

Organizing, Implementing, and Celebrating Your Annual Fund

*E*veryone is familiar with annual fund drives from the point of view of someone being solicited — by the local zoo, by churches, and by schools, for example. Most people who are approached to give have no idea of the work involved in running the campaign they are being asked to give to. But putting an annual campaign together from the soliciting side involves a number of specific steps and a whole lot of planning.

This chapter is where you discover just what an annual fund drive is, what the ins and outs of creating a successful annual fund campaign are, and how to effectively evaluate your results.

Understanding Annual Funds

Where major gifts and planned giving may provide much-needed financial spikes in your organization's life, perhaps underwriting new initiatives or programs, an annual fund is typically run to support an organization's annual budget, bringing in the money the organization needs throughout the year in order to fuel its work. An annual fund is often structured to receive ongoing support and gain a donor base; in that way it is different from a one-time gift a donor makes to your organization. With an annual fund you are using pledge cards to secure unrestricted, higher-level gifts that donors can pay in installments — monthly, quarterly, or annually. Unrestricted means that you can use the money as you want, to repaint the restroom or stock up on paperclips; unglamorous, but necessary expenditures. Additionally, donors may want to be recognized for their gift with a naming opportunity or to be included in a giving club for donors who contribute within a certain donation range.

Some big organizations hire fundraising consulting firms to help them determine whether expanded fundraising expectations are realistic. If you don't want to hire an outside firm, go out and interview a whole lot of prospective donors. Ask them to look at your mission statement and then ask, "Is this doable? Are our expectations out of line?" Using a focus group in this way takes a lot of legwork, but the result can be a tested fundraising goal with a number of people getting on board before the fundraising train leaves the station.

Your annual fund may be large or small — you may spend weeks or only days planning it. Either way, the system you develop and the planning you put into it are closely related — the more well thought out your plan, the greater the return on your annual fund investment is likely to be.

Annual Fund Buster #1: Plan? What Plan? If you think that you can simply work toward your annual fund all year long without a specific strategy in place, think again. Without planning, the funds that do come in will be spotty and short lived. With a carefully prepared annual fund plan, you know what you're spending, how much you anticipate raising, who your key players are, and how you need to evaluate the effectiveness of the various parts of your plan after you reach your goals.

Designing Your Annual Campaign

The annual fund is the center of all the fundraising efforts at your organization. The time you spend planning and implementing an annual fund plan relates directly to the success of the drive — spend the time now, put the systems in place, and go about your other fundraising efforts in an organized way. It beats the socks off of shooting blindly at the wall and hoping a certain percentage of donors will want to support your continuing efforts.

There are four must-have ingredients for a successful annual fund drive:

✔ Know your goals.

✔ Have a well-prepared team.

✔ Know which tools to use.

✔ Evaluate your efforts.

The following sections explore each of these important areas in more depth. By the end of this chapter, you'll have the blueprint for putting together a well-thought-out annual fund drive.

Setting goals

So what do you want to accomplish with your annual fund? Most organizations rely on their annual fund to bring in the money they need for their standard operating expenses, plus whatever they need to grow in the areas where they've planted seeds.

You and your board should put together a list of the goals you want to reach with your annual fund. For best results, you should appoint a development committee that is willing to devote itself to setting up, carrying out, and evaluating the annual fund drive. And don't forget — your board members should be givers themselves.

You should include these goals for your annual fund, as well as other goals related specifically to the mission of your organization:

✔ Bring in the specific amount of funds to reach the fundraising target goal (use a Gift Range Chart, as described in Chapter 5, to determine your giving levels and the number of gifts you need in each area in order to meet your goal).

✔ Surpass last year's budget plus inflation, and add new programs.

✔ Find new donors and upgrade existing donors.

✔ Enlist and train a dedicated volunteer corps.

✔ Identify potential higher-level donors.

Although it sounds easy enough — setting your goal and choosing the right vehicle to get you there — setting the goal can often be a struggle in organizations large and small. The reason? You don't establish your campaign goal in a vacuum. You need to budget your activities, adding the necessary percentage of increase for inflation over last year's budget — and consider how you want to enhance your programs.

Struggles may result between the planning committee ("This is the year we want to add services for the kids with no hair!") and the budget committee ("That's too much of a stretch for this year — let's try that next year!"). Ultimately you have a moment of truth when everybody has to come together and ask, "Can we do it?" In many organizations, that's a tough moment.

Reaching a consensus on your fundraising goal is a major part of setting up your annual fund — and it may take considerable talking, planning, and reevaluating. It also gives your organization the benefit of returning to its mission statement, taking a look at its priorities, and ultimately getting everybody working together for the good of the cause.

Assembling your team

In larger organizations, the executive director is in charge of leading the annual fund effort, with the help of an active board and development committee. In smaller organizations, the annual fund drive may be run entirely by volunteers. In churches, for example, a lucky volunteer often gets the lead role in the management of the annual fund. There's no particular way to do it — but you want a person who is aware of your mission actually leading the charge.

Choosing the team leader

As with other types of fundraising campaigns, the person in charge of your annual fund effort should be

- Passionate about your cause
- Able to see both the big picture and focus on details
- Capable of creating a plan, getting it approved, and inspiring others to work on it
- Recognized as a person with whom people like to work
- Trained in leadership — either in a volunteer or professional capacity
- Respected by your constituency

Putting your team in place

The fundraising team you assemble will have a direct impact on how well your annual fund meets its goals. Who will be on an annual fund team?

Your volunteer team may be part of your Development Committee — you should have at least a member or two represented — and they should be people who understand and feel passionate about the work that you do. Important attributes of a team member are:

- Able to communicate effectively
- Good at following through on what they say that they'll do
- Trained in basic fundraising skills

Use your board to help identify key volunteers who would be good annual fund team members.

Creating a successful team

You can help make sure that the time and organizing effort your annual fund team puts into the project pays off by making sure that individuals have what they need. Your annual fund has a better chance of being successful if you make sure that team members have:

- ✔ Regular meetings to discuss the goals, strategies, and plans for the annual fund
- ✔ Materials used to compile annual fund publications
- ✔ Resources for compiling materials
- ✔ Access to existing and former donor lists and donor histories
- ✔ Prospecting lists that show how the prospect is related to your organization and give some rationale for their ability to pay or their payment level
- ✔ A system for easily tracking prospect responses

Choosing your fundraising tools

Because you want your annual fund plan to make the most of your resources and be effective, take some time to think about the approaches on which you want to spend the most time. We rank them here, from most to least effective.

Meeting face to face

A national survey by the United Way indicates that seven out of ten people will say, "Yes" to a request from one of their peers when asked face to face for a donation. Our biggest problem as fundraisers is that we don't ask enough people in person.

In a smaller organization, face-to-face contact may not get the same return, but it could no doubt get a bigger response than the other approaches. Why is that? Because, as the old fundraising saying goes, "People don't give money to causes. People give to people with causes." The human element is extremely important — and a face-to-face meeting gives your donors the easiest way to connect with you.

The best people paired for a face-to-face meeting are those who are peers in the organizational structure. If you send a top-level manager in to talk to a CEO and the CEO makes a case for the organization, the manager may be left feeling that his donation or refusal could affect his job down the road. Better to avoid the situation altogether and select people for meetings based on their peer status.

When you are fundraising in the workplace, it's particularly powerful when a colleague in your department becomes the solicitor for your cause. This way, the person doing the asking is someone with whom others have an established relationship — there is already trust built there. The thinking is, "Oh, well, if Sarah thinks this is a good organization, it probably is!"

Making personal calls

Actually connecting, listening, and responding to another human being is the next best thing to being there. A telephone call carries the voice — the living, real connection of another person. This is something you shouldn't underestimate — especially when you are tempted to call that donor back after business hours so you can simply leave a message on his machine. (Don't feel bad — we've all done it.)

Your responsiveness in a phone conversation helps build the relationship with the donor, which helps bring the donor closer to your organization. Also, experience shows that people have more trouble telling a "live" person on the phone, "No" than they do ignoring a fundraising letter or a more impersonal solicitation.

Writing personal correspondence

Personal correspondence means a personalized letter written specifically for the donor. Of course, mailing experts use technology in such a way that even a group letter looks as though it was written for a single recipient.

Personal correspondence says to the donor, "You're important enough to me that I took the time to write to you personally." This also, like the personal phone call, carries a bit of weight in the psychology of "the ask." The letter is more impersonal than the call or the visit, however, because the real human contact is missing. Donors have the option of never opening your letter, pitching it sight unseen, or misplacing it in a pile of other papers.

A personal letter with a phone call follow-up makes the contact more direct and alerts you if the letter hasn't been received. Take the time to write the note by hand, and you'll improve your response rate.

Making online contacts

So where does e-mail fit into the picture? Is it as effective as a personal letter? More so? E-mail contacts that are personalized and are sent directly to the donor may elicit a quicker response than traditional mail because of their fast nature. Some nonprofit organizations are conducting huge e-mail campaigns to take full advantage of online fundraising. "Opt-in" e-mail, where donors give their permission for you to contact them online, helps guard against charges of spamming (sending out massive quantities of unwanted, unsolicited e-mail), and provides the donor with a quick and easy way to stay up-to-date on the happenings of your organization. See Chapter 16 for more about using e-mail effectively.

One flaw with e-mail is that it often offers no way for the recipient to take action. You can ask the recipient to mail in a check, but you provide no envelope or pledge form. Often hitting Reply to respond to a mass-produced e-mail message ends up at a dead-end address. You can improve results with this format if you do allow e-mail responses to go to a real person, or you provide a link to your site where a donor can make an online pledge with a credit card.

Sponsoring special events

If you can get somebody to come to your special event, you already have a foot in the donation door. Someone who cares enough to come to your event is already interested and able to provide something to your organization. Make sure that you capture all the important data about the attendees at your special events — from who attends to whom they brought or sat with and what comments they had about the evening. You won't have time to run around with a notebook recording these pieces of information, but noticing the specifics on your top dozen donors can help you target future fundraising plans. See Chapter 19 for information on planning special events.

Going door-to-door

As any Avon representative will tell you, cold door-to-door calling is an expensive and time-consuming venture. Of all the "personal contact" options, this one is the lowest on the ladder in terms of effectiveness. If the prospect opens the door (and they may not, if you're holding something that looks like a sales kit), you need to cover a lot of ground in less than 30 seconds. Can you make someone see the heart of your organization in that amount of time? It's not impossible, but certainly challenging and potentially dangerous if there's an unfriendly dog about.

Using direct mail

As we mention in Chapter 10, direct mail is a very sophisticated operation today because of the ability to buy and sort lists. Going to people who already know about you, such as existing donors, last year's members, attendees from events, or even people who have gone to or are givers to similar organizations, allows for much more powerful niche mailing. Your direct mail campaign may include an annual fund mailer (maybe in the form of a membership renewal), a brochure, postcards, newsletters, or catalogs.

Any time you do a mailing, whether of an annual report or a thank-you letter, it's good practice to include another solicitation envelope. Change your appeal but make the most of every contact.

Telemarketing

As we note in Chapter 13, call centers are still going strong as a vehicle in fundraising. It's a safe bet that telephone soliciting will become less and less effective, however, as more and more people use call-blocking devices (such as Caller ID or more sophisticated filtering techniques) to weed out the calls they don't want. One online survey reported that 98 percent of 1.78 million people responding were made angry by telemarketing calls. In general, consumers want more control over who contacts them; for that reason, over time, telemarketing will become obsolete.

Getting on TV and radio

As you may have seen, TV can be an effective means of generating support. The tsunami in Indonesia brought an outpouring of support that was funneled through the American Red Cross. Television and radio also give a sense of authenticity (whether that's warranted or not is another matter); viewers and listeners often think that if they see it or hear it in the media, it must be true. Television and radio can be a great friend to your mission. Particularly if you have a noteworthy cause that has ties to current issues and events, you can use that exposure to help gain recognition for your organization, which translates directly into more dollars raised for your cause.

Media such as radio and TV is expensive, and often prohibitive for nonprofit budgets. Try instead to get human-interest coverage on local cable channels or place stories in news programs. Or try a prerecorded online broadcast from your Web site. It's free, and reaches many of the same people as advertising does.

Rating your organization

Does your organization have all these items in place? In Table 18-1, we present a way to rate yourself that encourages you to think about each of these areas and rate your organization on a scale of 1 to 10 (1 is "We haven't even thought about it yet!" and 10 is "Been there, done that, and it's working great!")

Table 18-1	Rate Your Organization: Fundraising Tool Effectiveness		
Vehicle	*Included in Your Annual Fund Plan?*	*Rating Value (1 to 10)*	*Next Step to Take*
Face to Face			
Personal Calls			
Personal Correspondence			
Special Events			
Door-To-Door			

Vehicle	Included in Your Annual Fund Plan?	Rating Value (1 to 10)	Next Step to Take
E-mail and E-newsletter			
Online Broadcasting			
Direct Mail			
Telemarketing			
TV and Radio			

Annual Fund Buster #2: Bad timing. Evaluating where you are in the fundraising cycle is important before you embark on a planned annual campaign. Is your board ready? Do you have leadership for the campaign? How experienced are your volunteers? Do you have the budget? These and other issues can have a lot to do with the success of your campaign — or the lack of it.

Putting the Plan in Place

After you've identified your goals, chosen your team, and evaluated the fundraising tools at your disposal, you are ready to get down to work. The first step is to identify prospects. Then you need to make sure that you have the materials you need for support. Finally, you need to ensure that your volunteers are trained and ready. After all that is done, you're ready to launch out into your community and begin your annual fund drive.

Understanding your approach: Donor research and planning

The annual fund campaign targets three types of donors:

- ✔ Prospects who have never given to your organization but have interests or involvements that make them qualified candidates
- ✔ One-time donors who can be approached for a repeat gift
- ✔ Repeat donors who can be upgraded to a higher-giving level

lse the donor research strategies in Chapter 6 to find out more about the pecifics of researching your donor audience.

chedule at least one prospect brainstorming session with your annual fund team and selected board members. Everybody should be ready, willing, and able to come up with names of potential donors that the annual fund team can use.

One of the items you should research during this phase is the percentage of people helped by the work that you do. Specifics ring true in the mind of the donor. For example, saying, "Your donation of $150 last year helped us warn a classroom of 30 preteens about the dangers of smoking" is much more effective than a simple thank you.

Choosing your materials

What will your annual team members need to support them in their donor contacts?

- ✔ **Brochures:** Brochures, flyers, or other publications explaining your annual fund. Also, provide any ID pieces your organization uses to promote itself and explain its programs. If your organization publishes an annual report, give it to your annual fund team members to help them understand what the funds are used for during the year.

- ✔ **Your case statement:** The all-important case statement (see Chapter 3) gives a clear picture of your mission and explains why you — and only you — can offer the services you provide in the way that you provide them.

  Come up with a new case statement for each annual fund you do. Nobody wants to see the same information served up year after year. The donations from the previous years should be making some difference, after all. Tell donors how their donations have helped and how you plan to use this year's donations. Be sure that you communicate the continuing need — and your unique response to it — with enthusiasm and interest.

- ✔ **Donor information sheets:** Your annual fund team members also need information sheets on donors giving them donation history and pertinent background information. These sheets are in addition to the donor list.

- ✔ **Pledge cards:** Givers to an annual fund often like to break their gifts into installments, which makes it easier for them to give larger amounts and makes it easy for you to allocate income out through the balance of your fiscal year.

Annual Fund Buster #3: An uncommitted board. A lukewarm board isn't going to bring in large checks — and it also isn't going to be able to do the day-in, day-out follow-up required to run an effective annual campaign. Be sure that your board understands its role in the fundraising function of your organization before you launch an annual fund drive.

Evaluating (and Celebrating) Your Annual Fund Drive

Going through a debriefing process can be helpful not only to give your annual fund team some closure, but also for next year's team, providing information on what worked, what didn't, and where improvements could be made.

Your evaluation of your campaign can include the following questions:

- ✔ Did we meet our financial goals?
- ✔ Did we meet the goals we had for the number of prospects and donors contacted?
- ✔ What was our response rate in direct mail and telephone solicitation?
- ✔ Which fundraising tools were most effective?
- ✔ Was our team prepared and provided with the tools they needed?
- ✔ How effective was our annual fund leadership?
- ✔ What were the three biggest factors in the success of the drive?
- ✔ What were the three biggest challenges we faced?
- ✔ If we were starting this campaign again today, what would we change?

After you finish your evaluation, don't forget to take time to celebrate! Celebrating is an important part of the annual fund process. You need to thank all your volunteers, recognize extraordinary efforts, and praise people all around. After all, the seeds you plant today may germinate and grow into the annual fund team you have tomorrow.

Chapter 19

Planning a Special Event

. . . .

In This Chapter

▶ Maximizing the benefits of special events

▶ Planning your special event

▶ Evaluating the event

▶ Organizing an online event

▶ Recognizing those who helped

. . . .

*W*hen you say "special event," people often think of black-tie, high-society events with fancy catered food and a fine orchestra. Although this type of event certainly exists and is held regularly (and with finesse) by major organizations, this type of event is by no means the most common special event that nonprofits host.

Put simply, a fundraising special event is an experience that brings people together and raises awareness for your cause and offers an opportunity to ask for donations. The event could be anything from a celebrity car wash to a walk-a-thon to a kissing contest to an evening of ballroom dancing.

Consider the following sampling of special events:

✔ A Jog-for-Health event that raises money for prenatal care

✔ A dog wash for the local humane society

✔ A gala event for the chamber orchestra

✔ A silent auction for a private school

✔ A Thanksgiving feast at the homeless shelter

✔ A black-tie auction for a local arts group

In this chapter you discover how a special event, done well, can raise visibility for your organization that can mean substantial fundraising bucks down the road. The key is to have a person who wants to champion the event, a committee that plans and executes it, and enough time to find the right event and pull it together.

Whatever the activity, the appeal of the event for your participant is in the opportunity for belonging, and the fact that the activity is something the potential donors see as a social activity that sounds like a fun use of their time.

Benefiting from the Event

The single biggest benefit of a special event is raising awareness. Through your publicity efforts — and hopefully by word of mouth — people in your community become aware of your organization. Raised awareness benefits you in a number of ways:

- ✔ Increase prospective donor list
- ✔ Involve donors as volunteers, forming a closer relationship with your organization
- ✔ Media coverage
- ✔ Fundraising, depending on the type of event — expensive events may yield less financial gain

How big does your special event need to be? Only as big as your budget and community supports. Because the focus of a special event is more about building awareness, the selection of the event itself is more important than the money spent.

Planning, Planning, Planning!

As with most things, the secret to a good event is in the planning. If you want your event to be truly "special," detailed and thorough planning is a must because your results could be sunk by a single misstep. If you're ready for the event and do it well, you maximize awareness in your community, build goodwill with your volunteers, have fun, and raise money. If you're not ready, an event that unravels can give the community the impression that your organization doesn't manage itself well, which can be a devastating perception for agencies trying to build credibility.

Planning your special event involves making a number of decisions right at the start:

- ✔ Who takes the lead? Which volunteers serve on the committee?
- ✔ What kind of event do you have? Who does it reach? How do you reach them?

✔ What do you want to accomplish? Are you raising awareness, money, goodwill, or all three?

✔ Can you afford to do a special event at this time?

Some events become annual events and grow precisely because they are annual events. For example, some organizations have an annual silent auction or dance. The anticipation and repeat promotion of the event from year to year helps the community recognize the organization and the cause.

Putting together the best team

The right leader (one who is enthusiastic, engaging, persuasive, and passionate) can energize your volunteer group. People want to help, and the event becomes a major team-building activity.

With the wrong leader — someone who looks at the event as a chore, someone who is already overcommitted, lacking the time or energy to take on another duty — the event looms as a continual albatross around the neck of your organization. Postpone your plans for a special event until you have just the right leader to forge ahead with heart and soul. A lukewarm event drains your organization's financial and volunteer resources and becomes a negative experience that nobody wants to associate with.

Select a committee chair who

✔ Has the time to commit to the effort

✔ Has people skills to motivate others

✔ Understands and is able to communicate the vision

Your special event committee should consist of volunteers who

✔ Love to get out there and promote your cause with enthusiasm

✔ "Get things done"

✔ Can work as a team to pull the event together

Provide enough lead time before the event (see the section, "Setting a timeline for your special event," later in this chapter). The committee should meet monthly at first to solidify the plan and keep it in motion. As the event draws near, the committee may meet weekly to ensure that all aspects of the event are under control.

Selecting an event

The type of special event you choose is also important. Is the event itself linked logically to your organization's mission? Will the people who care about your cause sit up and take notice of the event? An event to benefit a street outreach group for homeless teens makes sense as an informal, outdoor concert with casual attire, sidewalk vendor foods, and local bands. That same event, done in a ballroom with people dressed to the nines, will leave your donors wondering why the funding of this high-priced event isn't going to your constituency, instead. But if you're fundraising for the opera, a black-tie affair fits your potential donors' interests and net worth.

Especially for smaller organizations, the perception raised by the fundraising event you choose is an important consideration. If you are a small group that makes quilts for AIDS patients, people may wonder how you could host a $150-a-plate dinner with high-profile entertainment (unless, of course, the event is heavily sponsored, which we get to in a minute). Be sure that the message you send to your participants fits the message you want to send; don't leave them wondering whether the money they donate to your cause goes to fund that annual fundraising gala.

Here are some guidelines for choosing the right event:

✔ Look for an event that is a logical fit with your organization's mission.

✔ Think about who you want to attend — and why.

✔ Know the return you want from the evening.

✔ Consider how you can get exposure from the local press for the event.

✔ Be aware of the budget for special events and stay within your means.

Involve the people you serve in your special event. One mental health association nearly always includes in the audience people who have received their services. At first other audience members did a double take to see clients in the audience, but the inclusion of clients in the celebration shows that the organization means what it says about the rights and dignity of those they serve.

Deciding the where and the when

After you select the event leadership and the event itself, you need to decide where and when you want to have it. The "where" should also be logically connected to your organization. Why have a school special event at a location other than the school? The "when" should be selected after careful deliberation on the wants and needs — and schedules — of your target audience. Here are some questions that can help you answer the "when":

✔ What time of year fits logically with your organization's mission? A program that raises donations for holiday gifts for kids may have its special event the weekend after Thanksgiving, when the holiday buying season officially begins.

✔ What else is going on in town at that time? What other obligations may your audience have? If you schedule your fundraiser when the big city orchestra hosts its black-tie ball, you may lose some of your higher-level donors.

✔ Do you know of a time of year when you're likely to get more help than others? If many of your volunteers go to Florida for the winter, you may wind up having that Valentine's Day dance all by yourself. Remember that your volunteers are an important part of the overall success of the event — both for the word-of-mouth publicity they offer and the team-building experiences they have.

Equally important may be the where. Ask yourself these key questions:

✔ Where in your town can people get to easily and park near? Logistics can kill your event. If people can't get to the event easily, they won't come.

✔ What locale fits the event? If you're throwing a black-tie event, it can't be at a soup kitchen in the inner city. If your event involves art, a museum or theater makes sense. Make sure that the venue matches the mood and is a destination that is attractive to your potential donors.

✔ Is the location in your budget? Renting a swank country club for a black-tie event might be swell, but can you afford it? Your potential donors don't want to see you bleeding money for the sake of a fundraiser. Look for people to donate a locale or swap it for free, positive publicity.

Setting expectations

Clearly, making a mountain of money isn't a realistic expectation of your first fundraiser. When you get your special events committee pulled together, spend some time discussing and carefully thinking through the goals for your event. Realistic goals help you set a realistic budget. How will you measure your success? You may want to set goals in each of these areas:

✔ Number of people attending

✔ Cost per person

✔ Coverage in the local media

✔ Number of volunteers involved

✔ Amount of money raised

✔ Happiness quotient

Happiness quotient? How can you rate people's happiness with the event? Simple. Set a scale of 1-5. People with a happiness quotient of one left the event looking seriously bored or disgruntled. People with a happiness quotient of five left euphorically happy, singing the praises of your organization all the way down the walk. Include volunteer and staff reactions in the happiness quotient too. The 1-5 scale is not a scientific method of tracking event results, but the "good feeling" that results from a successful event may be the single biggest lasting effect your efforts make in the year to come.

Budgeting for the special event

Don't forget the budget. Even if it's mainly to generate awareness and goodwill, the event shouldn't break the bank.

If your organization has a history of special events, you probably already have a hefty allotment for this year's event. If you are putting on a first-time event or are trying a new event that presents new costs, you need to be mindful of the upfront investment involved in setting up services and reaching your target audience.

As your special events committee works with the budget, be sure to prepare for expenses in each of the following areas:

- ✔ Facility (rental fees, insurance, permits, lighting)
- ✔ Equipment (tables and chairs, audio-visual equipment, tents)
- ✔ Services (catering, housekeeping, transportation, security)
- ✔ Entertainment (speakers' fees, performers' fees, bands)
- ✔ Publications (invitations, flyers, posters, tickets, banners, thank-you cards)
- ✔ Decorations (table centerpieces, flowers, balloons)
- ✔ Recognition (gifts, cards, discount tickets, plaques, pins)

Remember, even if you do have a healthy budget for special events, you don't have to use all of it. Try to attain sponsorship for as many components of the event as you can — from the napkins to the catering to the limo service for your entertainers. You may be able to get a single corporate sponsor to underwrite your entire event, or you may be piecing together sponsors for each step along the way. Be sure to reward their generosity with acknowledgments in your publicity and at the event. Whether your sponsors are one or many, they are worth the time, research, and effort it takes to cultivate them. A low-level sponsor now, treated well, may turn out to be a major sponsor and part of a long-term alliance down the road.

Setting a timeline for your special event

How many months in advance do you need to plan your special event? If you can begin a year early, do it. Many organizations begin planning for next year's event the same day they evaluate the one they just had. If you do a repeat event every year, this is a fairly simple process. If you're starting from scratch and putting together a new event, you need all the time you can get.

Suppose that you're going to put on a gala, with catered dinner, a speaker, and dancing. You hope for the black-tie and evening-gown crowd. If you process the staging of the special event, you can break the pieces down into a timeline that helps you stay on track and get everything done in a comfortable timeframe. The timeline presented here is for a special event that will occur in July of the next year:

- ✔ **August:** Begin planning; select committee; hold your first committee meeting; select the speaker and theme. Follow with monthly committee meetings (with more frequent meetings as you get closer to the event) to keep the momentum.

- ✔ **September:** Divide tasks among the committee. Contact the speaker. Determine the location and equipment needed. Remember to consider permits, security, and insurance.

- ✔ **October:** Draft the agenda for the evening. Be specific, writing down what you want to happen from start to finish in 15 to 30-minute increments.

- ✔ **November:** Identify potential sponsorships and create a plan to pursue them.

- ✔ **December:** Identify potential participants from your donor list and the community at large. Begin to pursue sponsorships.

- ✔ **January:** Contact foodservice, housekeeping, and entertainment vendors.

- ✔ **February:** Approve the menu; select the music.

- ✔ **March:** Print invitations, flyers, and tickets. Finalize your publicity plan.

- ✔ **April:** Do a reality check.

- ✔ **May:** Start publicity; organize your volunteers; send invitations (the last week of May).

- ✔ **June:** Coordinate all elements of the event; assemble groups; practice a run-through; do a last-minute function check of the facility: housekeeping, service, sound system, and entertainment.

- ✔ **July:** Put on the Event! Don't forget follow-up activities such as sending thank-you notes to volunteers, hosts, and donors, and beginning to lay the groundwork for next year's successful event.

With sufficient time and detailed planning, your event should come off without a hitch. Relax and enjoy it!

Recognizing Success

The place is empty. Confetti covers the floor; dishes and flatware and crumpled napkins cover tabletops. Soon the crew arrives to disassemble the furnishings and the tent. It's all over.

The result of special events can be all over the board, and the amount of money you raise in your special event may turn out to be secondary to the goodwill you generate. Because goodwill is hard to rate, you may walk away from the event wondering whether you hit your mark.

You can use the goals you set to help you determine whether you reached the desired objectives. You can also watch for longer-term positive results by being alert for the following:

- People are smiling as they leave.
- Your event is mentioned — in a positive way — in the paper in the morning.
- People mention to you that they heard about your event.
- You get an increase in calls and/or visits.
- People signed the guest book to get on your mailing list or filled out a pledge card at the event.
- You feel that the community has a better understanding of who you are.
- Participants send thank-you notes.
- People ask you whether you plan to have the event again next year.

When the dust begins to settle and you have recovered from the stress, take more time to evaluate your event. Learning from this one can help you run the next one more smoothly. Here are some of the questions that you — and your special events committee — can ask as you evaluate:

- Did we meet the goals we set in the beginning?
- What kind of publicity did we get?
- How many new people did we reach?
- What was our per-plate (or per-participant) cost?
- Did we raise any money?

Is it possible to have a good event without raising any money? Yes! Although you may put on your special event with the objective of raising substantial funds, the more direct benefit is the exposure that you get and the awareness you raise. The money comes, over time, as a result of these other increased benefits.

Same time next year? Depending on whom you ask, some event planners feel that it's important to have the same event several years running to help "brand" the event in the mind of the community. Although this approach works well for some organizations (especially those who know that they have selected an event that fits well with their mission), an argument can be made for not repeating an event that clearly didn't work. If your event was a royal flop, don't buy into the argument that you really need to give it three years before you see any kind of return on your investment. In general, a good rule of thumb, especially for organizations on a shoestring, is to do more of what works and do less of what doesn't.

Organizing an Online Event

These days it's possible to hold interactive events from your Web site. You can hold a seminar where you present information about your cause that interests your donors. Or you can hold an online event with a special draw, such as a celebrity chat where attendees can submit questions and watch and hear the big name respond in real time.

Online events won't be as splashy as a black-tie dinner, but they are virtually free ways to keep your name in front of people on a much more regular basis.

Using online seminars to inform and persuade

Does your organization collect funds to save the rain forest? What about giving an online travelogue presentation about the rain forest and its various birds and beasts? Are you an arts group preparing for your Christmas show? Create a mini-documentary about the behind-the-scenes work at rehearsals and share it with your volunteers and donors.

Using a video camera, presentation software, and a volunteer with a good presentation presence you can prepare informational online broadcasts that people can play back at their own leisure next time they visit your site. Complete the program with a pitch for funds and a link they can hit to make their donation then and there. Consider including a mention of this broadcast in your next e-newsletter or e-mailing campaign directing people to a link on your site they can click to play back the event.

Chatting online with celebrities

If there's somebody with a big name who you can get to support your cause, but who doesn't have the time to travel to an offline event, consider setting up an online chat. This format allows you to get a famous name associated with your cause to chat with your donors online. Designate somebody as a moderator and, if possible, allow visitors to request an audio recording or transcript of the chat when it's done. When you send them the saved chat, include a pitch for a donation.

It's beyond the scope of this book to go into the technical ins and outs of setting up online meetings and chats, but trust us; it's not that difficult to do. Go to the online expert in your organization, or ask a local Web design group to donate their time to set it up for you. With a simple-to-use online meeting product such as NetMeeting from Microsoft, you'd be amazed at what you can do.

Saying "Thank You!"

Do you think that you want to do another special event next year? Then don't forget the last step! Say, "Thank you!" to all involved. As anyone who has ever been through a special event can tell you, the "thanking" is no small feat. It requires your heart-felt recognition for the various parts of the whole, from the person stuffing the invitation envelopes to the catering manager to the volunteer who desktop-published the flyers in her spare time.

How do you thank participants? Here are a few ideas (remember that the ladder of effectiveness ranges from personal contact to impersonal contact; but the biggest "thank you" comes from you, personally):

- A personal visit to the volunteer to say, "Thanks!"
- A phone call and a follow-up letter
- A personal letter to the helper
- A "thank-you" luncheon for all involved
- A group "thank you" in the next agency newsletter (this is a good idea to do in conjunction with another form of recognition)

It's easy to leave out a name or two in your thank-you list, but not acceptable. As you go along, make sure that everyone involved in the planning keeps a list of people who have helped throughout the planning for the event. Then when it's all over, just pull out your list and go through the thank yous, one by one.

Chapter 20

Building Buildings, Nonbuildings, and Futures: The Capital Campaign

. . . .

In This Chapter

▶ Deciding to run a capital campaign

▶ Designating who should lead your capital campaign

▶ Following through each step of the campaign

. . . .

*W*hen you think growth, think capital. Capital means *big* money, enough to build a building or provide income for your programs for many years to come. A capital campaign is the biggest campaign your organization can ever undertake. This campaign is a massive, all-out planning effort to secure large amounts of money for a specific purpose.

This chapter gives you the basics of planning and implementing a capital campaign — the Big Kahuna of fundraising campaigns. Of all the advice we can give you on this topic, here's the most important: Be sure that your organization is ready for this step; a premature capital campaign may do more harm than good. Better to organize a capital campaign when you can reach a meeting of the minds between fundraisers and planners and when you're strong and sure; then you're almost guaranteed success.

Gearing Up for the Big Campaign

Generally, the capital campaign is the one you use to bring in special funds over and above your operating budget (which is the money-eating animal that gets fed by your annual fund). A capital campaign raises the funds for the new wing of your hospital, the new program for teen mothers, or the funding of an endowment that supports the chair of your Philosophy department.

Most capital campaigns share the following characteristics:

✔ The campaign encompasses a massive, organized fundraising effort.

✔ The campaign is designed to raise a specific amount for a specific need.

✔ The campaign cycle stretches over a long but specific timeframe.

✔ Lead gifts make up half of your fundraising goal. Lead gifts are dependent on face-to-face solicitation. (We talk more about lead gifts later in this chapter in the section titled, "Identifying lead gifts and challenge gifts.")

✔ Donors pledge large gifts to be paid over a multiyear period.

Big gifts create big names. Not coincidentally, big names create big gifts. Use naming opportunities to attract and recognize your high-level givers, giving them a publicized stake in your organization's mission for today and tomorrow. And just think — each time your high-level donors come to visit their name-sake building, they are reminded of the importance of their generous gifts.

Like ice cream, capital campaigns come in several common flavors, which the following sections describe:

✔ Bricks-and-mortar campaigns

✔ Endowment campaigns

✔ Project campaigns

✔ Combined campaigns

Running a capital campaign every year is the fundraising equivalent of forcing your giving well to run dry. Capital campaigns should be, by their nature, rare. That's why making the decision to run one should be very carefully thought out.

Building bricks-and-mortar campaigns

The *bricks-and-mortar capital campaign* is probably what most people think of when they hear the term capital campaign. A bricks-and-mortar campaign raises money for tangible things, such as a new wing for your hospital, a new school, a new library, or improvements to a community center. Whether you're renovating an old structure or building an entirely new one, a capital campaign brings in the high-level funds you need to meet that goal.

Many funding entities these days exclude bricks-and-mortar capital campaigns from their giving agenda. Check to see whether a foundation or other source of money is receptive to a capital campaign proposal before you bother to write it up.

Raising funds before a building is built is much easier than raising funds to pay for it *after* it's built. The reason? People love to be part of a building dream.

Checking out endowment campaigns

You can also consider an *endowment campaign* as a variety of capital campaign, but it's one in which raised moneys are used to invest in your future, instead of in a building. With an endowment, a donor pledges a substantial gift that is given over a period of several years; sometimes the interest from such a gift can sustain a program over several years. Many of the grantor foundations were built through an endowment of their own. This type of gift typically goes into a fund for ongoing support of specific programs.

Endowments (gifts left to organizations upon the death of a donor who had a special relationship with the organization and was capable of giving at a high level) are often the result of planned giving instruments or bequests.

The one thing endowments have in common is the requirement that they be at a high enough level to generate income from the principal. This can be done in different ways. One form allows organizations to make use of the interest earned each year on the endowment balance. In another form, an endowment might allow organizations to draw down on the endowment by a certain amount each year. In both of these examples, you need to start with a substantial sum in order to make the impact of the endowment meaningful. For example, the interest on a $50,000 endowment may only yield $1,000 to $5,000, depending on how it's invested. Certain costs associated with maintaining a small endowment could eat up whatever small payoff it provides year to year.

Putting together project campaigns

A *project campaign* raises funds for a program that requires a specific amount of money for a specific time — it's also a type of capital campaign, but one with a narrow focus. For example, suppose that you are currently serving 15 teenagers in your teen parenting program, and you need to increase that number to 25. In order to do this, you need more physical space, more funds allotted to the annual fund, more program materials, and more personnel. You can use much of the planning you do for a capital campaign to accomplish your goals in the more focused project campaign.

Running combined campaigns

If you want to see a combined campaign at its finest, look at any major university. Universities are quickly mastering the techniques for weaving together the goals of a combined campaign. A combined campaign orchestrates all your needs in a single plan — bricks and mortar, program goals, equipment, even the annual fund may all be interwoven with the overall combined campaign goals.

Selecting a Champion

In any capital campaign, leadership is everything. The person you select to head the campaign can often makes the difference between achieving your goal and falling short. The successful capital campaign is a thoroughly planned event that requires a leader with vision, experience, and the connections and means to secure the highest-level lead gifts possible. (Lead gifts are major pledges that come in early and really start your campaign rolling. We talk more about them later in the section titled, "Identifying lead gifts and challenge gifts.")

The best approach is to select a general chairman for the capital campaign committee from your board. You also need dedicated volunteers to serve on the committee as well. As you begin to select committee members, consider these characteristics:

- ✔ Commitment to the mission of the organization
- ✔ Position in the community
- ✔ Experience with the organization
- ✔ Ability and willingness to give

Each of these characteristics is vitally important. In a capital campaign, each of your board members must be a giving member. The members of the capital campaign committee will have more credibility if they are able to back up their requests with their own giving experience when they go face to face with potentially high-level donors. The ask, as we explain in Chapter 9, is more powerful if, when your committee member invites Bob to make a donation, she can say, "Bob, our board consists of 14 members, and we have each contributed between $3,000 and $50,000."

You may need to organize more than one committee to take care of each step of the campaign process because the planning and implementation of a capital campaign involves so many tasks.

Before you launch the capital campaign, you may want a capital planning committee to evaluate the institution's readiness for a capital campaign. This committee may hire an outside firm to do a feasibility study, and may also identify and cultivate prospective high-level givers. The study report is addressed to your leadership, and your campaign committee makes any decisions necessary to implement the plan.

Staging the Campaign

Planning is a particular priority in a capital campaign because of the campaign's sheer scope. Don't start before you're ready, or it will show in the results.

Planning for a capital campaign usually involves the following stages:

1. **Readiness:** Determine whether your organization is really ready to launch a capital campaign. You can do this yourself or use an outside agency to make sure that your basic fundraising structure is in place and functioning before taking on anything this massive and this public. The outcome of your capital campaign, whether you pass the goal with flying colors or fall flat on your face, can have an impact on the public perception of your organization for years to come.

2. **Testing:** Identify key potential donors of influence in your area and get their opinions on the readiness, practicality, and appeal of your campaign.

3. **Setup:** Put in place the basic organizing systems, such as research, record keeping, staffing, and so on, in preparation for the campaign.

4. **In-house preparations:** Finalize your case, develop materials, train committees, solicit challenge gifts, and recruit volunteers.

5. **Lead gifts:** Have your committee members acquire lead gifts from board members, individuals, corporations, and foundations.

6. **Public fundraising:** Publicly announce your capital campaign (when you are more than 50 percent to your goal) and build the public solicitation portion of your campaign.

7. **Completion and evaluation:** Focus on smaller gifts and bring the campaign to a close, evaluating the entire process, managing recognitions, and making suggestions for improvement in the next campaign.

Note that much of the work of the capital campaign is actually done behind the scenes during the first five stages of planning. The campaign only goes public in Stage 6, when you are more than 50 percent assured of reaching your campaign goal.

Testing the waters: Campaign feasibility

Testing for readiness is a major part of the success of the capital campaign. Is your organization ready? Is your board ready? Is the public ready? Many factors, both internal and external, affect the overall success or failure of your campaign.

Many organizations rely on consulting firms to do feasibility studies when they prepare a major campaign. Using people at a distance from your organization enables those interviewed to be open and honest in their responses. If a person from the organization asks questions like "Do you think that our organization is ready for this campaign? Do you think that the goal is realistic?" — someone closely affiliated with your organization may not feel free to answer candidly. You can also rely on the objectivity of the consultant to recommend whether now is the time for a major campaign; someone who is excited about the prospect in-house may push for a capital campaign before the time is right.

A *feasibility study* helps you

✔ Determine whether your case statement is solid

✔ Evaluate your board readiness

✔ Test the overall campaign goal

✔ Test whether donor record-keeping systems are ready for a capital campaign

✔ Test the markets for giving and the working Gift Range Chart for to the campaign.

Even if you're a three-person shop, do a feasibility study before you launch a major campaign. Although your study may not be something coordinated by a national consulting firm, you still should test your case statement, your goals, and your gift range chart with a number of high-level donors.

Don't worry: It's okay to go out to your stakeholders and say, "Here's what our board is talking about. Does this sound feasible to you?" Take along a questionnaire and do the interview in person. It builds the relationship and makes the donor feel as though she has really helped.

This type of interview accomplishes another goal as well: The interview and the questions you ask often give you a sense of which pitches are most and least desirable in the minds of your donors. The interview gives you an idea of which appeals to leave out of the overall plan.

Sometimes a feasibility test lets you know that you're trying to do too many things at once. The recommendation may come back that you need to divide your campaign up into smaller segments. If this happens, don't despair: Instead, look at it as an opportunity to celebrate a greater number of successes.

Setting your goal

Like everything else, setting the goal for your capital campaign may be the subject of long and hard debate. You hear the clashes between risk takers and stability — you see the different priorities and definitions of a number of people who care about the organization and want to see it grow in the right direction. The financial goal for the capital campaign is wrapped up in the vision and agenda of many individuals, so be prepared for much discussion before you finalize the capital campaign goal.

When you arrive at a consensus about the amount of money you need to raise and the realistic possibility of attaining it, test the number. In your feasibility tests, in interviews with donors, ask people "Do you think that this is a realistic amount?" Listen carefully to the responses and evaluate them. If you get too many "Nos," go back to the discussion table with the responses and reevaluate your position.

Here's a sample listing of capital campaign goals:

- ✔ Solicit large amounts
- ✔ Stretch out pledges over multiple years
- ✔ Use challenge and matching grants
- ✔ Include corporations and foundations
- ✔ Stress lead gifts

 The best-laid plans — especially when construction is involved— overrun their boundaries. Be sure that you create a contingency fund to take care of overages on projects and unexpected expenses. As a ballpark figure, plan on putting aside between five and ten percent to handle those unexpected construction overruns.

Identifying lead gifts and challenge gifts

A *lead gift* is one of the first few — and biggest — gifts you can expect during your campaign. These gifts take a lot of time and cultivation and are developed and solicited strategically, over months (or perhaps years). A relatively low number of lead gifts comprise a high percentage of your overall fundraising goal. According to the Center for Philanthropy at Indiana University, Purdue University at Indianapolis, the numbers break down like this:

- ✔ The 10 to 15 top gifts comprise the top 34 percent of your total.
- ✔ The next 75 to 100 gifts make up the next 33 percent.
- ✔ All other gifts make up only 33 percent of the total.

A Gift Range Chart (see Chapter 5) helps you plot out the number of major gifts you need in order to make your fundraising goal. The gift range chart is extremely important in capital campaigns, as well, and can help you determine not only how many of each type of gift you need, but also the number of people you have to approach in order to reach that goal.

Those first few gifts of a capital campaign are important pieces of your overall capital campaign strategy. So just who will be your first lead givers?

- ✔ **Board members.** You must have a giving board in order to run a successful capital campaign.

- ✔ **High-level donors.** Your major givers in other areas of your fundraising program will also be those who are likely to step up to the plate with a substantial gift in your capital campaign. You need to think of gift incentives, such as naming opportunities and other forms of recognition, as well as a revitalized case that helps donors see why now is the right time to give that large gift.

- ✔ **Stakeholders in business and philanthropy.** Lead gifts may also come from the corporate or philanthropic community. Companies may be interested in sponsoring a portion of your campaign by providing a challenge gift that inspires others to give at a higher level. See Chapter 22 for more about soliciting corporate gifts.

One of the most effective vehicles in a capital campaign is the challenge gift. A *challenge gift* is one in which a lead giver (an individual, a corporation, or a foundation) says something like, "I'll give you $100,000 if you can get it matched by July 1, 2007." This enables you to go to other prospective high-level donors and say, "If you give now, your money will go twice as far." Because of the matching funds, a donor that gives $25,000 will get the good feeling of knowing that his gift actually takes you $50,000 closer to your campaign goal. See Chapter 21 for more about challenge gifts.

This decade will see one of the largest transfers of wealth that it's possible to imagine. Estimates of the amount that will be transferred from one generation to the next run as high as $14 trillion! When this type of generational transfer takes place, you have a huge opportunity to solicit a major gift.

When you have your prospects identified and your goals and approaches in place, your fundraising for these larger gifts involves all the techniques discussed in Chapters 7 through 16 of this book. However, your prospect list is typically more targeted, and the win for your efforts can be bigger, though the time you spend in cultivating these big-hitter relationships can involve months or even years.

Going public

Suppose that you've completed the campaign plan and the consultants have told you the time is ripe for your capital campaign. So you pull your committees together, begin prospect research, gather your materials, and secure all the necessary lead gifts. You're already two-thirds to your goal and you're certain you're going to make it. Now what do you do?

Sit back and coast to the finish line? Nope. Now's the time to go public with your campaign.

A successful capital campaign is a big boost for the morale of your supporters and the public perception of your nonprofit organization. It says a number of things to the public at large:

✔ This organization knows what it's doing.

✔ This organization is responsible with its money.

✔ Other people believe in this organization — look who's giving!

✔ This organization is worth a lot — look at the size of its goal!

✔ This organization is doing good work.

Each of these messages is important in a dollars-and-sense kind of way. Because fundraising is more about relationships than it is about money, and because relationships are built on trust, which is built on credibility, you have a great opportunity to further the trustworthiness of your organization. The more trustworthy your organization, the more people will want to identify with you. So what do you need in place to take your campaign to the public?

✔ A spokesperson (this may be your committee chairperson)

✔ Visual aids (something like the big United Way thermometer comes to mind)

✔ Printed materials (brochures, pledge cards, flyers, and so on)

✔ E-mail lists and a Web site

✔ Media contacts, such as radio, television, and the Internet

✔ Donors willing to say why they believe in your organization

Make sure that you prepare for going public in your campaign plan so that you've budgeted the necessary funds, prepared and printed the necessary materials, and established the ground rules and the organization for your publicity effort. See Chapter 12 for more about working with the media.

Following up with your capital campaign

Your campaign has been a success. So, how do you wind down the campaign? Follow-up to your campaign includes major celebrations, which should be part of your publicity component. Have dinners to thank the volunteers — and invite the media. Hold a ribbon-cutting ceremony for the new wing — and invite the media. Make a fuss over the first new teen mom to graduate from your job training facility — and invite the media. After doing all this work quietly, the time has come for you to pat yourself on the back in a very public way.

As you bring the public campaign to a close, you need to organize a number of things to make sure that the gifts promised are delivered and the goodwill created continues:

- ✔ Effective and quick responses to gifts from all donors
- ✔ Timely follow-up with thank-you notes and receipts
- ✔ Accurate accounting and data tracking
- ✔ Evaluations and reports on various stages of the campaign
- ✔ An open letter of thanks to the community, published in the local papers, for support in reaching your now-successful campaign goals

Debriefing everybody

Especially with something as big and far-reaching as a capital campaign, learning from your successes as well as your mistakes is important. What went right in your capital campaign? What would you avoid like the plague in future?

Before you disperse your committees, ask them to meet one last time for a debriefing. Prepare a questionnaire related to the individual tasks you assigned. Ask people to rate their own effectiveness as a team and to list any suggestions that they would make for the next team to step into their shoes. Ask them about likes and dislikes about the process, and glean any important insights for the next capital campaign team that comes along.

Finally, summarize all the information you gather (and archive it for the future) before closing the book on the capital campaign fund altogether. Remember that the effects of your work, resulting in long-term pledges that will pay over a number of years, will be coming in for many months to come. The knowledge that you gained helps others begin where you left off and can take your organization into the future.

Chapter 21

Securing Major Gifts, Planned Gifts, and the Challenge Grant

*Y*ou're sitting on Mrs. Lewis's divan. Your mouth is dry. This is the moment you've been preparing for, for months.

You had to lunch together and follow-up conversations. You've exchanged personal correspondence repeatedly. You know her dog on a first-name basis. From your relationship to date you expect Mrs. Lewis to be a major giver in one way or another. Now is the time to see how substantial her support will be.

This chapter explains the important role of the big-time giver to your organization, whether that person (or in some cases corporation or foundation) presents you with a huge check, or offers to match other donors' contributions with a challenge grant. We also explain how to go about dealing with planned giving, a scenario where an individual provides for your organization in the will. Not everyone has the means to give that $5,000, $20,000, or $100,000 gift, but those who do — and who have an interest and a heart for your mission — can help you greatly through one of these three mechanisms.

In this chapter, we provide a basic introduction to the major gift and the planned gift concept. We encourage you to talk to planned gift specialists for particulars on how to develop a planned giving program that is right for your organization.

Finally, we explore the potential of challenge grants, one of the most effective fundraising tools around today. The challenge grant is a funding that is offered — sometimes anonymously — contingent on "matching" funds being raised.

Making a Perfect Match

The fact that your organization's mission and the interests of the donor are compatible is the most important facet of securing a major gift. The giver's ability to give is important, yes; but more important is her interest in giving, the position of her heart on the cause you represent, which makes for a win-win situation.

This matching of causes is one of the principal reasons why knowing the heart of your major giver is of primary importance in securing major gifts. Die-hard fundraisers who are more interested in getting the money than they are in building relationships seem to have a "grab the money and run" philosophy, but that approach only works (and not very well) in lower levels of giving. After you begin talking to a donor about a major gift — $5,000, $10,000, or $15,000 — other things, like mission and fit, become more important.

Although you don't want to insult somebody by asking for an outrageous amount of money, donors are often flattered that fundraisers think that they are capable of giving at such high amounts. Asking for more than you expect also gives you another benefit: It gives you the opportunity to accept less, which lets the donor know that it's okay to "bargain down," and you can suggest a lower amount with which the donor may be more comfortable.

Deciding on the major gift amounts for your organization

The word "major" is relative. What is a major gift? To a small organization, it may be $5,000. To a university, it may be $5,000,000. To a tiny, shoestring agency, a major gift may simply be a gift that is bigger than the norm.

Consider what would be a major gift in your organization. Take a look at your overall operating budget and ask yourself: What type of gift would be a major help to us? Five percent of the operating budget? Ten? Two?

Deciding on the amount that represents a major gift for your organization can help you plan to solicit for that amount. It also keeps you from settling for a $2,000 gift when you really should be moving your givers toward $5,000.

As you decide on the level of major gifts for your organization, ask yourself the following questions:

- ✔ Who are our major givers likely to be?
- ✔ Who will work on building relationships with our major givers?
- ✔ Do we have any givers now who can be cultivated into major givers? If so, who are they?
- ✔ Does our board have expertise in this area? Do we need to have board training on how to ask for major gifts?
- ✔ Is our board currently giving at a major gift level? If not, why not? If so, who are our highest givers?
- ✔ How do we recognize our major givers?

A major gift is defined differently for a capital campaign than for your annual operating campaign. In a capital campaign, you strategize with big gifts at the top — in that category, $1,000,000 is a major gift, but $10,000 wouldn't be. See Chapter 20 for more information about capital campaigns.

Getting to the heart of the all-important major giver

In Chapter 8, we tell you all about the major giver — who he is, what he wants, and how you can make sure that the donor-agency relationship is a positive one.

The most important thing to remember about the major giving prospect is that you work with him or her over time. The relationship is one that grows through years of involvement. Your organization establishes a relationship with Mrs. Edna Lewis, for example, by following these steps:

- ✔ Identify her as a prospective major donor.
- ✔ Qualify the donor by determining her interest in your organization and her ability to give.
- ✔ Cultivate the donor and bring her ever closer to the heart of your mission.
- ✔ Ask, listen, and respond to her needs.
- ✔ Request the major gift.
- ✔ Acknowledge the gift and continue the relationship by letting her know how her gift is making a difference to the people you serve.

The give and take in a major campaign

The major giver in a capital campaign gives a lead gift that can make a huge difference in the progress of your fundraising effort. A major gift, one of the lead gifts for your campaign, may be a substantial amount of money, such as $25,000, $50,000, $100,000, or more. When you ask for lead gifts in a capital campaign, remember that you are looking for a few gifts that comprise 40 to 60 percent of your total.

Those people who are regular and large donors to your annual fund are the best candidates for major, lead, and challenge gifts.

Be prepared for your major giver to want to contact a tax advisor or lawyer before agreeing to a pledge amount. In fact, if she doesn't suggest it, you should, as a donor service. Some major givers may want to draft a contract to stipulate certain aspects of the agreement. Work with your organization's legal team and your donor's tax advisors to come to an understanding. It's in everybody's best interest.

Corporate giving and cause-related major gifts

Corporations are a source of some major gifts; but more and more, corporations give when the gift, its purpose, and any publicity associated with it aligns with the mission of the corporation. This is called cause-related marketing. For example, a waterworks company may want to sponsor the water tanks at the aquarium at the zoo, and may want to attach the company name to the tanks in some way. This is not only a way to build their community-spirited image, but they also get lots of exposure as those crowds stroll by.

Companies that are dependent on research often endow chairs in the subject matter they care about in a university. A company that deals with healthcare needs may donate money to the Red Cross. Cause-related giving is happening more and more between for-profit and nonprofit organizations. Alliances, partnerships, and sponsorships are here to stay.

Valuing the relationship: Stewardship in action

What kind of reporting method do you plan to use to let your major giver know that her donation is going where you said that it was going to go? Each individual major gift is a campaign in itself — each individual deserves to be met with, listened to, and valued. After you receive the gift, nothing changes. In fact, it's more important than ever to include major donors such as Edna Lewis in the loop. She has become a part of your organization through her donation. She should be part of the communication flow when there is news to report and glad tidings to share. This helps the donor know that this is about more than money and makes her glad she gave to your organization as generously as she did.

Your annual report is one way you can report the use of donated funds to your donors. But for high-level givers, personalized letters with specific information about how their gift was applied are a nice touch. For example, your letter could say, "Your generous donation helped us provide training for 15 more teen moms than we helped last year." Or, you could write, "Because of you, Edna, Sarah was able to finish high school, take a computer course, and get an entry-level job at a small publishing company. Her daughter, Haley, is healthy, caught up on her shots, and happy in our day-care center while her mom works."

Personalized attention makes the major giver glad she's in a relationship with you. And in addition to respectfully honoring the continuing relationship, it keeps the door open for a planned gift in the future.

Creating a major gift strategy

What can you offer major givers in return for their generosity? In reality, they are looking for specific things from your organization. They want to know that your organization

- ✔ Cares about the issues they care about
- ✔ Values them as individuals
- ✔ Appreciates their gifts
- ✔ Practices good management
- ✔ Plans intelligently
- ✔ Selects good people who represent it well
- ✔ Presents an image they want to align with

Set the ground rules for major gifts before you need them. Come up with naming opportunities and other forms of recognition. The rationale? Know what you want and you can attain it.

Get your committee together, and use these tips when developing your major gift strategy:

- ✔ Brainstorm a list of major giving ideas.
- ✔ Get board approval before you proceed.
- ✔ Create ideas you can live with for quite some time — you can't remove the name from a named gift at the drop of a hat.

✔ Don't be afraid to stretch a little — set your sights high. (Remember that yesterday's major gift, which may have been $10,000, is today's small potatoes.)

✔ Consider whether corporate sponsorships or in-kind contributions can be in your major gift strategy.

As you put together your major gift strategy, remember to think about how to reward your donors when they enter into this high-level relationship with your organization.

Some of the ideas you can include in your strategy are:

✔ **Keep in touch with your high-level donors often.** Mail them newsletters. Call them up on the phone. Send an e-newsletter. Follow up in other ways, too.

✔ **Recognize your high-level donors' gifts.** Host a special dinner for your high-level donors. Take the individual donor out to lunch. Invite your donors to be part of an elite giving club.

✔ **Consider a naming opportunity.** Create a complete list of items that are available for naming and keep careful track of who is offered, and who accepts, these naming opportunities. Make sure that two different staff or board members do not promise the same naming item to two different donors. Naming opportunities are best planned carefully and used slowly, which helps preserve the importance of the naming item and keeps you from making a potentially embarrassing mistake.

If you do use naming opportunities, decide ahead of time how much must be donated in return for the naming. Is it $40,000 for a garden, $20,000 for a fountain, and $10,000 for a bench? Make sure that the naming items are planned, approved, and listed as available before you begin publicizing your major gift plan.

Preparing for Planned Gifts

And at the very top of the fundraising ladder, you find the planned gift. A planned gift is a long-term, high-dollar gift that may come to your organization in the form of a bequest, property, insurance, or one of several planned giving instruments.

Some fundraisers build entire careers around the concept of planned giving, as well they should. This highly specialized area requires continual education on current tax laws, financial instruments, best practices, and application and development of gift strategies.

Planned giving is one of the hottest areas in fundraising right now. Because of the huge transfer of wealth that will take place over the next two decades and the aging baby-boomer population, smart ways to preserve and hand down assets are in demand. Planned giving instruments give donors ways to protect their holdings, provide for their families, and leave a legacy to an organization with a mission they believe in.

Getting the gift that keeps on giving

A planned gift is the Big Kahuna — the gift that truly keeps on giving after your donor has passed away. It can range from a simple bequest to a complex trust. As you might expect, this level of gift comes from a smaller percentage of your complete donor list — generally three percent of your total number of supporters have everything it takes to be a planned giving donor.

When we first heard the term *planned gift,* we thought "That's odd — aren't all gifts planned?" The phrase "planned gift" actually refers to the high level of planning required — by fundraising officers, financial advisors, tax attorneys, and more — to develop just the right giving plan for a high-level donor who wants to leave a major gift to a charitable organization.

Planned gifts

- Provide estate planning for donors
- Can give donors income and possible estate tax savings
- Are not necessarily large and are sometimes given during the donor's lifetime
- Can provide an income to the donor or to someone designated by the donor
- Can improve the relationship between the giver and your organization while the donor is still alive
- Involve the donor's tax and financial advisors

So who is this person planning to benefit your group after he or she passes away? A potential planned giving donor will be

- Engaged with your organization at a high level
- Interested in making a difference for the organization long term
- Able to make a large donation (either now, by investing funds in a planned giving instrument or later, when the ability to get at the funds for their own use [called accessibility and liquidity] aren't issues)

The most important rule of a planned giving program: The needs of the donor come first. Your donor places high trust in your helping her find, evaluate, and select the right planned giving instrument for her needs and financial situation. Although you are working to secure a gift for your organization, remember that the gift must be the right "fit," and the donor should have his own advisors review and respond to the planned gift plan before the contract is signed.

Differentiating planned giving from other gifts

If you have a good, healthy donor program in place, in which you are cultivating donors, bringing them ever closer to the mission of your organization, and upgrading them to higher gifts each year, a planned giving program is a matter of education. It's a logical next step.

Planned giving is only about 40 years old. A change in the tax laws in the late 1960s concerning how charitable contributions are made led to the development of the planned giving instruments we have today.

There are three primary differences between planned gifts and other gifts:

- ✔ The size of the gift, which might be money, stock, insurance, or a home, property, or material goods.

- ✔ When the gift is paid. Although the gift is ordinarily paid to the organization upon the death of the donor, some planned giving instruments pay the donor and/or other selected recipients an income during the donor's lifetime, as well.

- ✔ The complexity of the gift. A planned gift is a transaction that requires the collaboration of tax advisors, lawyers, financial advisors, and fundraising professionals, all working together in the donor's best interest.

Your potential planned giver will want to ask his tax advisor over how many years he can allocate the deduction for his planned gift. Many people can't take the deduction all in one year. Make sure that your donor talks to his tax professional and gets all the answers he needs before you sign a contract.

Timing is everything: When to start

If you've just begun putting a fundraising system in place, or you're a one-person development office, you may be wondering how important it is to have a planned giving program and when you need to start it.

One big mistake organizations make with planned giving is in not starting it soon enough. When you create planned giving opportunities, you are generating gifts that will come to you later. Prepared organizations always have a handle on who their top-level donors are and what kind of potential gifts are "in the pipeline," which means future planned gifts as well as projected donations from other campaigns.

How do you know when you're ready to start a planned giving program?

> ✔ You have an established donor base.
>
> ✔ You have demonstrated good stewardship consistently.
>
> ✔ You have the resources (on your board or through a consultant) to offer the high-end support a planned giving program requires.

Many nonprofit organizations rely on the pro bono services of tax or legal advisors to set up and maintain a planned giving program. Traditionally only the larger organizations (museums, symphonies, universities, and so on) can afford a full-time staff member who specializes in this area.

Gearing up for planned giving

How many times have you heard us talk about the mission of your organization? Although we can assume that you have a crystal-clear mission and the publications to support it, before you embark on a program that takes you into the deep waters of planned giving, you need to be certain that you have the plan — and the people to work it — in place.

You need three important things to get a planned giving program going:

> ✔ A board that's ready for planned giving
>
> ✔ A plan to implement a planned giving program
>
> ✔ The professional resources to help you investigate, set up, and maintain the program

Do you need a planned giving committee on your board? Not all organizations are set up the same way, but some boards organize a planned giving committee to decide important things like what the responsibilities of the members will be, how funds will be invested, what the board's legal responsibilities are, and how the invested funds will be used. Other boards simply have a development committee that has the responsibility for overseeing the planned giving program, and the board of the endowment handles investment issues.

Starting with your board

Making sure that your board is ready is an important part of putting a planned giving program in place. If your organization has a good reputation in the community and is led by solid, respected leaders, it may be time to explore the planned giving option. Open the topic for discussion with your board and ask a local financial expert (if you don't have one on your board) to explain the various planned giving instruments and their individual features. Pull together a focus group to discuss the pros and cons of a planned giving program. You might also want to do an informal survey among some of your closest donors, saying, "We are thinking about starting a planned giving program for the people closest to our mission. Do you think that people would be interested in a program that. . . ."

Because planned giving is such a highly specialized area, nonprofit organizations considering a planned giving program for the first time need to get educated about the process before they begin. Look for classes in your area that offer the basics of planned giving (a financial services firm in your area may offer classes on planned giving instruments).

Creating a plan for planned gifts and choosing gifts for the plan

The largest part of preparation for a planned gifts program is in determining your goals and guidelines for the solicitation, acceptance, and administration of the gifts. You will need legal and financial advice as you prepare the guidelines. Your planned giving committee will draft policies that determine

- The type of gifts you offer
- The income offered to donors
- The legal and ethical responsibilities of the fundraiser
- How you preserve the confidentiality of the donor
- How assets will be distributed
- Allowed investments

In planned giving, a number of different vehicles can be used — which is one of the reasons that having a well-trained, knowledgeable, and up-to-date consultant or staff member is vitally important. The person who works with donors on planned giving possibilities needs to know her stuff. She needs to be able to answer questions about the various instruments, use her resources to find the solutions to complex situations, and make recommendations in the best interests of the donor. Here are some of the more popular planned giving instruments your organization will be working with as you begin to explore planned gifts:

- Wills
- Charitable gift annuities

   ✔ Charitable remainder trusts

   ✔ Insurance and interest gifts

Here's a rundown on each of these different gift types:

   ✔ **Working with wills.** A will is the simplest and most common form of
      planned giving instrument. Because most people are familiar with wills,
      this is the easiest instrument to explain and to market. In working with
      your organization to draft their wills, donors can protect their depen-
      dents, reduce their estate taxes, and control the way in which their
      assets are distributed — and to whom. Some donors like leaving
      contributions to charities in their will for the reason that the gift is
      revocable — if the donor changes her mind later, she can revise her
      will and erase the gift. In other gift forms that are based on contractual
      agreements, this is not the case.

   ✔ **Assessing annuities.** In a charitable gift annuity, the donor makes a gift of
      cash or assets to your organization and your organization agrees to pay
      an income to the donor and/or her beneficiaries until the donor's death.
      Your organization invests the donated funds and pays out a fixed income
      to the donor. The benefits to the donor include receipt of tax-free income
      and income, capital, and estate tax benefits. The ACGA (American Council
      on Gift Annuities), a national organization of charities founded as the
      Committee on Gift Annuities, educates charities about gift annuities and
      other planned gifts. You can find suggested charitable gift annuity rates by
      going to their Web site at www.acga-web.org/giftrates.html. Most
      charities rely on the ACGA to help them determine the payout rate for
      charitable gift annuities.

   ✔ **Tackling trusts.** The *charitable remainder trust* is a three-way relationship,
      arranged between a charity and a donor through a trustee, who manages
      the account. Using this type of instrument, the donor sets up a trust for
      the donation, which pays out upon his death. This benefits the donor by
      reducing the donor's estate tax and providing income and capital gains
      tax benefits. A *charitable lead trust* is slightly different from a charitable
      remainder trust in that an annual payment is made to the charity for a
      number of years specified by the donor. At the end of that time, the prin-
      cipal is returned to the donor or paid to a designated beneficiary.

   ✔ **Investigating insurance and interest gifts.** Donors can also will an organi-
      zation the proceeds of an individual insurance policy. The charity collects
      the gift upon the death of the donor. If the premiums are continuing, typi-
      cally the organization pays the premiums and the donor sends in an
      annual contribution to provide for these payments. Insurance policies
      are fairly common planned giving instruments. In some cases, you can
      use a two-fold system: A charitable remainder trust purchases an insur-
      ance policy on the person who donated the money in the first place. The
      charity gets the money in the trust, and the insurance proceeds go to a
      designated heir selected by the donor.

State regulations on annuities and trusts vary, so check the regulations in your area before beginning such programs. You can get a listing of state regulations by going to the Planned Giving Resources site at `www.pgresources.com/welcome.html`.

Marketing the plan to the giving public

When you announce, "We now have a planned giving program," your next task is to educate your donors about what that means, how it benefits them, and how they can best take advantage of it. How can you educate your donors about your program?

- ✔ Mention it in your newsletter.
- ✔ Send a flyer to prequalified donors in a targeted mail campaign.
- ✔ Write personal letters to individual donors.
- ✔ Create a new planned giving brochure.
- ✔ Send an e-mail message to online donors.
- ✔ Advertise in publications with your audience base.
- ✔ Announce it at a donor recognition luncheon.
- ✔ Provide information about your program on your Web site.

Marketing tips for planned giving

Part of getting your program going is to let people who advise their clients about such programs know about it. How will speaking to professionals help your program? Education is the key. If tax advisors, lawyers, and financial experts in your area know about your program, they can recommend it to their clients, saying, "You're in an estate tax rate category in which you can designate the money for a charity you care about; otherwise, that same money is going to be paid to the state and federal government for estate and inheritance taxes." Who wants to pay money to the state when they could be leaving behind a legacy with an organization they care about?

Here are a couple of ideas for marketing your program to professionals effectively:

- ✔ Get out in the community and make presentations. Go to lawyers' and accountants' offices — two groups who will be interested in what you are offering their clients — and explain your planned giving program and the instruments you offer.

- ✔ If you live in a small-to-middle-sized town, go to your local banker and ask, "Who are the local lawyers in town who deal with most of the big gifts?" Follow those leads to have discussions with the attorneys in town who deal most often with planned giving.

TIP

Web resources for planned giving

The National Committee on Planned Giving, the professional group for planned-giving professionals in the United States, lists various position papers related to planned giving instruments on its Web site at www.ncpg.org.

In addition, check out *Planned Giving Today*, a publication for Canadian and U.S. gift-planning professionals at www.pgtoday.com.

You can also find a number of resources for planned giving at www.pgresources.com, including a listing of state requirements for charitable gift annuities.

Check out articles about planned giving in the research library at www.charityvillage.com.

TIP

One key to launching a successful planned giving program is to publicize it to the right audience. If you approach a mid-30s audience with a planned giving strategy, they are going to say, "Great. Let me get back to you in another 25 years." If you introduce your program to a select group of high-level givers who are also retirees, sooner or later they are going to begin coming to you and saying, "I'm putting together my will. . . ."

Making Money Go that Extra Mile: Challenge Grants

In Chapter 11, we explain the ins and outs of grant proposal writing. Challenge grants also involve grant proposals, but with a twist: In this proposal, the donors of the grant spell out the terms and conditions of the funding. The donor states that he/she/it will give a substantial gift, if the giving public will match it. This provides a huge incentive for potential donors to make their dollars go much, much farther.

When you apply for a challenge grant, you say to your potential funders, "This is a program that covers not only all the standard grant proposal ingredients but also a plan for securing matching funding, projected amounts, intended sources, and measurable outcomes." You want to communicate, "You have the possibility here to be the whole inspiration for this new initiative. It's your challenge grant that will make it happen."

Here are a few examples of situations in which a challenge grant can make a difference:

- ✔ A wealthy patron of your church says, "Boy, I'd like to see us get a new organ for this place. I'll put up $15,000 if you can get other people to match it."

- ✔ The Forever Fund at the United Way was created with the intention of providing an endowment for the continuance of the organization. The fundraising effort floundered until the Lilly Endowment came along and gave a huge challenge incentive.

- ✔ A challenge grant helped to start community foundations. Not only did that challenge grant raise a huge amount of money, but it also created community foundations that weren't there before. In 10 years, more than 50 new community foundations were formed that otherwise wouldn't have been there, all stimulated by challenge grants from large foundations like Lilly and Kellogg.

Challenge grants do three positive things:

- ✔ **Challenge grants spotlight your organization and provide an endorsement from a major player.** The person or entity giving you the challenge grant is most likely someone in the public eye — the publicity they receive for their philanthropy will benefit you both. For your organization, this alliance means respectability — the "good fundraising" seal of approval.

- ✔ **Challenge grants help people feel that their money goes further.** If a foundation gives you $10,000 to start a new family life program and you match it with another $10,000, everybody giving to your campaign can feel that a donation went twice as far.

- ✔ **Challenge grants enable you to honor and reward the giver of the challenge grant.** This person is a "mover and shaker" and probably one of the closest constituents you have in your organization. The recognition will help him feel good about his gift and have the satisfaction of knowing it was his generosity that enabled the whole program to work. This inspires others to want to make challenge grants in the future, as well.

Who wouldn't love a challenge grant? The idea is to leverage potential funds to make the money go further — it truly builds a community of giving that can have payoffs far into the future.

Before you open up to the possibility of challenge grants, discuss the idea with your board. Feel out any resistance. Most likely, your board will okay the idea and want to participate. Often the first challenge gifts you receive are from board members themselves.

Understanding the mechanics of challenge grants

Both corporations and foundations are currently playing major roles in giving challenge grants, because it leverages their money. Their initial investment may be doubled, tripled, quadrupled, or more. One recent challenge grant began with a $5 million grant and raised more than $40 million total. The corporation got publicity and credit for initiating a $40 million contribution. This is potent stuff.

But not all your challenge grants are going to be multimillion-dollar affairs. In church fundraising drives, the arts, social services, and education, challenge grants take the money further than the original gift. In each of these areas, the grants are usually related to something new or to the enlargement of an existing program.

Live events such as public radio fundraisers, often accept a challenge grant from a listener or corporation of as little as $1,000 that must be met in the next hour. If you have access to such media, look for the mini-challenge, short-time-period grant opportunity.

As you look for ways to get a challenge grant going, keep the plans quiet. Top-level donors will be interested in getting in on the front end of a big deal — advertising your intent may diffuse the excitement. Work it all out, approach the selected donor with the idea, "We're designing this program and we think that you would be perfect to lead the campaign with a challenge grant of $5,000."

Designing your proposal

When you design the proposal for your challenge grant, it's important to keep a key concept in mind: You are giving this person (or funder) the ability to empower lots of other people to give. This is a powerful thought and the major difference between a traditional grant proposal and a challenge grant proposal.

When you begin your challenge grant campaign, you want your potential matching donors to realize that this is a way to increase the effectiveness of their gift. You also want them thinking, "Gosh, we'd better do this — we certainly don't want to be left out!"

If you are leveraging a challenge grant to secure funding from another source, be prepared to provide proof of the challenge. A letter from the individual or entity, signed by the appropriate responsible parties, should suffice. Some organizations may want to see financial statements as well.

Generally there is no designation in a challenge grant proposal for the way in which the gifts come in — the idea is to get the amount matched.

Challenge grants nearly always have a deadline. This is a practical and helpful matter — the deadline gives you a timeframe for your campaign. This enables you to put some urgency into your fundraising letters, "If we don't raise the matching amount by September 24, 2008, we will lose half of the challenge grant."

After you're given the challenge grant, how do you motivate people to give? You secure great gifts from people and groups that donors admire, with the promise that donors can extend the reach of their gifts by contributing now.

Chapter 22

Approaching the Corporate Giver

· ·

In This Chapter

▶ Examining changes to the corporate giving landscape

▶ Understanding why corporations give

▶ Locating the perfect corporate donor match

▶ Approaching corporate donors

· ·

*N*ot all major givers are individual philanthropists who are interested in furthering your mission and earning tax benefits and other perks at the same time — corporations are a source of major giving on an international scale. Whether they give from their corporate foundations or with corporate sponsorships, corporations generally want more than a simple "feel-good" for their part of the bargain.

Philanthropy is good business. Favorable public opinion is a sought-after goal in both the for-profit and nonprofit sectors. Aligning with a good cause helps build the community "feel-good" quotient and benefits the company by boosting goodwill, perhaps increasing sales, raising visibility, and creating a sense of benevolence and involvement that may help it attract and keep good employees.

Understanding the Attitudes Behind Corporate Giving

You can't really know how to approach donors until you understand the reasons that they give. Individuals may have hundreds of reasons for giving. Corporations can be a little more straightforward: a blending of practical and altruistic reasoning.

Watching how September 11 changed corporate giving

Corporations made a stellar showing post 9-11, giving more than $621 million, a huge 40 percent of all the moneys pledged. Compare that to 5.3 percent of all giving in the year 2000 coming from the corporate sector, and you can see that corporations made a big shift in 2001.

Why did these businesses give? Yes, the majority of those giving after 9-11 had a presence in the New York City area and surely knew that things on Wall Street had to get up and running quickly, or there could be an impact on their operations. And yes, there was tremendous publicity value for stepping up to the plate so

quickly at these difficult times. But surveys conducted after 9-11 show an interesting shift; one such study conducted by RoperASW showed that 80 percent of consumers would consider switching brands because of cause-related support by a company.

Short term after 9-11, corporate giving went down because the coffers were temporarily bare. But long term, corporate giving has begun to be seen as part of business, part of getting and keeping customers, and not just a nice-to-have warm and fuzzy perk.

Many corporations give in the interests of cause-related marketing, a way to associate themselves with the good guys of charity to spiff up their own public image. They get free publicity, and free goodwill. People may buy more of their products over their competitors when they hear of their good deeds. Some even find that giving is a way to influence politicians regarding legislation related to their industries.

But many corporations give above and beyond the basic promotional possibilities, and different companies give for different reasons. Some may indeed have altruistic motives as well as having the desire to "give back" to the community. In addition to self-promotion, corporations give major gifts because they want:

- ✔ The community to think of them as people friendly (or arts friendly, or health conscious, whatever the case may be).
- ✔ Their employees to see that they care about improving their community.
- ✔ To help organizations that do work related to their particular industry (for example, a medical supply company may make a major gift to a medical school).
- ✔ To give a seal of approval to the cause.

Finding the Right Corporations

Finding the right corporation is like finding the right mate. Not every corporation fits with your organization. You have to find a match in interests, priorities, and self-interest.

For this matchmaking effort, put on your business hat. Remember that with a corporation (as with every donor for that matter but even more so with corporations), giving is an exchange — something for something. Corporations want to get something out of the relationship, so consider what you have to offer and who may want to "buy" what you have.

Using the local community hook

Which corporations give in your area? When you start looking for the names, you'll see them everywhere: on theatre programs, in the paper, at the park, and in the schools. Keep a notebook with you so you can jot down names of local businesses that support nonprofits with missions in your area of service. It's worth a look and some focused research when you begin building the part of your program that targets corporate giving.

If you have corporations represented on your board, you may already be receiving corporate gifts. As you start your planning for a corporate fundraising strategy, get together a focus group of these corporate representatives and ask what they would most like to see in a presentation about your organization. And don't forget to ask each attendee for the names of three people they think that you should contact as you begin a corporate fundraising campaign.

A local giving case in point

In 2004, Bank of America Charitable Foundation created a program called Neighborhood Excellence Initiative to address the need for a national company to find ways to fund local communities. They specified three components: Neighborhood Builders, Local Heroes, and Student Leaders. The program challenged local leaders to identify the needs of the local communities, identifying the most productive local nonprofit groups. The program has successfully provided both funding and leadership training for local nonprofit staff.

In its first year the program gave 60 different U.S. organizations in 30 different markets grants of $200,000 each. Each grant included leadership training to help local nonprofits become better leaders in their own communities.

Local corporations can be the best source for in-kind donations. For example, a national supermarket chain with a branch in your town might just donate food for a fundraising event. Your best bet for such a local in-kind donation is probably the manager of the local branch store or office, who has some latitude to donate to local groups.

Discovering where the CEO's heart lies

You have managed to get a meeting with the new CEO of Acme Paper Company. You go there nervous about meeting with such a powerful person but confident of your cause. You have done your homework and know that the company Mrs. Anderson headed up previously was a big giver in the healthcare sector, but now that she's with Acme Paper, you hope she'll follow their tradition of supporting animal-rights-related causes.

As you are ushered into Mrs. Anderson's office, you are relieved to see pictures of dogs everywhere . . . until you find out that those pictures belonged to the outgoing CEO, and Mrs. Anderson is allergic to dogs.

Often a company gives because the person in charge has a certain interest. If the head of the local bank is an opera nut, you might find a sympathetic ear for your community operetta group. If you can get to the CEO and have him or her turn you over to the person at the company who heads up corporate giving, you have a good shot at getting some kind of gift; it's a brave corporate giving manager who will disregard the CEO's recommendation.

Watch the social pages of your local newspaper to see if the CEO is showing up at theater openings, hospital fundraisers, or local horse shows. If you are an arts group, organization that helps pregnant women get healthcare, or animal rights activist, you may have the hook that will get your foot in the CEO's door. (After all, just because Mrs. Anderson is allergic to dogs, doesn't mean that she doesn't have half a dozen cats at home!)

Finding out what serves their interests

With a little strategizing, it's not hard to figure out the types of logical connections between business and a cause that make sense for corporate giving. Here are just a few:

- A pharmaceutical company gives money to fund a new community clinic.
- A software company donates free computers to schools, loaded, of course, with their own software products.

✔ The local car dealership gives to a program to put a stop to drunk driving.

✔ The large smelting plant that used to have issues with polluting the air gives money to fund an environmental study.

Ironically, even if corporations seem to be part of the problem — for example, the liquor industry without which there may not be alcoholism donating to a campaign against drinking and driving — they can claim that if their products are used responsibly, they're the good guys.

After you identify companies with which your cause could have a logical connection, you've found a likely corporate donor.

Approaching a Corporate Donor

Every corporation and every industry has different concerns, but they are all in the business of making money. So why are they giving money away? Because they see some kind of profit in doing so. Approaching a corporate donor isn't that different from approaching any donor. You determine

✔ What their interest is

✔ What their giving track record is

✔ How you can help them participate in an area where they want to help, for whatever reason

But the corporate world does have a few unique differences that we discuss in the sections that follow.

Researching the corporation ahead of time

Chapter 6 is all about researching donors, and Chapter 8 is all about approaching folks for major gifts. If you're serious about looking for corporate donors, read those chapters along with this chapter for more about researching.

With that said, take these special tips about finding a corporation/giving match. First, corporate giving usually comes from one of two sources, and they are slightly different:

✔ Company-sponsored foundations are separate entities under the law from the corporation they are linked to. Their giving typically is allied with the corporation's interests. They usually operate on endowments, with contributions from the parent corporation on a regular basis. Their endowments might grow when the corporation is profitable and shrink when things aren't so profitable. These entities are governed by regulations for private foundations.

✔ Corporate direct-giving programs are a part of the corporation itself and as such don't have to meet regulations for a private foundation. In this set up, the company typically can use up to ten percent of its pre-tax money to make contributions to charity, though most give more like one percent on average. These programs have no endowment per se but work off company profits. Often there is an employee matching gifts program and in-kind gifts program as part of the corporate direct giving set up.

The first step to finding the right corporation-giving scenario is knowing which kind of entity you're approaching. If the corporation has a foundation, you can go to foundation directories such as The Foundation Directory Online, or the Foundation Finder at The Foundation Center Web site (www.fdncenter.org). If they have a direct giving program, typically information can be found on the company Web site, or try the Internet Prospector's Reference Desk (www.internet-prospector.org) for corporations.

Some corporations have both a company-sponsored foundation and a corporate-giving program. Go to http://fdncenter.org/funders/grant maker/gws_corp/corp.html to search The Foundation Center's Web Sites of Corporation Grantmakers to find corporation foundations. The site also provides a list of links that will take you directly to Web sites of corporation grantmakers to speed your corporate giving search.

The difference between promotion and giving

Corporations give, but they do it in the name of promotion. Give a million, and it makes the front pages of the papers. (Unless Bill Gates just happened to give a billion that day, and then your corporate gift may be buried on page three.) Give a million, and your name is aligned with a cause. Give a million, and you become the national spokesperson and corporate sponsor of a program to combat the societal ill you are helping to fight. It makes sense; it makes money; and it makes friends.

But is it wrong?

Throughout this book we point out that you can't and shouldn't second-guess the motives of your donors, assuming their intent isn't illegal. If you do, you spend all your time and energy qualifying the reasons behind the gift and not acting responsibly in alignment with your responsibility to steward the gift. Corporations give, and that benefits your organization. If their promotions are in alignment with your mission and you can work out an equitable exchange, everybody wins — most of all, the people you serve.

The next piece of the corporate-giving puzzle is to figure out the types of programs that corporations support. This is very similar to the way you find the right foundation to support your cause. Each corporation or corporate-affiliated foundation publishes information about the type of programs they fund. Look on their Web site or contact them for a copy of their guidelines. The guidelines tell you whether the foundation leans toward the arts, health-related causes, education, community-focused issues, or whatever. Then go for the ones that seem a good match to your cause.

Knowing your value to the donor

Don't ever forget that your organization has something to bring to the table in the corporate-giving exchange. For example:

- ✔ You lend an image of goodwill and credibility to the corporation.
- ✔ You offer tax advantages for corporations donating pretax dollars.
- ✔ You provide a way for corporations to attract good employees who share their charitable interests.
- ✔ You help to improve the community in which the corporation exists and its employees live.

When you approach a corporation for a major gift, you are working with some-body who understands the value of this relationship better than most. You can use that to feel confident approaching corporate givers in a businesslike way.

If you're having trouble finding the right initial contact at a company, try searching their Web site for the corporate affairs or community relations department. If the company doesn't, as far as you can tell, have such depart-ments, start with public relations or marketing.

Putting together your presentation

When you're applying for a corporate grant, you have to jump through all the hoops that other kinds of donors put you through. Specifically, you should:

- ✔ Research the specific guidelines the corporation publishes for submit-ting applications.
- ✔ Meet all deadlines and include everything the guidelines require.
- ✔ Build a compelling case for your organization by including your case statement brought up-to-date, your accomplishments, and your ability to govern your activities professionally.

Don't forget the financials. Businesspeople are used to seeing balance sheets and budgets, and they expect to see that you are a viable business with some business savvy in your operations. If you have strong corporate types on your board, stress that. Include their resumes, or at least a short biographical paragraph on each of them, with your application. Try to get one-on-one personal meetings with your key board people and the corporation representatives if possible.

Following up in a businesslike way

Any good businessperson will tell you, good follow-up is respected in the corporate world. Of course you should look for guidance about likely timeframes in the corporate or corporate foundation's application guidelines, but if the estimated time of response has come and gone, follow up with a letter or phone call. You can inquire as to whether any additional information is needed. This contact could cause your application to get unearthed from a pile of applications and get some attention ahead of less proactive applicants.

After you get one corporate gift don't stop; continue to notice the corporations in your area that are giving to organizations in your particular field, be it the arts, education, health, human services, or civic affairs. Look for those sponsorships, and keep that data, and be sure to feed it back into your ever-expanding research file. One day in the not-too-distant future, the file may lead to an exceptional major gift.

Chapter 23

Building and Growing Endowments

Did you ever read an old Victorian novel where the hero lived off his trust fund or inheritance, and you always wanted to know how to get yourself one of those? An endowment is kind of like that: It provides a nest egg of funds, and your organization lives off the profits from the nest egg.

Endowments come in different types, and setting up and managing one has its own ins and outs. In this chapter you discover what an endowment is, whether it's right for you, and what's involved in getting and keeping one.

Endowing the Future

Where a gift of $200,000 to fund a new wing of your AIDS clinic is great, it's a one-time gift that gives and then stops giving. The whole idea behind an endowment is to take advantage of the profits a substantial amount of money can generate, without ever emptying the treasure chest itself. This process involves a lot of lawyers, paperwork, and administration. But if you're the right kind of organization, endowments can set you up for a more secure future.

Understanding an endowment

An endowment is simply a donation of funds that brings with it a stipulation that it be invested; the principal stays intact and the organization feeds off the investment returns. A small amount of the principal may also be paid out each year (perhaps 4 percent or so), in turn making the original money go much farther, which makes everybody happy. Note that an endowment can also consist of other assets, such as property or securities. Trust funds, memorial trusts, and asset base are other terms you'll hear used for endowments.

There are typically two types of endowment, restricted and unrestricted. Here's how they differ:

- ✔ The interest on *unrestricted endowment funds* can be used in any way the organization's board sees fit, on any program or administrative cost.

- ✔ *Restricted endowment funds* are earmarked for a particular type of spending, meaning that either the major donor stipulated how the money would be spent when giving the gift (this kind of gift is called *donor designated*), or the organization specified that the fund would be focused in one area when setting it up.

In addition, the length of an endowment can vary. An endowment may be permanent or term. Here's how these lengths differ:

- ✔ A *permanent endowment* is intended to exist in perpetuity, which is a fancy way to say that it is meant to last forever and the endowment funds themselves are not meant to be used up or sold off. Only income dollars can be spent.

- ✔ A *term endowment* can be set up with an expiration date. When you reach that date, some or all the principal can be spent.

You may also set up a *quasi endowment*. This means that your organization sets up some funds to function as an endowment, instead of the endowment being set up from donor funds.

Finding the right fit

Endowments aren't for everybody. Universities and community foundations are the prototypical endowment candidates (though not the only ones), because they share the following characteristics that normally make an organization a good fit for an endowment:

- ✔ They have been around a while and are expected to be around for many more years to come.

- ✔ They have a reasonably guaranteed constituency. Where your community arts project may fade away if the founding members lose interest or move away, people are likely to want to provide a college education for kids for a long, long time.

✔ The mission is broad enough. A community foundation that serves the community's needs, no matter what they may be, can adapt its mission as times change.

An endowment also typically involves a big chunk of change. Some organizations have endowments in the millions, making the investment of that money something with heavy-duty earning potential. If your group can't spend a lot of time trying to raise a million dollars because that would tap out all the giving power, leaving you without the funds to run day to day, an endowment probably isn't the best place to put your fundraising efforts.

In fact, many endowments are at least started with one huge gift from one source. But you can add to the endowment over the years. A lot of foundations are funded by endowments, and they in turn could become donors to your cause. The Lilly Endowment, for example, is entirely separate from the giant pharmaceutical Eli Lilly and Company (in fact one of their rules is that they don't give to healthcare-related organizations at all). Lilly family members established it as a way for their family to give back to society for their success.

Deciding whether you can build an endowment

How do you know if your organization has what it takes to build an endowment? There are a few key elements to look for:

✔ You have to have a completely committed board and staff that will stick with you through a lengthy process of endowment building.

✔ You have to have a very clear mission and a strong fundraising program already in place.

✔ It helps to have an endowment figurehead, somebody who is very visible and who attracts money and support.

✔ You have the resources to provide sound investment advice and management and a demonstrable investment strategy to attract donors.

✔ You have access to the kind of heavy hitters that it takes to seed an endowment with substantial gifts upfront.

✔ Be an organization where the long term is important. When you build an endowment, you are selling people the idea of your group's longevity. Many donors want to see that the money they give results in a program or visible change today. If you can make people get excited over the idea of just ensuring your continuation, you can get them to give. But never forget: for them to be excited about you continuing tomorrow, you have to show them that you are doing great things today.

Trolling for Endowment Gifts

In an ideal world you pick up the phone one morning, and Mr. Gray, a local billionaire, tells you he's giving $2 million to your group for an endowment, no strings attached. You thank Mr. Gray profusely, hang up, and shout, "Yes!!"

In the real world, though, it isn't impossible that your organization will just receive a large gift out of the blue, large enough to form the basis of an endowment. However, if no single gift drops in your lap, you have to go about building an endowment in a methodical way.

Getting your board to buy in

The first step in building an endowment is to get everybody in your group to agree that an endowment is the right way to go. They need to commit to a long haul, and everybody has to feel comfortable that you can continue your other forms of fundraising and keep all your core programs and functions running, while also raising an endowment.

Then set a goal of getting a handful of significant donations as the start of your endowment. People give money to endowments when they see that there's already a solid financial base. To that end, find out whether your board members themselves have contacts who are able to give such large gifts. And don't forget foundations and corporations as potential major gift givers. See Chapter 8 for more about how to approach foundations and corporations.

After you have a few large gifts as the centerpiece of your endowment, plan and run a long-term campaign to solicit additional gifts.

Explaining the value to donors

Some people are down on endowments. Why? Because they think that an organization that has some financial security may be less responsive to its constituency. Also, if you exist to solve a problem, ensuring your long-term existence suggests that you'll never solve the problem.

In reality, though you gain some autonomy from the giving whims of the public with an endowment, you will never be truly separated from them because you, as a nonprofit, have a stated mission that you must follow. Also, most problems we tackle never go away completely, or if they do, they leave another gap we can move to address. If a cure is found for a disease, there is still the issue of fair distribution of that cure to populations that need it most. If we lower the number of homeless people in our town, we still need to be sure that the population trains for and maintains jobs to keep them off the street.

The financial independence provided by an endowment, in reality, lets your people focus on solving problems, not on raising money. You have the tools and time to innovate in the way you tackle challenges. And with very few exceptions, an endowment is not a blank check. It is a cushion that allows you to focus on the more important issues.

Making your endowment part of your entire fundraising effort

It may take many years to get an endowment in place, so don't count your endowment dollars before they hatch. In the meantime, you have to keep your other fundraising efforts, such as your annual fund drive and special program fundraising, going. Be sure that you have enough staff or volunteers to handle all your fundraising activities. Also, be sure that donors understand the different types of funding you are now seeking. If possible, encourage them to support both the ongoing costs of your organization and its long-term sustainability.

A good print resource for more detail on endowment building is the book *Nonprofit Essentials: Endowment Building* by Diana S. Newman (Wiley).

Managing an Endowment

You have reached your goal and have stacks of endowment dollars in the bank. Now what? The people who gave you this money showed a great deal of trust in your organization. To take the best advantage of the generosity you've been shown set up the endowment. That means good administrative processes, a strong investment strategy, and responsible stewardship.

Living off the profits for years

When the major portion of your endowment is in place, you should establish the infrastructure of people and processes that will administer it. Often groups work with a lawyer to set up a formal trust or foundation with a trustee to administer it.

It's a good idea at this point to create an endowment policy document that lays out policies regarding:

✔ Accepting gifts

✔ Gift restrictions

✔ Donor recognition

✔ Investing strategy

✔ Spending policy

Strong policies and management structure give people confidence in the stability of your endowment.

If you have restricted endowment funds, don't forget that somebody has to ensure that any income from the endowment is used in strict accordance with that restriction. Spending the funds any other way is illegal. (See the section below, "Seeking professional help to manage the dollars.")

Seeking professional help to manage the dollars

Most endowed organizations have an investment manager on staff to deal with the investment strategy, but even those with staff typically rely on outside resources to help. Investment companies such as Merrill Lynch can help with your investment program. You'll also want an independent accountant keeping close tabs on the endowment funds — how they're earning and how they're used.

There are software programs available that you can use to manage your endowment fund. MIP Endowment Management (www.mip.com), Endowment Management Suite (www.FindAccountingSoftware.com) and Fundriver (www.feg.com/Fundriver/Fundriver.html) are a few that are worth checking out.

As you set up your investment strategy, keep in mind that many organizations are now looking at alternative investments that themselves support the organization's mission. For example, you might invest in environmentally responsible companies or funds if your own mission is to clean up the environment. Go to http://as.wsaccess.com to check into Wall Street Access Alternative Investments.

Where do you go from here?

Getting and running an endowment is not for the faint of heart, but if you think that your organization is ready for one, here are some more sources to check out:

The National Association of College and University Business Officers (www.nacubo.org) offers various conferences and seminars on endowment management. Check their Web site to see if there's something of use to you.

Commonfund (www.commonfund.org) maintains a list of seven principles of endowment management, covering topics such as risk management and selecting a fund manager.

Foundation & Endowment Money Management (www.foundationendowment.com) provides current articles on all aspects of endowments. They also provide a list of useful links to sites about philanthropy and foundations.

The Nonprofit Hub (www.nonprofithub.com) is another useful site to visit. There you can find links to endowment advice and professionals who specialize in working with endowments.

Check the laws and regulations regarding endowments and trust law in your state to be sure of your obligations. When you're dealing with this large a sum of money, having solid professional help and advice from both a legal and financial perspective is a must. Setting up and administering an endowment is like running a good-sized business. Professionalism is a must. But the return on your investment of time, energy, and resources can be the long-term financial security of your organization and its work.

Part VI
The Part of Tens

The 5th Wave   By Rich Tennant

"I know you're passionate about your fundraising, but I wish you wouldn't refer to my family as your donor-in-laws."

In this part . . .

*I*n typical *For Dummies* fashion, this part of the book lists a collection of ten items, grouped around a particular subject. Each lists information that's useful to any fundraiser, such as great opening lines and checking out the future of fundraising. Read whichever ones suit you best.

Chapter 24

Ten Predictions about Fundraising

*L*ong before our calendars clicked over to the year 2000, we heard predictions of what life will be like in 2005, 2010, and beyond. Today, you hear predictions of how advanced technology may affect your life. What will fundraising and philanthropy look like in the future? This chapter aims at giving you some short-term predictions based on our experiences and reasonable expectations.

Individual Giving Will Grow

Each individual giver could be worth more to you. According to a 2005 study by the Target Analysis Group, there are two trends for the price of one vis-à-vis individual givers. First, givers' own median income is up; and second, their individual donations are bigger. This increase may be a reflection of the wealth of an aging population, which you'll read more about in this chapter. But the fact that many people who are making better money are willing to share their gains with charities and other groups is a positive sign for the future.

Corporations Will Jump on the Cause-Related Marketing Bandwagon

Corporations have begun to realize that aligning themselves with a cause can't only up their image among the buying public, but also can offer lucrative benefits in marketing punch. When you approach corporations in the future, consider the marketing angle of your proposal; for example:

- Think of a company-sponsored event that would get their name and logo out there in a positive way.

- Could you interest the corporation in a promotion where a portion of what they get for their products goes into your coffers? They get new customers and higher sales that far outweigh the amount they hand over to you from their sales.

- Would the company like to place your logo on their promotional materials, attracting the buyer who has sympathy for your cause, and pay you a royalty for the use of your name?

These types of comarketing ventures will get more and more popular as corporations look for a quid pro quo for their charitable efforts.

HUGE Amounts of Wealth Will Be Transferred

Estimates are that a minimum of $40.6 trillion and as much as $136 trillion will transfer over the next 50 years from all adults alive today to their heirs, charities, taxes, and other recipients. Scholars base this prediction on assumptions about the huge baby boomer population that is entering the point in their lives when estate planning, the drafting of wills, and the passing on of wealth will become critical issues. The numbers are also based on assumptions about the U.S. stock market and the dramatic appreciation of investments that have taken place during the past 20 years. Also enhancing the situation is the fact that modern technology and communication have made stock ownership and other assets that appreciate or grow in value over time available to a huge part of the U.S. population through online brokerages and other mechanisms. More than 40 percent of the population has a stake in the stock market, up from barely 30 percent just 25 years ago.

Givers Will Become More Savvy

Through the Internet people have gained access to a wealth of advice and information. Legal sites provide articles and even ready-to-buy kits for making out wills, creating trusts, and planning for your estate. Books abound about how to handle your money, many giving advice about the tax advantages of giving or structuring your estate to leave bequests to charities or other causes. In short, givers may become more and more savvy about when and why to give, so you will have to do your homework to keep up.

That's not to say that people will go it entirely alone. A huge cadre of professional lawyers, accountants, investment advisors and estate planners are beginning to cultivate a vast new market of potential givers. These individuals are providing the expert advice that creates new contributions to the nonprofit sector.

The various giving mechanisms we cover in this book will be the tools that these professionals use, and their personal relationship with clients will have a major impact on fundraising and philanthropic giving.

Early indications are that the use of private foundations, the setting up of trust accounts with community foundations, bequests in wills to philanthropic organizations, and the creation of the various trust instruments spelled out in Chapter 21 are proliferating.

So it seems likely that this growing accumulation of wealth and increasingly informed donors could result in increased giving. If it does, the historic rate of personal giving as a percent of personal income may grow. It has remained at approximately 1.8 percent, on average, for three decades.

Fundraising Costs Will Be Scrutinized

The relationship between the amount of money given and the percent that actually goes to the charitable cause for which it was solicited has received growing attention.

In the summer of 2004, the U.S. Senate Committee on Finance Hearings focused on nonprofit governance and charity integrity. A report that same year from the Brookings Institute showed that only 11 percent of Americans felt that nonprofits spend money wisely. State governments are looking at nonprofit responsibility as well. In January of 2005, California enacted a Nonprofit Integrity Act that called for annual audits to be made publicly available.

For that reason, the importance of communicating clearly and honestly — how much money is raised, how much it costs to raise the money, and how much of the money is actually spent for the organization's mission — will become increasingly important for nonprofit organizations.

Without any question, however, the long-term relationship between a donor and the organization soliciting funds is the key ingredient in creating trust.

Many organizations are adopting a version of the Preserving the Public Trust Initiative started by the Donors Forum of Chicago. Adherence to the principles in this document helps to reassure potential donors of your standards and practices. You can get a copy of this list of fundraising best practices at www.donorsforum.org/publictrust/principles.html.

Nonprofits Will Go Commercial!

Burton A. Weisbrod, a Northwestern University professor, published a book entitled *To Profit or Not to Profit, The Commercial Transformation of the Non-Profit Sector* (Cambridge University Press). The author believes that the commercialization of many parts of the nonprofit world is inevitable. He cites decreases in governmental and contributed funding that force nonprofits to sell something — often in competition with for-profit organizations. Weisbrod points out that the nonprofit sector has been both criticized and acclaimed. He writes, "The rationale for its special tax treatment and subsidies rest on the belief that it provides services that are materially different from and preferred to the services that private enterprise provides." If demand for those services goes up and traditional funding sources are not available, then commercialization occurs.

Thus, the prediction is that nonprofits will dramatically increase their use of revenues other than voluntary contributions. As that happens, the interaction and relationship of nonprofits and the rest of the economy becomes more common. In some cases, the drive for revenue is bringing nonprofits into headlong competition with private enterprise. This is especially true for hospitals, universities, and some social service providers. For example, the nonprofit YMCA and YWCA in some cases find themselves in direct competition with for-profit recreational organizations.

In addition to competition between nonprofit and for-profit ventures, you're likely to see increased cooperation and blurring of the lines between them as well. For example, government may rely on nonprofits to implement certain government programs rather than attempt to do the work itself. Nonprofit universities conduct scientific research for the benefit of private firms. Universities also enter into major deals with private companies that sell athletic equipment and other products that could benefit from an alliance with the university's reputation. In other words, the private sector has already found a way to profit from the aura and reputation of the nonprofit sector.

Nowhere in the economy is it more obvious that competition and cooperation are taking place between nonprofits and for-profits than in the health care industry where nonprofit hospitals advertise for business, cooperate with for-profit ventures when advantageous, and ardently compete when necessary.

Even though a nonprofit may become more commercial or competitive, the nonprofit does not necessarily break faith with the core values or primary reason the nonprofit was created in the first place. The two can coexist.

Women Will Become a Bigger Force in Giving

Today, women own more than half of all investments in America. As they age, their salaries will increase, and in the same time period, they will inherit wealth from parents and spouses. In fact, 85 percent of women will control their family's wealth at some point in their lives, according to the Woman's Philanthropy Institute.

This means that you should spend some time and effort on understanding how to find and cultivate female donors. What types of causes do they tend to support? What kind of financial concerns do they have that may differ from their husband's, father's, or brother's? What will they want to leave as a legacy when they pass on?

Nonprofits Will Become For-Profit

The ultimate extension of commercialism is the conversion of nonprofits into commercial ventures. Although the Internal Revenue Service, through its regular auditing procedure, may suspend the tax status of a nonprofit and thus convert it to a for-profit venture, the more likely conversions will take place voluntarily by nonprofits who find that the nonprofit structure and the rules and regulations that go with it make it difficult to compete.

Conversion of mutual insurance companies and healthcare providers to for-profit status has become commonplace. These conversions are usually the result of decisions by management that the mission of the organization can best be met in the for-profit world. For example, conversion makes it possible for the company to seek different kinds of financing from the for-profit marketplace. In addition to voluntary conversions, some states have attempted to define nonprofits by requiring a certain percentage of revenue to be contributed income or that a certain percent of revenues received should be used for philanthropic purposes. Although no consensus exists on what's reasonable, it is clear that some nonprofits will find it necessary to convert to for-profit status.

Giving Goes Global

As the world becomes a smaller place, and disasters on the other side of the world seem to be very close to home, you'll see more giving on a global level. The Indonesian tsunami relief effort in 2004/2005 caused unprecedented giving, as did charitable giving in response to the World Trade Center attacks in 2001. People from around the world put geography aside as they are shown the disaster by every kind of media, from video clips on the news and the Internet to blogs and photos.

In fact, in 2004 there was a 16 percent median growth in new donors to the international relief sector, according to one Target Analysis Group study. This growth was no doubt largely due to the Asian tsunami.

Disasters such as these will continue to draw millions of dollars to their causes. That makes it all the more important that you have a strong, consistent donor base that plans to give you a gift year after year, even if they also give to the Red Cross or other group in times of unique disaster.

E-Giving Will Grow

E-giving has begun to have an impact and will become commonplace in the decade ahead. Click-and-mortar will be the combination for successfully marketing nonprofit causes. In other words, it will be important to have a conveniently located brick-and-mortar location where the nonprofit function takes place. But a click on the Internet is likely to be the simplest and easiest way to get a contribution.

This is even truer for time-sensitive disaster relief, where people feel that they must contribute today to be part of a bigger effort to get help where it needs to go right away. The ease of quickly donating on the Internet plays into this kind of urgency.

Chapter 25

Ten Great Opening Lines

Try these lines when you meet a prospective donor.

"Have you seen our new baby elephant?"

Get the donor hooked, right away. What does he care about? What interests him? Capture his imagination as soon as you can, and he'll be waiting for your next word.

"Hi Mrs. Jones, I just left a meeting where we were discussing . . ."

This natural comment can lead right into whatever you want to address with Mrs. Jones — a new program, a building, a campaign, whatever. You don't want to flounder around here, or leave the impression that you are making it up just to create a graceful transition into what you really want to talk about, so only use this statement when it's true. You may, of course, change it to "I was just thinking about . . ." or "We were just talking about planning. . . ."

"Recently I visited the people putting on the program you sponsored. The program was phenomenal! I really think you should see it sometime."

Not only does this line get the donor's imagination going, but it also recognizes him for his past donation and invites him to see the results.

"Now, how can I help you?"

This may get a baffled look and the comment, "I thought that you wanted something from me!" But it does open the door to the idea that fundraisers really do help donors find positive and proven ways to facilitate good in the world and meet their financial planning goals, as well.

"Research shows that giving is good for your health."

Said to the right people (like a group of doctors), this opening line gets people listening right off the bat. Why? First of all, we want it to be true. Second, it tells donors right up front that their philanthropic endeavors will benefit them. If nothing else, the donor will continue listening just so he can look for an opportunity to disprove you.

"You have no idea how much good your last gift did for our organization!"

Recognition is a good thing — especially when there's something substantial you can say about the results of the donor's past contributions.

Misrepresentation is never the best policy. Don't get in to see a donor under false pretenses. Acting like you're conducting a survey at a festival when you're really looking for an opportunity to promote your organization only creates distance between you and the prospective donor. Use your opportunities, certainly, but do it in a forthright manner.

"More people go to zoos today than go to all sports activities combined."

This is a "Gee Whiz!" statement that really gets people interested. What kind of "Gee whiz!" statements can you come up with about your own organization? Take an afternoon and research trivia or statistics related to your area. The Internet offers great tools for this. The interest you'll gain — and the conversations that happen — will be more than worth the expense of your research time.

"Seven out of ten Indianapolis families use United Way services in their lifetime."

This is another "Gee whiz!" statement that is based on fact and may appeal to both logical and emotional types. Know the good your organization has done and be willing to talk about it. Distill the facts down to three or four good opening lines that may interest the prospective donor and leave him wanting to find out more about what you do.

Personal visits are important. People find it very hard to turn down the person who is looking them in the eye.

"Hey — I just received this great picture! The new wing of the library is finished!"

Especially for people who have already given to your organization, seeing evidence of great new things is very heady stuff. Show donors a picture of the new elephant, display the newly purchased property, or of the recent turnout at the fundraising event you sponsored.

The Web isn't the same direct-contact medium as face-to-face visiting, but you can put images on your Web page that show happy people doing good work and suggest your prospective donor visit the site.

"Cute dog!"

Hey, what's the best way to a pet lover's heart? Like his dog! It may seem like an old salesmanship gimmick, but there's an important idea at the center: Identification is key. When your donor realizes that you and he share some common interests, he starts listening.

Index

• H •

• I •

• K •